Always the Fat Kid

THE TRUTH ABOUT THE ENDURING EFFECTS OF CHILDHOOD OBESITY

Jacob C. Warren, PhD

K. Bryant Smalley, PhD, PsyD

palgrave
macmillan

First published in 2013 by
PALGRAVE MACMILLAN®
in the U.S.—a division of St. Martin's Press LLC,
175 Fifth Avenue, New York, NY 10010.

Where this book is distributed in the UK, Europe, and the rest of the world,
this is by Palgrave Macmillan, a division of Macmillan Publishers Limited,
registered in England, company number 785998, of Houndmills,
Basingstoke, Hampshire RG21 6XS.

Palgrave Macmillan is the global academic imprint of the above companies
and has companies and representatives throughout the world.

Palgrave® and Macmillan® are registered trademarks in the United States,
the United Kingdom, Europe, and other countries.

ISBN: 978–0–230–34177–7

Library of Congress Cataloging-In-Publication Data

Warren, Jacob C.
    Always the fat kid : the truth about the enduring effects of
childhood obesity / Jacob Warren and K. Bryant Smalley.
        pages cm
    1. Obesity in children-Psychological aspects. 2. Overweight
children-Psychology. 3. Overweight children-Mental health.
I. Smalley, K. Bryant. II. Title.
RJ399.C6W37 2013
618.92'398—dc23   2012038482

A catalogue record of the book is available from the British Library.

Design by Newgen Imaging Systems (P) Ltd., Chennai, India

First edition: March 2013

10 9 8 7 6 5 4 3 2 1

Printed in the United States of America.

To Rita, Mark, and Erin
—Jacob

To Becky, Terry, Brandy, and Trinity
—Bryant

And to all the children and adults whose experiences
we describe in these pages.

Contents

CONTENTS

PREFACE

L ike so many others, we have seen the obesity epidemic sweep across our nation, and all our training cried out to us to *do something*. Our years of research experience in public health and psychology began to generate hypotheses for us to explore and gave us the methods to examine the issue from a social, cultural, physical, psychological, genetic, and even environmental perspective. We scoured the literature, spent years in the field talking with people, secured federal grants to support our work, and disseminated our findings like good professors should. As we did more and more research, we began to see a repeating theme: the consequences of childhood obesity were not limited just to childhood— something that up until now has largely been ignored by both the scientific community and the mainstream media—and we began to explore this phenomenon in more depth.

But while we are both university-based health researchers, the call to write this book was much more than professional. Our scientific training may have given us a framework from which to explore the enduring effects of childhood obesity, but our personal experiences are the true motivators behind what you are about to read. The first inkling we had about the long-term effects of childhood obesity came not from our research but from our own lived experiences. These experiences helped shape this book, and connected us to the topic in a way that nothing else ever could.

JACOB

My whole family struggles with weight—over the years we've all been fat and we've all been thin. I was an overweight child—bullied, teased, and insecure from kindergarten through twelfth grade. By the time I reached the end of my freshman year of college, I topped out at 230 pounds (at only five feet eight inches tall). I just didn't know if it was possible to lose weight and keep it off, so I never tried. The year that I hit 230 pounds, I got my own apartment and was living alone for the first time, and the freedom it gave me inspired me to make a change I'd wanted for years. I spent the next eighteen months on my weight-loss journey, dropping eighty pounds in the process without any surgery or drugs—I did it the good, old-fashioned way by changing what I ate and developing a consistent exercise routine.

During that time I learned a lot about myself, and realized that my weight served as the root of many things I had continuously struggled with throughout my life, but hadn't realized were influenced by my weight. My body image issues were obviously related to my weight, but the feeling that I couldn't pursue my dreams and achieve them was not so obviously connected. As I gradually began losing the weight, I came to understand that things like my lack of confidence and difficulty being assertive stemmed not only from the direct experiences of having been a fat child, but from the patterns, habits, and "truths" I had acquired while I was overweight.

Once I hit my ultimate weight-loss goal and reached 150 pounds, I was much more confident and comfortable with myself, but still noticed vestiges of my previous "fat self" peeking through. I figured it would just take time—I had been fat for twenty years, and I had to adjust to being a normal weight. After keeping off the weight for more than ten years, though, I started to get increasingly frustrated that the things I knew were associated with my weight hadn't evaporated—why was I still ashamed of my body? Still embarrassed to eat in public? Still insecure about being photographed? It was then that

I realized that it was permanent—that despite the fact that I had lost weight, *I would forever be the adult product of a fat child*; in essence, always the fat kid. It was as much a part of me as is the cultural influence of someone who grows up in a foreign country—instead of growing up French, I had grown up Fat. No matter what I looked like today, it didn't change who I was back then. Once I realized that, I was able to approach those hold-overs from a new angle, knowing how deep-seated they were, and begin to try to address them. As a public health professional, I could conceptualize what was happening to me in familiar terms and languages—I had a chronic condition that resulted from years of various childhood exposures ranging from physical to social. As a result, I had a syndrome of side effects, if you will. As Bryant and I explored this shared phenomenon during the early conversations that formed the premise of this book, we realized how much of an impact it was having not only on our own lives, but more importantly the impact it was having nationwide.

BRYANT

Jacob and I had very different experiences. While I was an overweight child, it didn't last my entire childhood—I was only overweight until the age of about twelve. Toward the end of my sixth-grade year I decided I'd had enough, and spent the summer exercising while I watched television. So simple, yet so effective: while I watched *The Price is Right* and Bob Barker implored me to spay or neuter my pets, I worked out on exercise machines. Three months of exercise and a well-timed growth spurt later, I went back-to-school clothes shopping. Out of habit, my family went to the store we typically shopped at for my "husky" jeans. As I tried on jeans and the sizes kept going down and down, I crossed my fingers and tried on a pair of "regular jeans"—and I'll never forget that feeling when they fit: I was officially no longer a fat kid. When I went back to school nearly unrecognizable in the fall, I could immediately tell a difference not only in how people treated me, but more importantly in how I treated myself.

I maintained my weight loss throughout the rest of my schooling and have seen the benefits that being a normal-weight teenager has provided. Like Jacob, though, I noticed carry-overs from the insecurities that had developed very early in my childhood. Following my clinical psychology training, I started to explore why this would be, and as Jacob and I began to approach this book we realized how developmentally intertwined our weight as a child is with so many aspects of our lives. The further we explored, the more we found— and the more we realized the intricate and widespread impact it was having on generations of children.

Our experiences were quite different, and have given us very unique perspectives on what it truly means not only to *be* a fat child, but more importantly what it means to *have been* a fat child. In this book, we have brought together decades of existing research with our own, and included that additional quality gained by two people who have lived what they are describing. We hope that it will help others who have experienced what we call "Fat Kid Syndrome" to see what impact it has had in their own lives, and help others realize the importance of changing the surging tide we are seeing of ever-fatter generations of children.

This book would not have been possible without our families. We thank *each* of you for your never-ending patience and support. This book would also never have come to be without the relentless efforts of our editor at Palgrave Macmillan, Luba Ostashevsky, who saw something in two researchers with a vision for a book that would push the envelope of the childhood obesity discussion and wasn't afraid to point out anything that would help make our message as strong as possible. We know our obsession with details was trying at times, and we appreciate your continued support.

INTRODUCTION

The Secret Word Is "Fat"

Let's face it. Children today are *fat*.

That word may make your skin crawl, as it has almost become a "dirty word" in our society, but let's call things what they are. As a generation, today's children are fatter than ever before. *One out of every three children in America is now clinically fat,* dwarfing the rates we have seen in previous generations. We have moved from Generation X to Generation XL.

Despite the ever-increasing presence of fat children, as a culture we have shied away from the word "fat"—we call overweight children "husky" or "big-boned," or the clinical-sounding "obese." All of these terms mask the underlying issues at play. Describing a child as "husky" or "big-boned" completely avoids the underlying truth. While the term "obese" is technically accurate, it has shifted the way we view being overweight from being a personal issue into the realm of being a medical *condition*.

But as we will discover throughout this book, obesity is a *behavior*, not a *disease*. The vast majority of overweight children are overweight simply because of diet and exercise behaviors that depend upon the choices made not only by them, but also by their parents and by society at large. By describing these children with a medical term such as "obese," we move fatness into the nebulous category of "disease," allowing us to give up responsibility. This only serves to reinforce the notion that obesity should be *treated*—that it is the responsibility of medicine, and not our own individual behaviors, to fix it. This is the same reasoning that in the past led us to give our children amphetamines to help them lose weight.[1]

It was not a *disease* that swept through America, but a wave of *behavior changes*. Obesity is a symptom of these changes, and up until now we have woefully underestimated the wide-reaching impact that this will have on future generations.

ALWAYS THE FAT KID: THE FAT KID SYNDROME

We frequently hear that "regardless of the cause," children are fatter than ever. That cause is, however, the key. In trying to find the cause of our children becoming fat, scientists and physicians have spent a lot of time, money, and energy on finding a perfect definition of "fat." When doing research, scientists rely on precision and cutoffs—absolutes are desired over shades of gray so researchers can place their subjects into boxes: fat vs. not fat. Then they can look at the other differences between their boxes to see what's tied to being overweight. Weight simply cannot be placed into a box—scientists can't look at you and tell you at what exact weight you will become "overweight." Finding a magic cutoff is simply unimportant: even without a clear boundary between normal and fat, we can look at our children today and know that weight is out of control.

Regardless of how you define it, being fat has long-ranging impacts on multiple aspects of children's lives both in youth and in adulthood—so much so that childhood obesity has become the single largest health concern facing children today. Because of their weight, children are now presenting with "adult" diseases such as adult-onset diabetes and atherosclerosis (a hardening of the arteries previously only seen in late adulthood). The problem has become so pronounced that people who developed adult-onset diabetes as children are starting to have *heart attacks in their thirties*. As a result of all of these unprecedented changes, for the first time in history our children are predicted to have a *shorter* life expectancy than their parents.

While the health effects are severe, we have yet to fully recognize the fact that obesity impacts much more than a child's physical health. Simply focusing on the physical health aspects of childhood obesity (as we have for over a decade now) neglects the degree to which weight impacts nearly all aspects of a child's life. One might assume that simply losing the weight takes away all the impact of obesity on a child. This is not true even for physical health risks, as considerable health effects remain regardless of the loss of weight.

Beyond physical health, being overweight as a child impacts the long-term mental and social health of the individual later in adulthood. Our personalities, fundamental views of the world, and the ways in which we view ourselves in relation to others are all shaped during the developmental periods of childhood and adolescence. Thus, a fat child forms a fundamentally "fat" way of interacting with the world. Even if an individual who was overweight as a child has been able to beat the odds and bring their weight to a normal range in adulthood, the personality and social interaction styles they developed as an overweight child carry over into their adult lives.

For example, overweight children who develop shame regarding their bodies will not suddenly view their adult bodies differently just because they have been able to lose weight. Similarly, an overweight child who learned that the best way to fit in was to make fun of himself and be the "butt" of jokes will likely continue this pattern as an adult (whether or not he is overweight in adulthood).

In essence, being an overweight child creates a lasting syndrome of physical health risks, mental health concerns, problematic behaviors, and personality characteristics—a "Fat Kid Syndrome," or a collection of diverse effects that will shape their future. The Fat Kid Syndrome will impact our future generations across many aspects of their lives if we do not focus on *preventing* childhood obesity. We must focus on preventing our children from becoming overweight in the first place, since targeting overweight children to reduce their weight will not prevent the full impact of childhood obesity. The responsibility for this lies with all of us, but particularly with parents, as we will see throughout this book. Not because childhood obesity is entirely their fault, but because parents hold the key to bringing about the necessary changes in their children's lives.

Always the Fat Kid is designed to raise awareness about what the full impact of childhood obesity is so as a society we can begin to recognize how much of an impact the childhood obesity epidemic will have on our children. We must take strides to reduce weight among children, but more importantly, we must work to prevent them from becoming overweight in the first place.

An ounce of prevention in this case is quite literally worth a pound of cure.

ONE

The Battle of the Bulge

By Numbers

Chances of a child being struck by lightning: 1 out of 1,000,000[1]

Chances of a child being in a car accident: 4 out of 100[2]

Chances of a child graduating from college: 30 out of 100[3]

Chances of a child becoming fat: 33 out of 100[4]

Chances of a fat child becoming a fat adult: 80 out of 100[5]

Think for a moment about these odds, and the amount of time and energy we put into either preventing or encouraging those outcomes. We ticket parents who do not have their children in seatbelts, and have extensive school-zone speed limit laws to protect them from motor vehicle injury. We have entire national systems in place to encourage education and support our children in attaining a college education, even putting a significant portion of our tax money into it—in essence mandating that it is our civic duty. In some states, we even *pay* for college to help as many students as possible to receive a college diploma. But we do very little to prevent childhood obesity, the most likely of these outcomes.

We have certainly arrived at the point where our children are experiencing near-irreparable harm as a generation, but we did not get to this point overnight. The causes of the continuous shift toward weight gain are deep rooted and incredibly complex, but much of the problem has come from a history of ignoring both the presence of the issue and its long-term impact.

THE WORST-KEPT SECRET IN AMERICA

Why has the seemingly innocuous bathroom scale become our enemy? It is always there in your bathroom, just waiting for you to call on it. It always tells you the truth, no matter how much you don't want to hear it. And it never, *ever*, tells someone else your secret weight. But we've become so weight sensitive that we want to hide from the scale—if we don't know our own weight, then we can't get upset about what it is. In essence, we can keep our weight secret even from ourselves.

About that "secret," though—*weight is not secret*. It is one of the most obvious and plainly visible facts about ourselves, no matter how hard we might try to mask it in dark colors, vertical stripes, or multiple pairs of Spanx. And by masking it, not talking about it, pretending it's not there, we have created an environment of weight ignorance. And weight is like a wild animal—you should never turn your back on it.

In the case of our children, we have most definitely turned our backs on the beast. The weight of our children has slowly progressed to the point of being a true public health crisis. Many researchers saw the problems coming years ago, but we were either unable or unwilling to consider the fact that we were truly harming our children—that it wasn't just a little extra weight, but something that was going to have a dramatic and systemic impact. The cumulative health effects are so pronounced that obesity is quite literally taking years off children's lives, and that represents an ultimate failure on our part as a society.

To help frame the rest of our discourse, let's first take a look at definitions of fatness for children. You may be surprised at how complex these definitions are, but as we move through this book it will help give us a vocabulary for both describing weight and for seeing what role misperceptions and simple semantics have had in sustaining our children's weight problems.

MEASURING FAT

So how do we actually determine if someone is or is not fat? In general, most methods separate individuals into four groups: underweight, normal weight, overweight, and obese. For our purposes, the two levels of "fat" are, of course, overweight and obese. In scientific terms, being "overweight" means that an individual is at increased risk for health-related complications because of their elevated body *weight*. People in this range are generally no more than 35 pounds overweight. Individuals past this range are considered "obese," meaning that they are at high risk for health-related complications (particularly diabetes and a variety of heart diseases) due to elevated levels of body *fat*. At the high end of obesity lies "morbid obesity," which indicates an individual is at *severe* risk for health-related complications and, more often than not, already has one or more medical conditions directly related to their weight.

There is no precise way to determine the exact point at which someone transitions from being normal weight to being overweight, or from overweight to obese. Weight is a continuum, and a person's "ideal weight" is as individual to them as a fingerprint. Unfortunately, the lack of a universal "cutoff" allows people to somewhat ignore the problem until it becomes extreme.

Much of the difficulty in classifying people by their weight comes from the fact that when looking at health, we cannot simply consider an individual's weight by itself; other factors, such as height and body composition (amount of muscle vs. fat), are essential in determining a person's ideal weight. Defining obesity is a tricky concept in general because of this, and countless methods ranging from newfangled "impedance machines" (which estimate your body fat by sending a jolt of electricity through your body) to submersion tanks (which determine your body volume and by proxy the amount of fat in your body by seeing how much water you displace when you are submerged in a tank) have been invented in an attempt to clarify the topic. As these methods are obviously not suitable for widespread use, a more simplistic method had to emerge. The main consideration with weight is that a method of determining if someone is overweight must be able to say that for a given *height*, that individual has too much *weight*. As a result, the most common method of measuring the appropriateness of weight is the body mass index (which is calculated directly from an individual's height and weight alone).

BODY MASS INDEX

Estimating what portion of an individual's weight is attributable to fat has been a target of science for over 150 years, long before obesity was perceived as a threat to the health of the population. In the first half of the nineteenth century, Adolphe Quetelet proposed what was then referred to as the "Quetelet Index," which was a simple ratio of a person's weight in kilograms to their height in meters squared. This method was among the first to attempt to take the individual's height into account when determining a "normal" weight. This index was coined the body mass index (or BMI) more than one hundred years later. Nowadays, countless websites offer "free BMI calculators" that claim to tell you what the ideal weight is for a person of your height, and "BMI" has started to become a part of our general vocabulary. While its utility in describing groups of people has been well-recognized, the BMI was never intended to be used to diagnose individual health. In essence, it was designed to tell us how overweight a *group of people* is, not a single individual. But because of its relative simplicity and its ability to combine height and weight into a single health indicator, it has become by far the most widespread measure of weight ranges currently in use.

To calculate BMI, you take weight in pounds, divide it by height in inches twice, then multiply by 703. For instance, the BMI for a 180-pound man who is 5'8" tall (or 68 inches) would be: $180 \div 68 \div 68 \times 703$, which would be a BMI of 27.4.

The range of BMIs considered "normal" has changed over time, and has only been concretely defined for adults (not children). Currently, adults with a BMI between 25 and 30 are considered overweight, and adults with a BMI of 30 or greater are considered obese. These cutoff levels were revised under the recommendation of the National Institutes of Health (NIH) in 1998, perhaps in response to growing concerns over the weight of the nation.[6] Prior to 1998, a BMI had to exceed 27.8 for an individual to be classified as overweight—with the change in BMI cutoffs in 1998 an estimated 25 million Americans who were previously considered normal weight were instantly reclassified as overweight to reflect the latest scientific evidence for the risk their weight was placing on their overall health. Prior to the new cutoffs, despite being at risk because of their weight, they were told they were normal and did not need to lose weight. This early misperception of healthy weight helped put in place a culture that was more accepting of higher weights, skewing our perception of what is "normal." Further reflecting the cultural nature of notions of ideal weight is the fact that some countries, such as Japan and Singapore, have even stricter BMI cutoffs than the U.S. *revised* standards; for instance, both of these Asian countries use a BMI of 23 as the transition point between normal weight and overweight.[7]

Let's consider the standardized overweight cutoffs in weight for an average-height man. For the average man who is 5 feet 9 inches tall, a BMI of 27.8 (the original cutoff) was about 190 pounds. For a BMI of 25 (the current cutoff), overweight is reached at 169 pounds (a 21-pound difference). For Japan's definition of a BMI of 23, overweight would be reached at 156 pounds, representing a difference of *nearly 35 pounds* between the original U.S. definition of overweight and the current Japanese definition. The cutoffs are constantly debated, but the variation that exists indicates the wide range of weights that are considered "normal" even using a *standardized* measure—it's no wonder none of us knows what an ideal weight really is.

As you can see, while it gives a nice, tidy number, BMI is not easy to interpret. Even beyond the relative arbitrariness of the cutoffs, one of the main challenges that the BMI presents is the fact that the number doesn't have any meaning in and of itself. If I know my BMI is 26, it doesn't tell me how much weight I need to lose, or how much my risk has increased. This severely limits its usefulness in everyday practice, but despite this fact it has become widespread not only in the research community, but also in the general public.

For lack of another option, in the remainder of this chapter we will consider an adult BMI of 25 as the cutoff for overweight and an adult BMI of 30 as the cutoff for obesity (as these are the federally defined criteria used in the United States today). BMI cutoffs for morbid obesity are less clear, and vary by agency, but typically involve BMIs of 40 or higher; a common definition of morbid obesity is also being more than 100 pounds overweight (regardless of actual BMI). These definitions only apply to adults though—measures of obesity in children are even more complicated (if you can believe that).

CHILDREN: FAT OR NOT FAT?

Measuring weight status in children is significantly complicated by the fact that children's bodies change over time. If a four-year-old has gained five pounds, is it developmentally related, or is it excess weight? When you think about it, it's even possible that the five-pound weight gain is not enough for where the child is developmentally. How can we determine if that child's weight gain, and therefore the underlying weight itself, is appropriate?

The first set of childhood weight standards was used in the United States in 1977 to help parents determine if their child was growing appropriately. They were based upon data that had been collected for decades by the National Center for Health Statistics within the Centers for Disease Control and Prevention (CDC). As the federal agency tasked with actively protecting the nation's health through prevention, CDC has been one of the most active federal agencies in addressing childhood obesity. CDC researchers are also responsible for monitoring the overall health status of the nation, and as such have unique resources and continuous research studies that allow them to best quantify where children's weights stand for the purposes of developing population norms. Based on their data drawn from tens of thousands of U.S. children, the CDC developed comprehensive growth charts that defined where any child's height and weight fell in comparison to others of their age.

Unfortunately, at the original construction of the national growth charts in 1977, childhood obesity was so far off the federal radar that a chart was not even created for BMI. At the time, all you could do was compare the weight of your six-year-old to the weight of other six-year-olds; you could not compare BMIs, which would take the children's height into account. While there were height-to-weight charts included in the 1977 release, they were not based on any scientific standard, such as the BMI, and were of limited utility. Again, at the time, federal officials were not focused on the need to establish overweight and obesity cutoff scores, so it simply did not happen. This oversight in the original 1977 charts left no true national comparison point that could be used to set a standard for childhood weight. These 1977 charts remained the "gold standard" for assessing healthy childhood growth for more than twenty years, during which time children as a whole became heavier and heavier (without any comparison point for us to truly measure what was happening).

As the childhood obesity epidemic began to grow, medical experts realized that the lack of an established system to classify the appropriateness of children's weights was dramatically impairing their ability not only to track the growing problem, but even to tell a parent if their child was overweight. In a vivid display of what can happen when scientists and policy-makers become so bogged down in the details that they lose sight of the big picture, the debate over the relatively straightforward question "When is a child fat?" has raged on for decades. In the process, the issue has become so obfuscated that it is absolutely no surprise that as a society we missed what was happening. Case in point: almost exclusively because of arguments over semantics (literally), *until the year 2010 there was* no *BMI that a child could reach that would lead them to be classified as obese using federal standards.*[8] The worst a child could be called was overweight, and even that label required unreasonably high levels of excess weight.

How did this happen? Well, the effort to define appropriate weight for children started out with the best of intentions. As of the 1990s there were no widely functional measures to determine the appropriate weight of a child; techniques that attempted to move beyond a child's simple weight relied upon methods that actually physically measured body fat using calipers (pincers that measure the thickness of the fat layer under the skin) or through other physical measures of the actual quantity of *fat*, not weight. This unfortunately left not only physicians, but also the general public, without an easy method to determine if their child had reached a concerning weight.

What to do? Naturally, form a committee. Mirroring the movement toward the use of BMI in adults (and thereby height-adjusting the associated weight), a federal expert committee was appointed in the mid-1990s to decide what official measure and what cutoffs of that measure should be used to determine at what point a child has reached obesity (with BMI identified as the most likely candidate). The panel included leading obesity experts and was populated and shaped by the American Medical Association, the American Academy of Pediatrics, the Centers for Disease Control and Prevention, the National Center for Education in Maternal and Child Health at Georgetown University, and the Maternal and Child Health Bureau of the federal Health Resources and Services Administration.[9] After much deliberation, the committee came to the conclusion that, despite its known limitations, BMI should be the official measure used to determine the weight status of children.

Ironically, in the first of many steps that would only serve to mystify the process, the committee tasked with creating an official federal measure for *obesity* got so bogged down in precision that they entirely rejected the use of the word "obesity" for *any* level of BMI (their own chosen measure). Stating that BMI is technically a measure of *weight* and not of *body fat*, the committee decreed that the traditional "overweight" and "obese" continuum used for adults should not be used for children, and instead created two levels of childhood fatness: "at risk for overweight" and "overweight." Their argument for not using "obese" to describe the highest BMIs? You couldn't be "sure" that a child at any BMI technically had too much body *fat*; there could always be a child with extreme muscle mass or another non-fat related issue that skewed their BMI.

Seriously?

So in their efforts to prevent the rare child who may technically have a high BMI but not have too much body fat from being classified as obese, the committee decided to *wholesale* reject call-ing *any* child obese based on their BMI. Keep in mind that, as we've discussed, BMI is the gold standard for measuring obesity in adults, for whom this effect is no different—you can just as easily have an adult who has a BMI above a certain level that does not actually have too much fat in their body. In a move not retracted until 2010, the federal government agreed with and implemented these defini-tions, supporting a functional ban of the use of the word "obese" to describe a child's BMI.

Potentially even more harmful than avoiding the word "obese" was the way in which the committee decided to set the standards for BMI. To address concerns regarding developmental appropri-ateness of weight gains, the committee defined weight statuses for children based upon how a child's BMI compares to other children their age, rather than just basing the cutoff on the actual BMI itself. So it became less about what a child's BMI actually is, and more about how that child's BMI compares to others their age (the logic being that a higher BMI might be appropriate at certain ages based upon the physical changes occurring during that developmental stage). At first glance, this seems reasonable, but it has led to the complete masking of the prevalence of obesity in our children—if a population is *already* overweight, how can you decide on a healthy weight based on an arbitrary cutoff created from comparisons to the same already overweight population?

To match the committee's recommendation of using BMI as the official measure of childhood weight, the CDC revised their 1977 growth charts in 2000, at which point a BMI-for-age chart was included for the first time. This came too little, too late though—when these first BMI charts were created, we were already well into the childhood obesity epidemic and our snapshot was of a popu-lation that was already too fat. While the growth charts included data collected since the 1970s, it also included data from the 1990s, well into the growing problem. Despite this, we considered the population "normal," leading us to severely underestimate the problem of childhood weight in 2000. This has helped directly lead to the disastrous results we are currently facing—until 2000, we had no BMI chart to show how bad things were, and once that chart was in place, things had to *continue* to degrade for us to notice it.

Combining the committee's recommended cutoffs with the CDC's 2000 growth charts (available at http://www.cdc.gov/growth-charts), the federal government officially defined a child as "at risk for overweight" if he or she was in the eighty-fifth percentile for BMI, meaning that the child was heavier than 85 percent of other children their age, and defined a child as "overweight" if he or she was in the ninety-fifth percentile, meaning they were heavier than 95 percent of children their age (in both cases taking the child's height into account by using BMI rather than actual weight). So with these measures in place, because of the decision to label the heaviest children as overweight instead of obese, in 2000 only 5 percent of children were designated as overweight and *none* were designated as obese. These definitions meant that a child could be heavier than 94 children out of 100, and not even be called over-weight. Even though there was an obvious problem with childhood obesity in our nation, these official definitions left the nation with-out a recognized population-level measure for obesity. In essence, at the federal level, childhood obesity did not exist.

Once the CDC defined childhood weight using these national, data-based measures, they quickly became nearly universally accepted and represented the official federal definitions of child-hood obesity. Or, rather, childhood "overweightness." Again, though, these definitions were based on an already overweight population, and the percentiles should have been much lower. Even more problematic was the message sent to parents that there was no such thing as childhood obesity: children were at worst over-weight, and much more likely only "at risk for overweight." When the committee decided on the label "at risk for overweight," they meant it to represent a group who could possibly already be over-weight, but could accidentally include some children who had an elevated BMI due to other circumstances (extreme muscularity, for instance). So they meant it to imply "your child's weight means that they could possibly be overweight." Instead, once the definition left the cozy ivory tower of research and hit the real world, it came to be interpreted by the public as stating "your child is *not* currently overweight, but could *become* overweight." The misunderstanding could not have come at a worse time and led parents to believe that their children who were at elevated risk for severe physical conse-quences were actually in a normal weight range.

Despite the obvious growing problem of childhood obesity and mounting pressure from the research community and physicians, the CDC refused to officially label children as obese based upon BMI for over a decade. It was not until the year 2010 that the CDC officially changed their labels, reclassifying children in the eighty-fifth percentile as overweight and those in the ninety-fifth percen-tile as obese. Finally, we had "obese" children, but by then it was far too late. With the revised definition, 30 percent of our children were overweight, and half of those were obese. So we went from 5 percent of children being overweight in 2000 to 15 percent being *obese* in 2010, just because of a faulty definition.

In a move that only served to further cloak reality from both par-ents and children, the same expert committee that recommended the use of the clinical terms "overweight" and "obese" issued the following guidance in 2007 (emphasis added in italicized text):

> Consistent with the 1998 recommendations, the expert committee urges clinicians to be supportive, empathetic, and nonjudgmen-tal. A careful choice of words will convey an empathetic attitude. Adult patients have identified "fatness," "excess fat," and "obe-sity" as derogatory terms, and obese adolescents *prefer* the term "overweight." Younger children and their families may respond

similarly, and *clinicians should discuss the problem with individual families by using more-neutral terms, such as "weight," "excess weight," and "BMI."* Therefore, *the expert committee recommends the use of the clinical terms overweight and obesity for documentation and risk assessment but the use of different terms in the clinician's office,* to avoid an inference of judgment or repugnance.[10]

So literally out of a fear of hurting someone's feelings and because *adolescents prefer it*, an expert committee with representatives from fifteen leading health organizations decided that no physicians should actually tell a parent or child that a child is overweight or obese: *directly avoiding use of the appropriate clinical terms*. Instead, they should use terms that do not nearly adequately convey the severity of the problem—"excess weight" sounds like you're a couple of pounds overweight, not that your chances of *heart disease* are significantly higher. Or, they recommend using the term "BMI," but as we've discussed, BMI is so difficult to understand it would be like explaining cancer using only the term "malignant neoplasm." It also becomes ironic when you remember our discussion of just a few paragraphs ago: even though BMI wasn't considered accurate enough to classify someone as obese until 2010, it's now recommended as a useful term to explain weight to parents.

The concern over "judgment or repugnance" is well-intentioned but misplaced. As we'll see later in this book, weight-related teasing and bullying does have a significant impact on self-esteem, but a *physician* using the proper clinical terms in a doctor's office is *not* bullying. In making the mandate to avoid these terms, physicians have placed the short-term remote potential for minimal psychological distress ahead of the long-term negative consequences associated with being an overweight child. In essence, they have decided that it is not worth it to address the problem head-on, and instead, it is better to veil the problem in politically correct language.

"NORMED" DOES NOT MEAN "NORMAL"

Growth charts have made it extremely difficult to understand where a child's current weight status places them. Not only do you have to know the child's BMI, you also have to know how it compares to others'—requiring access to the CDC charts and the ability to interpret them correctly. This is not that simple—as you can see in Figure 1.1 on the following page, these charts are fairly complex.

More importantly, these definitions come with severe limitations. As mentioned, the current definitions of overweight and obese for children depend upon how heavy they are *in comparison to everyone else*. The troubling aspect of these definitions is that they are based on population norms, meaning that the *more* overweight a population is as a whole, the *less* children will actually be classified as overweight or obese (since the definition is based on comparisons to others). This comparative nature of the definition of childhood obesity has disguised the gradual shift in children's weight, leading us to the point we have reached today.

To illustrate, the current definitions still rely on the growth charts established in 2000. Many argue that these charts are due to be updated and revised (particularly since the CDC has finally agreed to the use of the terms "overweight" and "obese" in relation to the charts). The natural tendency would be to go back into the population and determine the eighty-fifth and ninety-fifth percentiles. However, childhood obesity has tripled since 2000, meaning over 15 percent of children are currently *obese* based on 2000 population norms. In addition, 18 percent of children are non-obese overweight. Therefore, if the CDC were to update their charts using the same method they did in 2000 (classifying the eighty-fifth percentile as the "overweight" cutoff), the obese children would take up all of the 15 percent at the top, and *all children currently classified overweight would be reclassified as normal weight*! Figure 1.2 provides a visual of this effect.

FIGURE 1.1: CDC GROWTH CHART FOR BOYS AGES 2–20

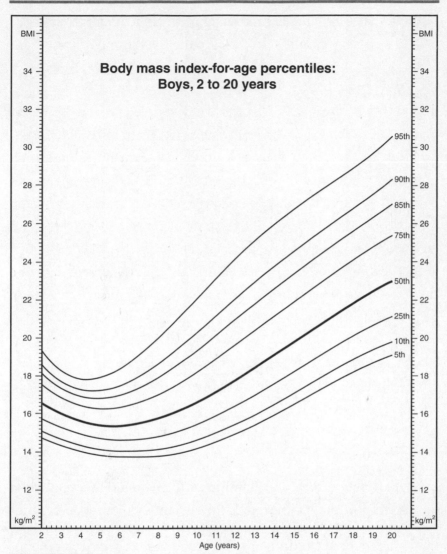

Published May 30, 2000.
SOURCE: Developed by the National Center for Health Statistics in collaboration with the National Center for Chronic Disease Prevention and Health Promotion (2000).

Obviously this does not accurately represent the weight of the population, which could be a large reason why the CDC has yet to update their charts, but nonetheless it points out a fundamental flaw in the way that childhood obesity is currently defined and

FIGURE 1.2: THE PROBLEM OF NORMS

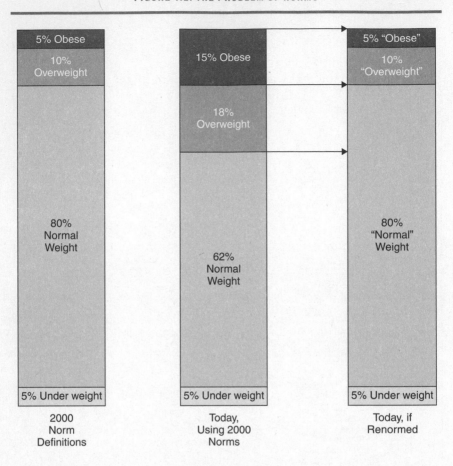

shows part of how the 2000 definition effectively hid the weight of a significant portion of children. If the current method of percentiles is used to define obesity moving forward, the weight a child would have to reach to be classified as overweight or obese will continually *increase* because the population as a whole is getting heavier. For instance, a child who was 20 pounds overweight in 2000 might have been in the ninetieth percentile, while a child who is 20 pounds overweight today might only be in the eightieth percentile, since so many more children are currently heavy. Thus, by updating the growth charts using this method, the CDC would reclassify many children as having a healthy weight, *despite their actual weight not changing.* This is a pitfall of using population norms to define weight status, one that will have to be seriously considered as definitions are updated. This effect does not occur with the methods used to define adult obesity—the BMI cutoffs of 25 and 30 do not vary based upon what is happening in the population; they are fixed cutoffs.

What makes this population-based method even more alarming is that these charts were normed in the midst of the growing obesity problem, meaning that the 2000 charts are *under*estimating the weight problem faced by our children (potentially explaining why so many more adults than children are classified as overweight/obese—it is not due to sudden weight gain right at the point of adulthood, when actual BMI scores are used to define weight status).

Despite its flaws, however, this method has become the "gold standard" for defining levels of fatness for children, due largely to the lack of another suitable method. To counteract this, many have proposed age-specific BMI values that can be used to categorize children as overweight or obese. By setting actual, non-moveable cutoffs, we can prevent the "creep" that can occur when you repeatedly "re-norm" weight based on an increasingly heavy population.

Another issue that emerges when using population norms for childhood obesity is that they do not align with the absolute norms we have empirically tested for assessing adult obesity. What happens when a child transitions from the child BMI population norms to the adult absolute BMI values? Currently, the childhood BMI growth charts stop at age 20, after which a "child" transitions to the adult measurement method. Consider the case of a 6-foot-tall boy who is 19 years and 364 days old. Based on the BMI growth charts, to be overweight he would have to reach a weight of 200 pounds. Compare that to *the next day*, at which point he is overweight at anything over 185 pounds (adult BMI of 25). In other words, as a 19-year-old he can be 15 pounds heavier than he can as a 20-year-old. What makes the situation even worse is that up until two years ago, when the CDC finally revised the labels of weight for children, in order to reach the overweight category that 19-year-old boy would have had to weigh 225 pounds. So in 2009, a 19-year-old 224-pound boy would not have even been *overweight,* but at the age of 20 would have been *obese* and would have needed to lose *forty pounds* to reach a normal weight. Most people think you don't become overweight overnight, and in general they are right—but in the case of children who have just crossed into adulthood, you actually can.

All these problems have compounded to make it very difficult for children and parents to know (accurately) where their weight stands, and what kinds of risks their weight is placing them at. The CDC's recent move to finally use the definitions of "overweight" and "obese" is an important step in the right direction toward help-ing demystify childhood weight. While it is definitely a good thing that these labels have been changed, it will take *generations* before the effects of the old labels wash out—those who were told they were normal-weight children will view the same weights as normal in their own children without significant educational campaigns to reset that mental picture of what a normal weight is. And it still will not change the fact that the line between classifying child and adult obesity has a strong disconnect that must be addressed.

Many people think that the "problem" with childhood obesity today is that we don't take weight seriously enough. While this is definitely a part of the problem, a more insidious process overtook us during which we did not even realize exactly *how* overweight our children were. Go back to that 6-foot-tall teenager and think about what kind of crazy system we had created in which one day he is normal weight, and the next he is more than forty pounds overweight. We weren't taking heavy children seriously enough because we didn't even know they were heavy—we simply didn't have an accurate idea of when weight became problematic. And it's no wonder—the system that was created, and for the most part the system we still have, is so complex and difficult to understand that weight gains passed us by unnoticed.

THE "MAGIC" TRANSITION POINT—WHO CARES?

So unfortunately, there is obviously not a clear, precise way to define what weight truly qualifies a child as being "fat." However, children who are *visibly* far above the weight they should be do not require a precise measurement—we know that children today must lose weight, and that we must break the chain that has led so many of our children to become obese in the first place. Rather than spending our efforts deciding if individuals are in the "border zone," we must focus on those children in the "danger zone" who clearly need help in returning to a normal range of weight. We must also focus on having children stay at a healthy weight from the beginning of their lives. As we'll see on the next page, the number of children who are not at a healthy weight is simply astonishing, and these numbers will have a ripple effect upon our population the likes of which we have never seen.

BY THE NUMBERS

Let's take a look at how BMIs have changed in recent years (knowing the limitations the BMI has as a measure). Compare, for instance, the following maps showing the rates of obesity in adults in 1990 as compared to 2010 (as measured by the CDC's Behavioral Risk Factor Surveillance System—BRFSS—which is used to monitor weight and other health predictors nationwide). In 1990, the *highest* rate of obesity seen in any state was 14 percent. In stark contrast, by 2010, the *lowest* rate seen in any state was 20 percent. This was mirrored by an increase in the average weight

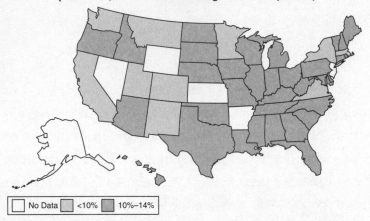

**Obesity Trends* Among U.S. Adults
BRFSS, 1990**
(*BMI ≥ 30, or ~ 30 lbs. overweight for 5´ 4˝ person)

No Data | <10% | 10%–14%

Centers for Disease Control and Prevention: Obesity Trends Among U.S. Adults Between 1985 and 2010. http://www
.cdc.gov/obesity/data/adult.html.

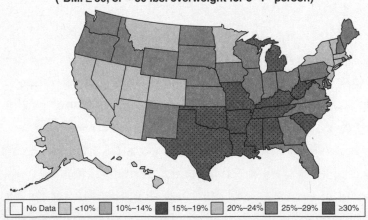

**Obesity Trends* Among U.S. Adults
BRFSS, 2010**
(*BMI ≥ 30, or ~ 30 lbs. overweight for 5´ 4˝ person)

No Data | <10% | 10%–14% | 15%–19% | 20%–24% | 25%–29% | ≥30%

Centers for Disease Control and Prevention: Obesity Trends Among U.S. Adults Between 1985 and 2010. http://www
.cdc.gov/obesity/data/adult.html.

of the adult American by 24 pounds between 1960 and 2002.[11] By 2015, it is estimated that 75 percent of all adults will be overweight, with 41 percent clinically obese.[12] That would mean that only one out of every four adults would be at a healthy weight—largely because of the generations of overweight children who will be reaching adulthood soon.

Similar trends are seen in children; in the late 1980s and 1990s, childhood obesity increased from 5 percent to over 15 percent, tripling in a remarkably short amount of time.[13] Currently, one out of every three children is overweight or obese. Given the similar trajectory seen in the adult population, this change is not surprising; in fact, its co-occurrence with the sharp increase in adult obesity may have masked its full magnitude—if rates had only been increasing in children, it would have been much more noticeable and intervention may have begun much sooner. We have clearly reached a crisis point, as these levels are beginning to impact the ability of our children to lead healthy, productive lives—lives that are, for the first time ever, getting *shorter* than those of previous generations.

LIFE EXPECTANCY

"Life expectancy," or the number of years an individual can expect to live, is a measure frequently used to discuss the health of a population. At the turn of the previous century, the life expectancy of a newborn in the United States in 1900 was around forty-seven years.[14] In 2000, thanks in large part to advances in immunizations and medicines, that number had steadily grown to almost seventy-seven years. In 2005, however, a group of researchers from the University of Illinois projected that the growth in life expectancy we had come to expect was slowing, if not reversing—they predicted that the obesity epidemic would conservatively *remove* up to three-quarters of a year of life from average life expectancy, and that the cumulative effect could end up shortening the lives of children to the point that

they can no longer expect to have longer lives than their parents.[15]
That might not seem like a significant change, but given the centuries of advancement that have occurred (excepting years influenced
by wars), any regression is, quite simply, historic. And a backslide
that shortens lives across a *generation*, not a single year, has never
occurred. So, unless the obesity epidemic is reversed, despite all
the medical advances, new medications, and cutting-edge vaccina-
tions we have developed, we will have regressed to the point that
our children will have the life expectancy they would have had a
quarter century ago.

This shift in weight will continue decreasing the lifespan of
our citizens. Consider for instance Table 1.1, showing the average
life expectancy of a variety of countries of differing technologi-
cal advancement and socioeconomic levels. Most people assume
that the United States has one of the longest, if not *the* longest, life
expectancies because of our leadership in medication development
and astonishing expenditures per capita in health care. This could
not be further from the truth—in fact, recent estimates place the
United States *fiftieth* in life expectancy worldwide. To truly put it in

TABLE 1.1: LIFE EXPECTANCY IN THE UNITED STATES AND
OTHER COUNTRIES[16]

Rank	Country	Life Expectancy
1	Monaco	89.7
3	Japan	83.9
8	Hong Kong	82.1
9	Australia	81.9
10	Italy	81.9
12	Canada	81.5
18	Israel	81.1
29	Jordan	80.2
30	United Kingdom	80.2
41	South Korea	79.3
45	Bosnia & Herzegovina	79.0
50	United States	78.5
59	Cuba	77.9
60	Libya	77.8

perspective, *life expectancy in the United States is currently shorter than in South Korea and in Bosnia and Herzegovina*, and the full effects of obesity on life expectancy have yet to be realized.

Our eroding life expectancy has been attributed nearly entirely to the staggering rates of childhood obesity. As discussed in later chapters, we are now seeing "adult" diseases, such as Type 2 diabetes, more and more frequently in children. Known by many as "adult-onset diabetes," it is tied almost exclusively to being overweight. Recent studies have even shown that the arteries of obese children look like those of *forty-five-year-olds,* and overweight children with diabetes are expected to start having heart attacks in their thirties to forties (rather than fifties to sixties).

CONCLUSION

If the situation appears so bleak, what then do we do? The first step is to recognize the extent of the problem, which we hope this chapter has helped you to do. The next step is to recognize how we got to this point. The following two chapters explore diet and exercise—and how changes to those behaviors have led to the staggering increases in childhood obesity.

TWO

Obesity Is a Behavior, Part One

Oodles of Calories

On her first day "in the field" at her new job as a community health coordinator, Amber was nervous to make a presentation at a local school. Her boss had sent her to one of the middle schools in the district's most rural area to talk to seventh-grade children about the importance of eating fruits and vegetables. Amber assembled the materials for the presentation she had been trained to deliver, putting lettuce, tomatoes, cucumbers, broccoli, squash, spinach, and onions into her basket and packing it with her portable hot-plate. She loaded up her Honda and headed to the remote school, her GPS barking orders along the way as she passed cornfields, tobacco fields, and countless other varieties of farmland. Having moved to the region from a very urban area, she thought it would be easy to explain vegetables to kids who grew up right next to major farms.

About the time her GPS lost all touch with reality and tried to navigate her straight through a cattle pasture, she arrived at the school. She headed to her assigned classroom and set out her supplies for the cooking demonstration. As the children arrived, she asked the teacher who the most outgoing student in the class was so she could partner with the student to get the class engaged in the demonstration. He quickly pointed out a spunky twelve-year-old who happily jumped to the front of the classroom to assist Amber, who started out with her standard spiel:

"Good morning, everyone! My name is Amber, and I am suuuper excited to be here today to talk to you about how important fruits and vegetables are! Real quick, everyone raise their hands who had a vegetable with dinner last night."

As usual, only a handful of children raised their hands. Amber continued: "Okay! Well you're all going to have some today. Can anyone tell me why you should eat fruits and vegetables?"

A shy young boy in the front row raised his hand. Amber smiled at him, using all her training to help the boy feel comfortable. The boy smiled back and quietly said, "to make you big and strong."

Perfect, Amber thought. "That's right! To make you big and strong, like Popeye! Who knows what Popeye eats to make him super strong?"

"Spinach!" almost the entire class rang out.

"That's right, spinach! And you may not know this, but spinach doesn't come from a can. It's actually grown in the ground and looks like this." She held up the raw spinach and passed it around the class. The children laughed, several of them muttering that they didn't want to eat leaves. "It actually is a kind of leaf, but it is very, very good for you. You can eat it just like that in a salad, or you can cook it and eat it that way. When it's cooked it looks like what Popeye eats, but I wouldn't eat it cold right out of a can—that wouldn't be very good! It's much better warm." Concerned eyes looked up at her. "I promise I won't make you eat any today; we'll be trying broccoli and cucumbers instead."

Amber smiled to herself, glad that she had gotten past the vegetable no one ever recognized. She decided to move to a familiar one to help get the class engaged. She turned to her energetic assistant. "We're going to start on the cucumber now. Can you pass it to me so I can start slicing it?"

The girl looked at her with panic in her eyes, her hand hovering tentatively over the squash. Under her breath, she whispered, "Ms. Amber, I don't know what a cucumber is…"

L et's address something basic, yet important. Food is good. *Really, really* good. We would venture a hefty bet that you've met very few people in your life who don't view meals as some of the best times of the day. There are entire television stations devoted exclusively to food, and they have quite an audience. And really, who can blame us for loving food? It satisfies the most basic need of the human body, and as such, our bodies have hardwired us to find it, savor it, and almost always look for more. Our propensity to gain weight is shaped by our evolution, and it's hard to combat a few million years of human evolution. In the early days of human development, obesity was protective—being able to pack on a few extra pounds helped us last through winters, droughts, and food shortages. Today, though, the majority of us do not struggle against such things and the desire to eat more than needed has far outlasted its utility.

As we all know, gaining weight is simple—just take in more calories than you burn. At first it seems like it's all about food intake, but it's not. There are two variables at play—food consumption and calorie burning—and both are dramatically impacting the weight status of our children. If you exercise the same amount you've always exercised but start eating more calories, you will gain weight. If you eat the same amount you've always eaten but become less active, you will gain weight. And when you look at what has happened with our children, they are eating more *and* exercising less—not a good combination.

All this leads to one main point: obesity is a *behavior*. It is not a disease or medical condition caused by a genetic defect, insidious bacteria, or toxic chemical. Obesity is really an accumulation of hundreds and thousands of bad decisions—nothing more.

We don't typically think of obesity in those terms, but that's what it is: choices and resulting behaviors. Our behaviors dictate our weight, and our unwillingness to control our own behaviors (or for our discussion, those of our children) are what have led to the problems we are facing today. Yes, there are those who have genetic conditions that influence their weight, but we can assure you that the human genome has not shifted enough in the past twenty years to account for the skyrocketing rates of obesity that we are seeing today. This change is not medical or genetic; at its most basic, this change has been a *choice*. We choose to be fat.

As it is not a medical condition, and more accurately reflects consequences of daily choices, obesity is viewed by some through the lens of impulse control and addiction. Unlike other problem behaviors such as drinking or drug use, though, we can't simply cut out eating—it is essential to our survival.

But this "addiction" is not new—we have always relied upon food in a way that is only rivaled by our need for oxygen. What underlies the sudden change in the addiction? The question is not "Why are we fat?" We *know* what makes us fat. The question instead is, "Why have our *behaviors* changed so drastically?" As such, we must focus on what underlies the *behaviors*, not the outcome.

FOOD—WHAT'S NEW?

We all know the many ways in which food rewards us and is used to reward our children—very few of us can say that we have never boosted ourselves with food. The soul-filling taste of fried chicken, the luxury of an expensive meal, or the silky heaven of a tangy slice of strawberry cheesecake. We all do it to ourselves, and unfortunately, the majority of us do it to our children. The associations between food and pleasure, praise, and approval are deep-seated, well-recognized, and hard to change. Food is an integral part of our culture through celebrations as well, tying strong emotions to food at a deep, subconscious level.

These relationships are not new, however, and can't be used to support the rampant spread of childhood obesity. Food has always been an integral part of our culture, and we have seemingly always used food as a reward. There are several factors that have changed recently, however, and the synergy of these changes have spiraled food consumption in the United States out of control. Some of these are familiar, such as the super-sizing of portions and the perils of processed foods, but several others have managed to slip into our very culture in a way that has harpooned us into allowing our children to eat more and more.

SUPER-SIZED PORTIONS

As most people have become aware, portion sizes today are often staggering in comparison to what they were twenty or thirty years ago. Put simply, the problem isn't *seconds*, it's *firsts*. The problem of food portions has become so large that when the USDA recently revised the infamous "food pyramid" they threw it out altogether—the USDA now uses what they call "MyPlate," designed to help individuals learn how to fix a healthier plate by balancing portion sizes.

This might seem drastic, but it was not an overreaction. Recent studies published in the *Journal of the American Medical Association (JAMA)*[1] found that between 1977 and 1998, in fast-food restaurants there was on average a 220-calorie increase *per meal*. Assuming a fast-food meal three times per week, this average increase would equate to children gaining *ten pounds per year* as a result of portion size increases. What's alarming is that portion sizes have continued to grow in the nearly fifteen years since data was collected for that study, further pushing our children toward obesity. Only recently have portion sizes seemed to track downward, and that has likely been as a result of the faltering economy and a demand for less expensive options, not as a result of actually wanting to control portion sizes for health reasons.

Why did we move to larger portion sizes? It's actually simple: the larger the portion, the more perceived value in the restaurant on the part of the consumer, even if the cost increases as well. Unfortunately, the increasing portion sizes at restaurants have also shifted our "normal" for portion sizes at home, where portions have been shown to be increasing right in line with restaurants (if not more).

As portion sizes have continued to grow, they have far exceeded the guidelines for portions set forth by the Food and Drug Administration (FDA) and the United States Department of Agriculture (USDA). In fact, some portions are staggeringly large. For instance, hamburgers are on average double the recommended size, cooked pasta dishes are six times as large as the recommendation, and cookies—one of our most common snacks—are on average *eight times* the recommended size.[2] The increase in portion size wouldn't be as important if people would eat less of it, but studies have shown that the more food a person is presented with, the more they will eat, even if they are no longer hungry.[3] And given that the 2,300 calories that can come from a super-sized hamburger combo literally take a marathon to burn off,[4] this becomes a very large problem.

More subtle increases in portion sizes have also occurred: when comparing new editions of cookbooks such as *Joy of Cooking* to their older counterparts, identical recipes result in *fewer* servings in the new editions; so an identical quantity of cookie batter that was marked as originally producing twenty-four cookies specifies only eighteen cookies in the new edition, thereby increasing portion sizes without the individual really being aware of it.[5]

What effect has this had on child diet? Regardless of location or origin, a child will eat the amount provided to them. Basically, if you give it, they will eat. Children cannot be expected to decide upon a healthy portion size; their basis of comparison (restaurants and the amounts of food eaten by their parents) is programming them to expect more than is needed, and their bodies will quickly adjust and send signals to over-eat due to millennia-old survival strategies. Interestingly, up until the age of three, children have been shown to have innate portion control mechanisms—they will eat a set amount no matter how much is provided to them. As children age, however, they are gradually socialized to eat more than needed through observing others and being instructed by parents to "clean their plates." This effect comes on so strongly that by the age of five, their intake is linked directly to the amount provided to them and their natural control mechanism is completely lost.[6]

While pressure is beginning to be exerted by local governments in particular to control portion size increases, just stopping the increase in portion sizes will not do the trick—we must look at decreasing them. That will not be popular on the part of the consumer, but if retailers discover that they can shrink portion sizes *and* prices (but maybe not quite as much as they shrink portion sizes), there may actually be more profit in it for them in the long run. Continuing to wag our collective finger at restaurants will not do the trick—where there is demand, supply will follow, unless we present a palatable alternative.

PROCESSED/PREPARED FOODS

One hundred years ago, eating food that was not prepared in the home was a luxury, requiring a trip to a restaurant or the hospitality of a friend. Just a generation ago, 75 percent of all food expenditures were for meals to be prepared at home (as compared to only 50 percent today).[7] Children today eat a large variety of meals made in various places—at home, in schools, in restaurants, and pre-prepared meals that are merely heated up at home.

The problem with this shift in food consumption stems from a fundamental lack of knowledge about what exactly someone is eating. When we eat at restaurants, other than the basic ingredients that are identifiable, we have no idea what, and how much, we are actually consuming. People find themselves eating quantities of ingredients they would never have considered eating if they had actually prepared that meal themselves. For instance, many restaurant meals at major chains contain more than 2,000 mg of sodium. That's nearly an entire teaspoon of salt *per person*. Similarly, large amounts of butter and oil are used that the consumer may not even be aware they are eating. Grilled entrees (thought to be healthy) are frequently made with heavy amounts of butter or oil that significantly raise the calorie and fat content of the meal. These preparation methods are not necessarily new, but as we increase our reliance upon restaurant meals, their impact becomes more pronounced.

While many restaurants now provide their nutritional information online (or more rarely within the restaurant—and frequently then due only to local laws), it is not generally required, and is not typically easily accessed when making meal choices. Even more troubling, studies have shown that these nutrition facts are often grossly underestimated, with one in five menu items being at least one hundred calories more than advertised.[8] This deceives a consumer into thinking they are eating a healthy option or choosing a healthy meal for their child when in fact it may have up to twice the number of calories advertised. This lack of information (and sometimes lack of *accurate* information) impacts what adults eat, and correspondingly what choices they make for their children.

A further complication of dining at restaurants is actually what many consider to be a strength—menu variety. At home, if parents cook grilled chicken with vegetables, that's all that their children can eat because that is the only food choice for that particular meal. When a family dines out, however, the children are presented with a variety of choices, most of which are not healthy. Even if the parents choose healthy options for themselves, without careful guidance (or, more effectively, strict rules) from parents, children are much more likely to eat unhealthy meals—after all, they typically taste better, and nowadays, peer pressure is even an influence ("That's what everyone else is eating, why can't I?"). Unfortunately, children's meals are rarely nutritionally balanced; in fact, studies have found that only 3 percent of fast-food kids' meals meet basic National School Lunch Program guidelines[9] (the criteria used to judge the nutritional makeup of school lunches), guidelines that have been criticized for *not being nutritious enough*. Children are therefore often left making decisions between bad and worse, rather than truly being able to choose healthy meals. While some restaurants now offer healthy side options to children (such as apples instead of French fries), without the guidance from parents to make those decisions, children will choose the unhealthy option almost without fail.

Similar problems arise from frozen dinners and other pre-prepared meals. To counteract the loss of taste that arises from not being fresh, such meals typically have additives (such as additional fat) to improve the taste of the food. Without carefully reading the ingredients and nutrition information of the meals, it is all too easy to end up eating ingredients and quantities that one typically would not eat. Again, as with restaurants, the variety of choices can be negative if the child's choice is not limited at the time of purchase, and children rarely have healthy options even if they were inclined to make a healthy choice. It is *critical* for parents to take a more active role in helping their children choose healthy foods, and if the parent also struggles with making healthy food choices (as do the two out of three adults in the United States who are overweight or obese), they must take the time to learn more about nutrition and what foods their children should be eating. Almost equally important is reestablishing the presence and role of parents in the meal process itself—up to 25 percent of adolescents have less than three family meals *per week*, severely limiting the ability of parents to help shape their children's meals.[10] Family cooking has become so rare that leading medical experts have even called for a return of home economics in an attempt to re-connect children with food and how it is prepared.[11]

FOOD DESERTS

Consistently, residents of low-income areas (ranging from inner city to the most rural locations) have been shown to have higher rates of obesity. For many years, this was assumed to be tied directly to socioeconomic status—healthy foods are more expensive and therefore less likely to be a part of the regular diet of the poor. However, as programs were planned to increase motivation to find affordable healthy food options, a trend was realized: not only could residents of low-income areas not afford food, frequently high-quality food wasn't even available.

Much attention has recently been paid to this problem, and such locations have been dubbed "food deserts." A food desert is a location where a grocery store or supermarket is not readily available, effectively "forcing" people to make unhealthy food choices by getting their food at fast-food restaurants or convenience stores. In these food deserts, even if the will to eat healthy foods is there, the supply is not. Food deserts can involve living more than ten miles away from the nearest source of fresh foods—a daunting distance to travel and transport food for individuals who may rely on public transportation (or in the case of rural areas, where no public transportation is available at all). This problem is widespread and growing; currently, nearly 14 million U.S. residents live in food deserts (see Figure 2.1—food deserts shaded in gray).

While access to healthy foods has always been low in certain areas, changes in the retail market have led many supermarkets and grocery stores to close, leaving more areas than ever unable to access fresh foods. When paired with the explosion of fast-food restaurants seen in recent years, it is not difficult to see how food deserts have contributed to increasing rates of obesity. When the only choice for food is McDonald's or a gas station, nutrition is not exactly easy to find.

THEY'RE GRRRRRRRRRRRRRRREAT! (AND FULL OF SUGAR)

Advertisers have always worked to get us to buy things—watches, cars, almost anything you can name. As prepared foods became an increasing part of our culture, food shifted from being a necessity to being an advertised product. This fundamentally changed the way we saw food; food (including entire meals) went from being a need to being something to be purchased.

FIGURE 2.1: FOOD DESERTS IN THE UNITED STATES

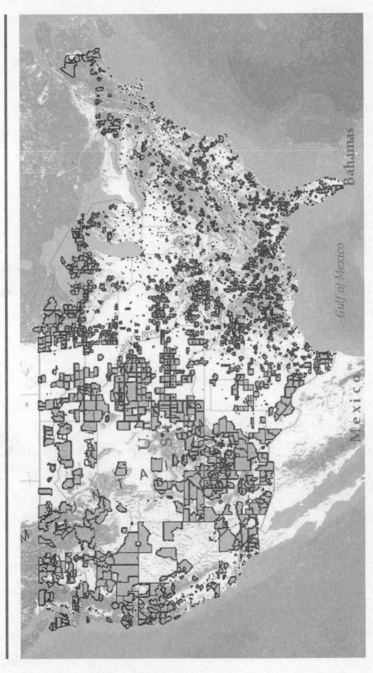

Map generated by the United States Department of Agriculture "Food Desert Locator." www.ers.usda.gov/data-products/food-desert-locator.aspx.

Food is no longer sustenance, it is a *commodity*. And as the commodity nature of food developed, so did the corresponding advertising—this new type of market led advertisers to create campaigns to get parents to buy branded food for their homes. We've all grown up with food advertising geared toward adults, particularly mothers, since they were the ones typically purchasing food. But food advertising has exploded in recent years—by the late 1990s, the food marketing system was the second largest advertising group in the U.S. economy (behind only the automotive industry), comprising nearly 16 percent of all advertising expenditures—more than all other household items combined. Food has become one of the most branded items in America, thanks in large part to its consistent, repeated purchase—food is one of the only things we all must purchase on a regular basis. If a food company can build brand loyalty in a customer, it can lead to hundreds of purchases. Quite simply, food expenditures represent one of the most coveted portions of spending, representing an industry that captures 12.5 cents out of every dollar spent in America.[12]

Food advertising itself is not as new as the current childhood obesity problem. Food has been advertised to us as long as it has been for sale. What has become rampant in recent years, though, is the relentless targeting of children with promotions, catchy jingles, and cartoon characters—anything that will entice a child to beg their parents to purchase a food item.

Children are the most specific target of food advertising—nearly two-thirds of commercials airing during Saturday morning children's programming are for food items.[13] Unfortunately, those food items are rarely healthy—some commercials even parody the fact that if you tell a child a certain food is healthy, they will no longer want to eat it. Children want bright colors and funny-voiced cartoon characters, and with children having more and more "screen time," advertisers quickly realized the immense power children could have over the food expenditures of their parents. After all, it's easy to say no to purchasing a toy—it is not a necessity—but parents have no choice but to purchase food for their children. And if a company such as Disney or Nickelodeon gets a kickback for allowing the use of their characters? All in a day's profit.

The American budget for purchasing food outside the home is at an all-time high—almost half of all food expenditures happen in restaurants, mostly at fast-food restaurants, and the advertising for these venues has increased from representing 5 percent of food advertising in 1980 to 28 percent by the late nineties. As our culture of convenience simultaneously emerged, the impact of fast-food restaurants on the nutrition of our children became unprecedented. In Eric Schlosser's groundbreaking book *Fast Food Nation,* the historic influence of fast food is thrown into dramatic relief. The book uncovers startling facts, among them: McDonald's trademark golden arches are more recognizable than the Christian cross, and there was a more than 1,800 percent increase in fast-food expenditures between 1970 and 2000.[14]

While some may feel that children are not as susceptible to marketing influences as adults, the data is overwhelming, and the precipitous increase in spending on food marketing to children is matched by a similar increase in childhood obesity. As laid out in a 2008 study,[15] in 1983, the *total* amount spent on television advertising to children across all companies was $100 million.[16] By the year 2000, the marketing of food products to youth had reached upwards of $15 *billion.*[17] Burger King alone spent $80 million marketing to children,[18] and Quaker Oats shifted $15 million to advertise just for its cartoon-driven Cap'n Crunch cereal.[19] In the following years, Cap'n Crunch went from being ranked thirteenth in cereal to being touted as "the number-one kids' presweetened brand in the ready-to-eat cereals category."[20]

This explosion in food advertising to children is irrefutably tied to the increase in childhood obesity. Remember, since 2000 when these advertisings began to reach their peak, obesity has *tripled* in children, right on the heels of this staggering increase in child-focused advertising expenditures. Now, fast-food companies alone spend around half a billion dollars per year marketing just their kids' meals.[21] Children are an exceptionally valuable market, with the potential to become lifelong customers if they can be hooked early enough.

One of the most prevalent marketing tactics used by fast food restaurants to bring children into their restaurants is the nearly ubiquitous kids' meals toys, accounting for 75 percent of the child-targeted marketing expenses of fast-food companies.[22] Those toys have recently become a source of controversy, though—in San Francisco, the Board of Supervisors recently put into place a law to ban the inclusion of toys in any children's meals that do not meet certain nutritional standards (even overriding a mayoral veto in the process). A class-action lawsuit against McDonald's filed by the Center for Sciences in the Public Interest (CSPI) is currently pending, in which CSPI, in cooperation with parents, is suing McDonald's over what they claim are illegal marketing techniques that "force" parents to go to fast-food places because of the demands of their children.[23] Such steps are considered radical by many, but are stark indicators of the perceived abuse of advertisers and marketers in targeting children. Experts have repeatedly called for regulation of food marketing to children, something that has been nearly entirely ignored at the federal level.[24] Some chains (including Jack in the Box) have already stopped including toys in their kids' meals, stating that they wish to focus on quality of the food rather than gimmicks to get parents to purchase them.[25] It remains to be seen how many other companies will follow suit, as such methods have been a staple of fast-food restaurants since the 1980s.

Happy Meal toys, funny clowns, and movie tie-ins have been proven very effective at promoting brand association, and in turn, increasing the demands that children make for eating certain foods. In a study completed by researchers at Stanford University,[26] children were presented with identical portions of identical foods, half wrapped in McDonald's branded wrappers and the other half in plain wrappers, and then asked which tasted better. The results were overwhelming, with children preferring food they thought was from McDonald's nearly across the board. One of the most striking findings was that this preference extended to non-prepared foods; children rated milk, juice, and even carrots as better tasting when wrapped in McDonald's wrappers. Further reinforcing the direct link between the role of advertising and this finding, the perceived preferences for "McDonald's" food steadily grew stronger in proportion to the number of television sets in the child's home.

Compounding the strong effect advertising can have on food choice for children is the fact that foods marketed to children rarely meet even basic nutrition guidelines. Across all food advertisements, the highest expenditures are tied to foods that are the most processed and packaged. Even in 1997, only partway into the rising epidemic, the most advertised foods were already cereals, candy, and gum—some of the most processed foods there are.[27] Assessments of food advertising, specifically on kid-centered channels, have shown that the vast majority of foods promoted are of poor nutritional quality; in an examination of all the types of food promoted by Nickelodeon, researchers at CSPI found that 88 percent of foods advertised directly on the station, 76 percent of foods in the station's affiliated magazine, 60 percent of Nickelodeon-character-associated grocery store items, and a staggering 94 percent of Nickelodeon-affiliated kids' meals at restaurants were of poor nutritional quality.[28]

What is the result of all this advertising? Does it really make a difference? The research has repeatedly shown that the more television a child watches, the less healthy their dietary habits are; studies have shown that children who watch more television have lower fruit and vegetable consumption and higher candy and fast-food consumption.[29] In brief, the advertising *works*. Such studies prove that advertising has an immense amount of influence on children, and marketers will continue to advertise to children as long as children are able to influence the spending of their parents.

Interestingly, marketing has been shown to have the potential to *improve* healthy food choices as well. In a study conducted by Sesame Workshop (the nonprofit behind Sesame Street) to investigate the potential positive utility of children's attractions to cartoon and other television characters, researchers offered one group of children a chocolate bar and a bag of broccoli, and asked them to select which they wanted to eat. Not surprisingly, 78 percent of the children chose the chocolate, with the remaining 22 percent selecting the broccoli (which in and of itself is surprising enough— we would not have expected such a high proportion to choose the broccoli!). What the researchers did next, though, shows the positive power that marketing influence can have—when they repeated the test with a new group of children, researchers placed an Elmo sticker on the package of broccoli and a sticker of an unknown character on the chocolate bar. Just by associating the broccoli with a well-loved character, the number of children who chose broccoli more than doubled, to the point that *half of the children chose broccoli over chocolate*.[30] Anything that can get kids to choose broccoli over chocolate is quite simply astonishing and presents an opportunity to capitalize on what has become such a negative factor in child food selection. While this has tremendous potential, it is much less profitable to the companies behind the beloved childhood characters, and it is unlikely that without significant public demand (or more likely federal legislation) any of this impact will end up translated to the national marketplace. The Sesame Workshop has launched an admirable campaign to use this effect (even taking the "radical" step of trying to teach Cookie Monster that "a cookie is a sometime food"), but its efforts are rooted in the company's underlying nonprofit focus and mission of improving the lives of children, something that is *not* the goal of most companies backed by multi-million dollar advertising campaigns with investors to answer to.

Some progress is being made in limiting the impact of advertising on children's food choices in larger companies—in a move supported by First Lady Michelle Obama, Disney recently became the first major media company to completely ban advertisements for unhealthy foods across its media empire, including on ABC's Saturday morning cartoons. While this is an important first step in the right direction, an unlikely concerted cross-network transformation would have to occur to completely remove the effects of advertising upon children's food choices. Such efforts will not occur spontaneously, and many groups continue to lobby the federal government for protective legislation. Unfortunately, the collective voice of a few concerned parents and groups is drastically outdone by the massive lobbying capabilities of these multi-billion dollar corporations.

THE COMMERCIALIZATION OF THE CAFETERIA: SCHOOL LUNCHES AND VENDING MACHINES

Prior to 1972, there was a federal law in place (the Child Nutrition Act) that prevented schools participating in the National School Lunch Program from selling any "competitive foods" on school grounds. Its intent? To ensure school children were receiving nutritious meals. After all, as a captive audience, it seemed unfair to not try and ensure that healthy options were available. In 1972, however, the U.S. Department of Agriculture passed an exclusion to the Child Nutrition Act that permitted sales of foods (including through à la carte menus, vending machines, and stores) as long as the profits went back to support efforts within the school or school system.[31] Originally, it was thought that increased snacking would be beneficial because it would "help round out meals and contribute energy to the diet."[32] At the time, childhood obesity was not even remotely on the radar, and no states were recognized as having more than 15 percent obesity in adults.

The nutrition content of school lunches has been tightly regulated for some time; the regulations include strict rules on what proportion of the meal can come from fat, how many vegetables must be on the plate, and what the overall calorie count for the meal can be. The latest revisions to the school lunch program even include requirements for the quantity of different *colors* of vegetables that must be served. Unfortunately, with the exemptions to the Child Nutrition Act in place, the regulations only apply to traditional, buffet-style school lunches that are subsidized by the federal government. Even in these regulations, the definitions of various "nutrients" used have been questioned by many. In what is likely the most absurd example, Congress recently voted to uphold *pizza's* standing as a vegetable in the school lunch program[33]—as long as a little extra tomato sauce was added. So pizza, a junk food, is still given to our children as a vegetable as long as it has lots of tomato sauce (and a tomato, by the way, is technically a fruit).

Once the exemption to the Child Nutrition Act was passed, allowing other foods to be sold in schools, we officially commercialized the nutrition of our children. In over 90 percent of schools, children are now able to purchase items other than the traditional school lunch on an "à la carte" basis, where they build their own meal and pay exclusively out of pocket (thus not spending any federal money on the meal and bypassing all federal nutrition requirements).[34] In addition, more than three-quarters of high schools and half of middle schools have vending machines so children can purchase food throughout the day, and a shocking 40 percent of high schools have food *stores* for children to purchase food.[35] These foods are not regulated at the federal level in any way, and children are able to purchase whatever they have the money to buy. Children are even able to purchase items with the lunch money provided by their parents (potentially intended for the nutritionally balanced, federally regulated meal). The nutritional detriment is not limited to these "extra" snack-style foods consumed during the day; à la carte sales in schools at lunchtime (where students can choose to get a cheeseburger and tater tots, for instance) have been shown to drastically impact the nutritional quality of the average meal, increasing saturated fat intake and decreasing intake of fruits and vegetables.[36]

These changes have almost universally been recognized as huge mistakes, but resistance to changing the policies back is immense—all because of the rationale behind the original exemption (that these policies generate profits for the schools to support or expand their programs). School systems sign lucrative exclusive sales contracts, and the perception is that the profits in turn fund many programs. Unfortunately, this has come at the expense of children's health. While many strategies to encourage "healthy choices" from vending machines have been tried, the fact remains that almost 75 percent of students purchasing items from vending machines buy sugar-sweetened beverages, buying on average 1.2 servings per day (amounting to hundreds of calories daily).[37] These purchases represent victories on the part of soft-drink manufacturers, who spend an estimated $3 billion *per year* in the United States on advertising alone,[38] frequently targeting youth to create lifelong loyal customers (think of Coca-Cola commercials featuring computer-animated polar bears and Pepsi commercials featuring pop icons). The advertising power of the two leading soda companies (Coca-Cola and Pepsi) is so large that when combined, their annual advertising budgets alone are more than the *entire* two-year budget of the World Health Organization[39]; there is no way for the voice of health-conscious parents and consumer groups to counteract the messages generated by such large companies. Some states have banned vending machines in schools, or allowed them only if they sell healthy options such as bottled water, but the debate over food choice in schools remains high. During times of budget cuts and shortfalls, it becomes a tension between money (and thus the ability to fund important programs) and health. We have reached a crisis point, however, and health *must* take the top priority.

While many point to this financial argument as the main reason for leaving vending machines in schools—because the funds "support" other programs—the mental image of money pouring into schools from these vending machines is quite simply a myth. Ironically, when you look at the revenue generated from vending machine sales in schools, only around one-third of the revenue ever makes its way to the school; the remaining 67 percent goes directly to the food/beverage company's coffers. Ultimately, vending sales only generate on average $18 per student per year for the school.[40] For an average high school of 750 students,[41] that is only $13,500 in revenue. So, we have sold our children's health for less than $20 apiece—a pretty raw deal.

BAD BEHAVIOR—PARENTS

You know how they say the best predictor of future behavior is past behavior? Well, one of the best predictors of a child's behavior is their parents' behavior. Generations have progressively adopted more and more unhealthy eating behaviors, and those behaviors are passed on as easily as genes to their children. In fact, half of children with an obese parent will go on to be obese themselves, and if both of a child's parents are obese, there is an 80 percent chance that child will become obese.[42] This is despite the fact that less than 1 percent of all childhood obesity is caused by actual physical problems,[43] meaning that the cause *isn't* genetic, it's *environmental*—linked to the environment that the child was raised in that effectively enabled their obesity. Given 67 percent of adults are overweight, it is no wonder our children are also struggling with weight, and the habits we have developed regarding food and exercise over the course of a lifetime pass right on to our children. In fact, it is almost surprising that "only" one-third of our children have become overweight or obese given that twice as many adults are.

Unfortunately, parents have simultaneously grown to feel incredibly uncomfortable discussing food and weight with their children, which has enormous ramifications. In a poll of nearly 1,300 parents of adolescents and teenagers, parents admitted that they are now less comfortable discussing weight with their teenagers than any other topic (including sex, smoking, drugs, or alcohol).[44] That's right—*parents are more comfortable giving their teenager "the talk" than they are talking with them about weight*. And unfortunately parents don't even necessarily think that weight is a problem—only 37 percent view it as being a large risk to their children, whereas 90 percent of medical professionals recognize weight as being *the* most important health topic parents should discuss with their children (more important than safe sex, smoking, drug use, and alcohol).[45] To a large extent, parents seem to expect their child's doctor to address weight if it is a problem; unfortunately, 40–50 percent of children's health practitioners (including pediatricians, pediatric nurse practitioners, and child-serving registered dietitians) do not end up recommending a weight control plan even for children identified as being over-weight,[46] and less than one-quarter of parents of overweight children have been told by a doctor that their child's weight is impacting their health.[47]

If parents are unwilling to talk with their children about weight, and why making healthy food choices is so important, then children will continue to make the same unhealthy choices they are seeing their parents make and will never learn the importance of making healthy decisions. Parents have no qualms telling their children to put on a seatbelt and need to get to the same point when discussing the importance of eating healthy meals. Their ability to do so is limited, however, by the medical community's complicity in veiling the obesity epidemic in "acceptable" language (discussed in the previous chapter).

It comes down to the fact that children are sponges. They absorb anything and everything they see someone else doing, particularly their parents. If Mom comes home from a bad day and treats herself to a giant slice of cake, that habit will be picked up on by her son. If Dad doesn't like broccoli, odds are pretty good that his daughter also won't (even if she might have under different circumstances). A proper relationship with food must be modeled for children, because it will be very difficult for them to change the way they view food once they have reached adulthood.

The most important influence that parents have is through their role as the provider of food—children can only eat what their parents provide for them. While we all want our children to be happy and to have everything they want, it is our role as their parents to make sure they have everything they *need*, including the ability to maintain a proper weight. This means sometimes having to make unpopular decisions such as not buying certain things at the grocery store, or restricting portion sizes. As this book will demonstrate, that temporary unhappiness protects against a lifetime of consequences of being an overweight child.

CONCLUSION

Childhood obesity comes down to a simple system that must be in balance—the balance of calorie intake and calorie expenditure. As a society, we have moved toward higher and higher intakes of calories, both in adults and in children. These moves that shape our children's dietary intake are guided by many things, including cultural habits, learned associations, aggressive marketing, and the increased availability of unhealthy foods. Outside the context of exercise, these factors alone would be enough to cause skyrocketing rates of obesity; however, as calorie intake has *increased*, the level of physical activity children are engaging in has *decreased*. Chapter Three examines the changes in society that have pushed us away from physical activity; as you read it, remember that the decreases in activity have been paired with increased food consumption, creating a system with no possible outcome other than rampant childhood obesity.

THREE

Obesity Is a Behavior, Part Two

Get Moving!

Imagine a 1950s scene of domestic tranquility: it's summer, and school is out. Dad is in the kitchen reading the paper as Mom cooks dinner, Billy is playing baseball outside with his friends, and Sally is playing hopscotch in the backyard. As dinner gets close to being ready, Dad goes into the yard to call the kids inside. Billy and his friends quickly settle on what the score is: five to three; and Sally remembers her new record: eight straight hopscotches without hitting a line or losing her footing. They both run inside, wash up, and head to dinner. Estimated pre-dinner-playing calorie expenditure: 250 calories through full-body aerobic activity.

Fast forward sixty years and Billy is locked in his room, playing first-person shooter games over the Internet with a squadron of friends he hasn't actually seen in days despite interacting with them for hours on end every day. Sally is in her bedroom texting friends next door rather than actually talking with them in person. Dad calls up the stairs for them, and Billy yells down that he's not at a save point yet and he can't leave his friends high and dry. Sally comes out of her room and down the stairs, texting all the way. Eventually, enough of Billy's friends have to go too that they mutually decide to pause the game and he runs downstairs. As soon as the meal is done, the family quickly disperses, Mom to her Kindle, Dad to his BlackBerry, and the kids back to what they were doing before. Estimated pre-dinner-playing calorie expenditure: five calories through intense exercise of the thumbs.

DECREASE IN PHYSICAL ACTIVITY

A number of factors have led to a marked decrease in physical activity in the past few generations. The decreased level of physical activity means that the average child's base caloric needs (the number of calories the body will burn in a day) have gotten *lower*, unfortunately without a corresponding decrease in caloric intake; in fact, as discussed in the previous chapter, caloric intake has actually *increased* substantially, making the decrease in physical activity even more troublesome.

In general, there has been a "lazy-fication" of our children. While school used to be intimately tied to physical activity, nowadays only about half of students are enrolled in *any* kind of physical education and recess is quickly going the way of the dinosaur.[1] Now, we'll be the first to admit that we don't always get the amount of physical activity recommended, but the overwhelming problem for our children isn't that they don't always get it, it's that they *never* get it. Recent studies have shown that nearly three-quarters of all children do not get the recommended amount of daily exercise,[2] and such sedentary lifestyles have been linked to more than thirty-five types of chronic health conditions.[3] The physical health consequences of lack of exercise are so strong that researchers have even described the steady decrease in physical activity as leading to "Sedentary Death Syndrome" to convey the intense impact that lack of physical activity has on health outcomes.[4]

Changing this trend of inactivity will require us to take a hard look at what is keeping children from engaging in exercise. Some of the key factors in the generational decrease in physical activity are discussed in this chapter. We have focused this chapter on some of the expected and unexpected causes that play the strongest role in activity/inactivity. Understanding these factors is crucial in addressing the alarming trend toward sedentary lifestyles seen in today's children.

TECHNOLOGY: THE NEW NANNY

People are busy—no one is disputing that fact. It grows harder and harder to keep children entertained and occupied with the increasing demands that parents face. There are more of both dual-job and single-parent households than ever before, and occupying children's time is becoming an increasing challenge. As technology has simultaneously grown more advanced, parents have increasingly turned to technology to fill the role of babysitter. Whereas children would previously have been told to play in the backyard while dinner was prepared, now parents sit them in front of a computer to surf the web or hand them a remote control and tell them to find something on TV.

While technology is not entirely new, the extent of its use certainly is—the sheer number of devices and electronic screens in the hands of children today is nothing short of astonishing: laptops, cell phones, iPods, tablets, e-readers... the list goes on and on. And with these devices increasingly able to fill an important babysitting role, parents have begun to rely on them to do just that. Even though many technologies offer an educational component that is used by some parents, the sheer amount of time that children are spending interacting with technology is staggering. And these screens are directly impacting our children's physical activity levels (not to mention their diet as well, as discussed in the previous chapter). So "screens" are doubly bad—directly tied to both unhealthy diet and lack of exercise.[5]

We're all aware that everyone, including children, are using media in more ways and for longer periods of time than ever before, but we all tend to underestimate the amount of time that children actually spend with technology in all its forms. In a recent report focused just on television use, Nielsen found that children aged two to five spend on average 32 hours per week watching TV or playing video games.[6] *That's nearly the equivalent of a full-time job.* For older children, it might at first seem to be better—they "only" watch on average 28 hours of TV, but these children also spend 7 hours per day at school and are still managing to pack in 28 hours of TV into their schedules (on top of the 35 hours a week devoted to school). Similar studies have found that on an average day, children spend three hours on the computer,[7] an additional hour playing games and watching media on their cell phones,[8] and an hour and a half texting.[9] To top off a typical day, a teenager needs about 9 hours of sleep,[10] but with the way technology has entered the equation, there are only 7.5 hours of room left in the schedule.

Taken in total, that is 9.5 hours of technology *per day*. There is actually even more technology exposure than shown below in Figure 3.1, as teenagers love to multitask and will frequently be listening to their iPods while working on the computer or texting their friends while watching television—the times listed are for single-technology use only; overlaps have been removed.

FIGURE 3.1: AVERAGE DAY FOR HIGH SCHOOL STUDENT

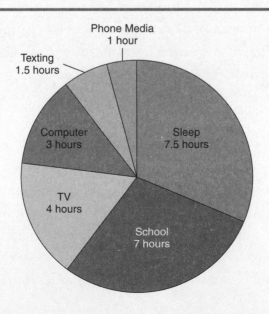

That average day should raise a lot of questions—where is exercise? For that matter, where are meals, family time, and extra-curriculars? In reality, certain activities occur more frequently on the weekends, leaving a brief buffer of additional time during the week, but technology is slowly pushing out all the other activities of the day. Just factoring in one hour to eat each day, the recommended 9 hours of sleep per night, and the recommended hour of exercise leaves children at a 27.5-hour day.

Quite simply, something's got to give.

While we will never be able to reverse the trends of reliance upon technology (it will only expand), we can find creative ways to build its use into something that promotes physical activity. Essentially, we can turn the problem into the solution. A passing fad a few years back was the bike-powered television; you could watch television while you exercised on a stationary bike, but had to maintain a certain intensity of exercise to power the television itself. Kind of catchy, but not very effective—it's not like you can't just use your regular television.

More successfully, Nintendo's Wii revolutionized the video gaming industry by incorporating movement into games in a way that has encouraged physical activity in places from schools to nursing homes. More recently, there has been an emerging market of app-integrated physical activity devices such as Fitbits and Nike's Fuel Bands that allow people to connect exercise trackers (such as pedometers and accelerometers that keep track of your body movements and intensity) to apps on their smartphones to track their daily activity. Not only does this provide feedback about the quantity and quality of physical activity, it can even allow for competitions with friends to see who can get in the most physical activity in a day. Some programs don't even require you to actively report your activity—your device can connect directly to your phone, which can then tweet your level of activity automatically. While such solutions may seem "hokey" to adults, for children who have grown up in an age of 140-character instant communication, broadcasting their daily activities may provide a significant boost to their participation.

A more straightforward solution, though, is simply putting back into place the expectation of physical activity. Having "unplugged time" in which children must do something, *anything*, physical rather than interfacing with technology is an important step. If parents would join their children in the unplugged time, this would also go a long way toward improving parents' health—their use of media is rapidly joining that of their children, and group exercise has been proven to increase the likelihood of success, thereby improving the entire family's fitness.

Yes, "unplugging" requires additional time and effort on the part of parents, but there is quite simply no way around it. As physical education programs become rarer in school settings, the only consistent opportunity for exercise will come at home. Additionally, if children only learn to exercise in the context of school, once they have graduated they will not have a model of integrating physical activity into "everyday" life—establishing the pattern of literally taking time to exercise will be a very important part of establishing the patterns and habits necessary for a healthy adulthood, as well.

While we are not out to paint television as evil, we want to leave you with a final point when it comes to TV—studies summarized in the *Journal of the American Medical Association*, the most prestigious medical journal in the United States, examined the impact of television viewing on numerous health outcomes (through its cumulative impact on diet and exercise), including diabetes, cardiovascular disease, and even death. They were able to determine that for every extra 2 hours of television watching per day, there are 176 more cases of Type 2 diabetes, 38 more fatal heart disease outcomes, and overall 104 additional deaths *for every 100,000 people.*[11] Is it the television itself that is killing people? Of course not, but because of what we are doing (and not doing) while we watch TV, we are literally sitting ourselves to death.

A CULTURE OF CONVENIENCE

An additional factor that people are increasingly aware of is our culture of ultra-convenience. Never before have we been so pampered and spoiled. Just to put it into perspective, think about the immediate access to knowledge that we now have—if I were to ask you who the twenty-third president of the United States was (Harrison, incidentally), fifty years ago you would have had to get up, get in your car, drive to the library, find an encyclopedia, and look up the answer. Thirty years ago, if you were lucky, you had your own encyclopedia, so you would walk to your bookshelf, pull out the P volume, and flip through the pages until you found the answer. Fifteen years ago, you might have walked over to your computer, booted it up, put in your Encarta CD, and searched for the answer. Ten years ago, you would pick up your laptop, bring up Lycos on the Internet, and type in your search query. And today, you would just reach in your pocket, pull out your cell phone, and, using voice prompts, tell your phone to Google it for you (illustrative, isn't it, that the name of a website is now a Webster-defined *action* verb?).

The same applies for food—while we once hunted and gathered everything we ate, now we don't even have to go to the grocery store to get food—it can be ordered from our cell phones and delivered right to our doors. We no longer have to *spend* calories to *get* calories, a very new development. While it's been a while since we hunted most of our own food, we have never before reached a level of such food availability (with such minimal effort).

It's quite simply astounding how far things have come, and this is reflected throughout our lives. Our cell phones are now remote controls, our light switches are virtual, and our televisions turn themselves on and off. We don't even have to put a tape into the

VCR to record our shows; they record themselves automatically onto our DVR. We no longer have to go to a bookstore to get a book or even go to Walmart to shop there. Our small, disc-shaped vacuum cleaners skirt across the floor, guiding themselves, our electric razors self-clean, and our showers automatically spray a cleaning mist when we leave the tub. Even our toilets flush and clean themselves.

As generations become more and more accustomed to immediate gratification and minimal effort, their approach to all things becomes impacted—shouldn't all things be this easy? Isn't there a quick fix for everything? This is a fundamental problem when looking at obesity because exercise is a chore—by definition, it is *work*. It involves getting up and making yourself do something that you technically don't have to do and typically don't even enjoy doing. Our society has reached a point for the first time ever where physical activity has become increasingly *optional*, and we are struggling to develop ways of incorporating it back into our lives.

THE DEATH OF RECESS

Think back to elementary school, and the hour of your day that was blocked out for going outside to play—to get fresh air, sunshine, and some physical activity, and learn how to interact with other people your age. The field days, Frisbee throwing, and time trials to see how quickly you could walk a mile. For many children, recess is their favorite time of day—a chance to help their bodies develop in coordination with their minds.

Nostalgic, isn't it? And like most things nostalgic, recess is rapidly becoming a thing of the past. Less than half of school children are enrolled in physical education courses, and less than one-third receive daily physical activity as a part of their educational curriculum.[12] In 2004, more than 40,000 of the nation's schools had no recess.[13] As budgets have continued to be cut and academic performance measures have placed increasing pressures on schools to raise their academic outcomes (or lose their funding), physical education and recess are often the first targets to go. After all, what do you "learn" in a PE class? That is, other than how to live an active, healthy life?

Nearly half of all schools report that they are eliminating or significantly reducing recess because of the constant pressure to improve school test scores.[14] This is not only removing children's options for physical activity, but also removing an important association—children no longer associate physical activity with being a part of a "typical" day—it only happens on special occasions (track and field day, special competitions, and so on). While there is no question that our schools have room for improvement in academics, what about the *health* of their students? Why is it acceptable to withhold funding from a school because the children are not meeting educational milestones, but not hold funding similarly hostage based upon a school's ability to meet health-based milestones? Health is no more out of the sphere of influence of schools than is academic achievement—genetics, family support, and environment play a crucial role in both. And as discussed in Chapter Two, because the health of our children has been "bought" by vending companies, the educational system is actually becoming a place of *risk* rather than a benefit for overall health. This trend will only continue if we persist in divorcing health from our most basic outcome measures in schools.

Some states are now requiring health report cards to accompany academic report cards. These "FitnessGrams" help explain where a child's health currently falls in order to help parents understand what might need to be done. While this program is *highly* worthy and has the potential to help educate parents about the health of their children, the ultimate irony is that they are originating from a source that is *decreasingly* focused on actually improving what is behind that "report card."

We understand that there are a limited number of hours in the school day, and that with federal regulations the way they currently are, PE and recess appear to have much less value to children than academic programs. Changing this perception will require policy advocacy by parents—we must stand up and demand that health be re-incorporated into a child's academic program. We regulate the food that is offered in schools based on the logic that children have no choice but to be at school and therefore we are morally obligated to offer healthy options for food (although Chapter Two pointed out the glaring holes in such legislation); why does the same argument not extend to physical activity?

A CULTURE OF FEAR—INJURY AND LIABILITY

A much more insidious influence on activity levels has been a steadily increasing culture of fear. We all want our children to lead long lives, and we all discourage activities that could be dangerous, but we have begun taking this to extremes. In the past, we would hand our children a bike and tell them to explore the neighborhood until dinner. They would ride off (without helmets, even), and not be back for hours, unreachable by cell phone or any other means than a loud shout or a scouting trip in a car. Children would walk themselves to school, jump on trampolines without confining safety nets, and play freely in front yards. Now parents are terrified of their children being hit by a car on the way to school, of breaking their arms on school playground equipment, or of being snatched out of their own front yards. The risk of any of these things occurring has not gone up; in fact, it has actually gone down, but we have become so afraid of any injury coming to our children that we have created the exact opposite effect—we are now harming our children in our desperate attempts to protect them.

Take our fear of kidnapping, for instance. Most parents use this specter as the primary reason for not allowing their kids to walk to school or play unattended in the backyard. In a landmark study conducted by the United States Department of Justice, they discovered that only around 115 children per year are kidnapped in what are considered "traditional" kidnappings (taken by a stranger or slight acquaintance with the intent to keep, ransom, or harm the child). To put it into perspective, your child has a higher chance of being killed in your car while driving to and from school than being kidnapped while walking to and from school.

This fear extends well beyond kidnapping, though, to the degree that parents are so petrified of *any* harm coming to their child (even injuries that may previously have been considered rites of passage, such as skinned knees and broken bones) that they are not allowing *any* activity that could lead to harm. If your goal is to never expose your child to the possibility of being harmed by physical activity, then you are missing an underlying truth—activity always involves danger, and that is just quite simply part of being alive. But the fear of injury has become so strong that *perceived* safety of a neighborhood (regardless of the *actual* safety of the neighborhood) has been shown to have a powerful impact on obesity—children whose parents perceive their neighborhood as being less safe are over four times as likely to be obese as children whose parents do not perceive their neighborhood as being unsafe.[15] This shows that parents are severely restricting the exercise behaviors of their children in attempts to keep them safe from immediate harm, despite the long-term negative effects (not to mention the simple truth that their children are much safer than they perceive them to be).

Another simple truth is that growth frequently depends on harm—the very act of muscle building itself requires damage. Muscles grow when they experience microscopic tears that are then rebuilt bigger and stronger. If we protect our children to the point that they cannot even engage in the activities necessary to build stronger muscles, we are *directly* harming them in ways that have lifelong consequences. Generations of children have engaged in sports that are now being labeled "high risk" and for decades have played on what is now considered "unsafe" playground equipment. Danger is a part of life, and the sooner parents accept this, the better able they are to protect their children against real risks.

Sports

Parents are increasingly concerned about safety in sports. For instance, there has been much recent attention paid to the high prevalence of concussions in soccer (particularly among girls). Yes, soccer and other sports can be dangerous. All of us likely have been hurt or at least have relatives that have been injured playing sports. But in addition to the direct exercise benefit, sports teach valuable skills, including teamwork and dedication, as well as how to handle success and failure. If the risk of injury becomes real and pressing (such as in the case of repeated soccer concussions), something does need to be done to limit the possibility of injury. If that means discontinuing the sport, then that is something parents must decide. But parents must then find a suitable alternative that allows their children to still be active—just cutting off an activity altogether is like removing your child from school because they happened to fall out of a classroom desk.

Playgrounds

Our mounting fears have led to crushing parental pressure to change playgrounds and alter the way our children play in those playgrounds. Common playground equipment pieces (such as monkey bars and merry-go-rounds) are increasingly vanishing from our playgrounds because they are suddenly perceived as "high risk." In New York alone, by the mid-1990s more than half of all monkey bars had been removed from playgrounds because of safety concerns, and in Chicago they were all gone. Seattle similarly took aim at its jungle gyms,[16] citing concerns over safety and liability.

Research has consistently shown that the more varied the equipment of the playground, the more activity children will engage in.[17] While we may be marginally decreasing the risk of low-likelihood, short-term physical harm when we remove equipment, as with everything else we've discussed, we are increasing the risk of much more likely long-term damage to kids' health.

Ironically, many parents feel that their children are safer playing at home, and therefore keep them from public playgrounds (after all, those large climbing contraptions seem dangerous, right?). In fact, studies have shown that injuries sustained while playing on *home* play equipment are more severe than those injuries sustained at public playgrounds. If a parent follows the facts, to truly decrease the odds of physical harm they would limit their child's activity even at home (something we obviously don't want to encourage). We cannot continue to be petrified by non-life-threatening (or even non-life-impacting) injuries. Cuts, scrapes, bruises, and, yes, even broken bones, are part of growing up. There is no point in keeping our children away from potential harm just to deliver them to a shorter, less-fulfilling adult life. Is a child more likely to break their arm falling from a set of monkey bars than they are falling off the couch? Yes. Does that mean we should ban monkey bars? *No*.

As playgrounds continue to be pillaged to remove anything perceived as risky, the mob has yet to stop and ask for evidence of the effectiveness of these measures. In an ultimate irony, some experts say not only is there no consistent evidence that implementing "safe" playgrounds decreases risk, but it may actually *increase* the risk of injury.[18] Their argument? Evidence of increases in broken bones in both England and Australia after implementing safer playground equipment. The likely culprit? A decreased perceived risk of the activities. Parents and children are more vigilant when they perceive the risks, but when there are shock-absorbent, protective floors and low-height equipment, the perceived risk is less, and therefore, so also are the safety measures. While this has been debated, the fact remains that while there is equipment on playgrounds that could be made safer, it is impossible to make an injury-free playground.

In increasingly absurd moves, many schools are caving to parental pressure to ban certain games and activities that are simply *perceived* as dangerous, regardless of any evidence to the contrary. The most recent casualty? Tag. What is likely one of the oldest games on earth (even played by animals, including gorillas,[19] wolves, and coyotes[20]) is facing an onslaught of opposition based upon the unreasonable fear that children may injure themselves as they run into each other. This fear has led to tag being banned in schools across the nation, in cities in Wyoming, Washington, Kansas, South Carolina, Oregon, and California.[21] If these trends continue, what will be next? Walking down the hallways?

Additional concerns over liability have led to increasing removal of playground equipment and other activity options by schools, businesses, and local governments. The lack of available playgrounds has a direct impact on activity—children who have access to playgrounds engage in nearly an hour of additional activity per week, just due to proximity.[22] This doesn't represent an average across just children who go to the playground, but *all* children in the neighborhood. The mere proximity of playground equipment has been shown to be directly correlated with more physical activity and lower rates of obesity.[23]

The playground safety movement has unfortunately limited the accessibility of equipment—in their admirable quest to improve safety, advocates inadvertently created standards that were simply unaffordable, leading to the closing of numerous playgrounds in communities without the funds to bring the playgrounds up to code. The 2006 revisions of the American Society for Testing and Materials (ASTM) playground safety standards reached a voluminous fifty-five pages, making it nearly impossible for communities struggling through the worst recession since the 1930s to keep their playgrounds open.[24] Because of these guidelines, mandatory or not, continuing to operate a playground that does not meet guidelines opens communities to escalating liability. The only possible outcome: the slow death of the community playground. The issue truly has come to a head: we all want our playgrounds to be safer, but the option rarely comes down to "do we update our playground equipment or not?" Concerns over liability forces the question to become "do we update our playground equipment or close the playground altogether?" So is it worse to have a playground at which someone may be harmed, or no playground at all?

GET OVER IT

Let's be direct—children will get hurt playing. *And that's okay.* To some extent, children are *supposed* to get hurt—it is how we learn what is safe and what isn't, how far we can go, how much we can push our bodies to do. It's almost like a vaccine—getting mildly hurt engaging in normal childhood activities helps protect children against future harm. Researchers are increasingly concerned about our recent obsession with safety, arguing that helicopter parents are robbing their children of their ability to be self-sufficient and to navigate risks themselves. Once you think about it, this makes perfect sense—if our children grow up in a world where anything dangerous or strenuous is to be avoided, how will they learn to face danger and overcome it? How will they know that they can accomplish things that might result in harm, such as vigorous exercise? While we fear risk-taking play in our children, early childhood specialists have even argued that the desire in children to engage in risky play with potential injury consequences is so deep-rooted it is evolutionary—that children who face such fears early in life have improved coping skills and self-efficacy (a sense of being able to accomplish what is desired).[25] For a child who is not allowed to face

such things, thereby decreasing physical activity and ability to overcome adversity, how will they ever be able to tackle their problems
with weight?

We are not arguing against safety standards, or against the need
to create as safe an environment for our children as is reasonable—
what we argue against is the propensity to want to create the safest
environment *possible*. The negative impacts of such an environment on long-term health (and emotional development) are much
too costly. We must accept that our children are exposed to harm
on a *constant* basis. We must make informed decisions as to what
harms are worse: unlikely immediate harms, or much-more-likely
distant harms. As a society, we have always focused on the immediate rather than the long term, but that is precisely how we have
reached our current obesity crisis.

FOUR

It's *Not* Just a Little Baby Fat

Physical Impact in Childhood

The doctor pulled the chart from the caddy next to the exam room door, preparing to enter the room. From his morning schedule, he already knew what he would see: yet another teenage girl who was morbidly obese and unable to lose weight. As a bariatric surgeon, he never imagined his practice would be expanding down to those so young. After all, he wasn't a pediatrician, and never thought he would be increasingly pulled in that direction. He flipped through the chart to review the details, braced himself, and walked in.

"Hello Melanie, and Mrs. Carlson. My name is Dr. Jimenez. I understand you are interested in learning about bariatric surgery?"

"Yes, Melanie has been trying to lose weight for years, but it just isn't happening. I read something online that says that weight-loss surgery is safe for children, so we wanted to come and talk with you."

"Before we start talking about surgical options, has Melanie tried diet and exercise programs?"

"Yes, it seems we've tried everything, but nothing works. She'll lose ten or fifteen pounds, but then it comes right back and then some. It's just so hard because I don't have any control over what happens when she's in school—I don't know if she's getting the foods she should and how much other food she's able to get without me knowing."

"If you were to be interested in weight-loss surgery, we first require that you go through a six-month weight-loss program supervised directly by me so we can see if we can reach weight-loss goals naturally before undergoing major surgery." Dr. Jimenez braced himself; he had grown accustomed to the types of reactions

*this typically generated (despite being the widely accepted standard
of care for pre-bariatric patients).*

*"But she needs to lose weight now! She's already diabetic, and
we haven't been able to get her blood pressure under control for the
past two months. Can't we just go ahead and figure out how to move
forward with the surgery? It would be so much easier than continuing what we've been doing…"*

*"Mrs. Carlson, I know you're eager to improve your daughter's
health, but there are many other things that can be done to avoid
major surgery."*

*"Listen, Dr. Jimenez—this is the twenty-first century. Can't you
just fix it? Isn't that what doctors are for, after all?"*

C ommonly paired with the popular media's discussion of the
childhood obesity epidemic is a description of its negative
health effects. These effects are extreme and expanding,
prompting growth in weight-loss surgeries such as the one discussed
above as parents, desperate for a "quick" solution, increasingly turn
to what were previously considered alternative methods.

Some of the health effects we'll examine (such as diabetes and
high blood pressure) are more familiar, but there are other significant health impacts, such as metabolic syndrome and sleep-
disordered breathing, that are less commonly known. Throughout
this chapter, keep in mind that we are not discussing long-term,
adult health consequences—these diseases are already present in
children who are overweight. They are direct threats to life and
well-being. Many of these diseases have never been seen before in
children, and we truly have no basis for comparison to determine
exactly how much of an impact these conditions will have later in
their adulthood. Despite this, it is clear that obesity-related conditions that are presenting during childhood are creating at least a
simultaneous "epidemic of cardiovascular risk in youth,"[1] and in
many other health conditions as well that pediatricians are simply
not accustomed to encountering.

As today's overweight children reach adulthood, we will begin to see a much clearer picture of what the true impacts will be. While we may not know the full impact, these conditions will profoundly impact their risk of many diseases, in particular heart disease (already the number one killer in America). The magnitude of the obesity epidemic on children's health is reflected in the significantly higher use of medical care services, including laboratory tests, among obese children (whether a doctor has told them they are obese or not).[2]

These effects combine to significantly impact not only quality of life, but also its very duration. The impact of childhood obesity on daily functioning is so dramatic that obese children are similar to children with *cancer* when we examine how much their health has impacted their quality of living.[3] When you see all of the immediate deleterious health effects of being an overweight child, it should come as no surprise that our children are also living shorter lives. When combined with the adult health consequences and the emotional and social consequences we will discuss later in the book, the full scope of the obesity epidemic becomes clear, and the devastating effect it will have on our children finally comes into full light.

Here we describe some of the leading and some of the more surprising health effects that are being seen in children. There are many more, and even more will continue to emerge as the epidemic grows, but even just the few highlighted over the next several pages paint a bleak physical picture.

DIABETES

Diabetes mellitus is one of the oldest chronic diseases known to man. The condition occurs when the body is not able to properly control the amount of sugar in the blood (glucose). This can occur because the body is unable to produce the natural glucose stabilizer insulin altogether (as in Type 1 diabetes) or because the body either no longer produces enough insulin to keep up with the body's needs or the body has started to ignore the insulin (as in Type 2 diabetes). Type 1 diabetes typically happens when the particular cells in the pancreas that produce insulin die or cease to function, and represents only about 5 percent of all diabetes cases.[4] People with Type 1 diabetes must regularly inject themselves with insulin to control their blood sugar. In Type 2 diabetes, the body is not able to keep up with the need for insulin and in a fashion simply falls behind, leaving too much sugar in the blood. Type 2 diabetics sometimes rely upon oral medication to stabilize their sugar but have the opportunity to decrease their need for medication by making changes to their diet to keep high-sugar foods from spiking the amount of glucose in their blood. While there are many factors that increase someone's risk for Type 2 diabetes, overweight/obesity is a primary risk factor—the more fatty tissue a person has, the more resistant his or her cells become to the glucose-controlling effects of insulin.[5]

Previously, Type 1 diabetes was referred to as "juvenile diabetes" and Type 2 as "adult-onset diabetes." A child diagnosed with diabetes in the 1980s was by default assumed to be Type 1 diabetic because Type 2 diabetes was typically diagnosed only in those forty years of age or older.[6] Because of the childhood obesity epidemic, however, these labels are no longer accurate—now, over 3,600 children a year are diagnosed with Type 2 diabetes.[7] Beyond the physical effects described here (and in more detail in the next chapter), a diagnosis of Type 2 diabetes comes with severe consequences, even doubling risk of death in a given year.[8]

The main complication is that too much sugar in the blood is actually toxic—it causes damage to the eyes, kidneys, nerves, and the circulatory system itself. This can in turn lead to blindness, kidney failure, and circulation problems that can ultimately result in amputations (although these outcomes are not typically faced until adulthood). Peripheral nerve damage not only causes tingling and numbness, but also decreases a person's ability to detect injury to their extremities (which can then progress to more extensive injuries).

Because of the unpredictability of Type 2 diabetes, a child diagnosed with the illness must begin a strict regimen of glucose monitoring and dietary changes to ensure the disease does not become more severe. Quite simply, it changes their life forever. Multiple times a day, the child must have their blood tested to ensure their blood sugar is in an appropriate range. Sugary foods and drinks must be avoided, because the accompanying buildup of sugar can lead to dangerously high levels of blood glucose and result in coma, organ failure, and even death. The intense level of care required by diabetic children is creating previously unencountered problems in school settings, where school nurses are now responsible for ensuring that diabetic students within the schools have the care they require. This is greatly complicated by the fact that childhood Type 2 diabetes not only progresses more rapidly than adult Type 2 diabetes, but also becomes resistant to medications faster. Common treatments have also been shown to have a 20 percent rate of serious adverse events in children.[9]

While the consequences of diabetes are severe, the one ray of hope in combating childhood Type 2 diabetes is that for obesity-linked diabetics, bringing weight to a normal range will often cause the diabetes to go into remission. Similarly, for children at risk of developing diabetes, losing weight can completely prevent its onset. Type 2 diabetes is therefore the rare illness that is for the most part both curable and preventable. This gives parents unprecedented power to *reverse* or *prevent entirely* an illness that could impact their child for the rest of their life.

HYPERTENSION AND HEART FUNCTION

As with diabetes, being an overweight child dramatically increases the risk of being diagnosed with another disease previously seen almost entirely in adults, high blood pressure.[10] For overweight children, their chances of developing the disease are tripled,[11] and recent trends show hypertension among children is increasing in ways that directly parallel the obesity epidemic.[12] When a child's blood pressure is higher than normal, it places too much strain on the circulatory system, causing it to work harder and put unnecessary stress upon the body's blood vessels. The consequences of high blood pressure in children include enlarged heart ventricles, seizures, strokes, and congestive heart failure[13]—very serious complications previously seen almost exclusively in adults. Even beyond hypertension, overweight adolescents have decreased heart function because their increased body mass places so much strain on their heart.[14]

Hypertension has become so common in the United States (an estimated one-third of adults have hypertension[15]) that we have lost sight of the seriousness of the condition, particularly in children. The figure on the next page shows the "treatment algorithm" recommended by the National Institutes of Health for the treatment of childhood hypertension—anyone looking at the complexity of this chart can see how much of an impact the disease has. To highlight the gravity of the diagnosis, consider for instance the presence of "assessing for organ damage" in nearly every line of treatment. For *children*.

After being diagnosed with high blood pressure, children must follow a strict, low-sodium diet to prevent progression of and complications from the disease; frequently, families must work together to implement a dietary plan that everyone follows. As with diabetes, if a child is able to bring their weight to a normal range, the hypertension can often remiss.

FIGURE 4.1: PEDIATRIC HYPERTENSION TREATMENT ALGORITHM[16]

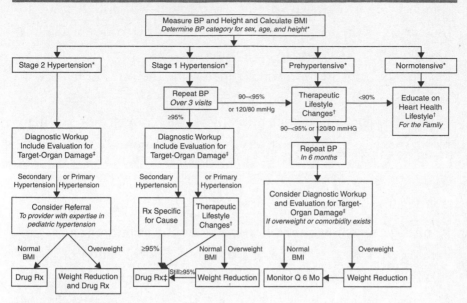

*See source for more details
†Diet modification and physical activity
‡Especially if younger, very high BP, little or no family history, diabetic, or other risk factors

In a discussion that harkens back to our earlier examination of body mass index (BMI), the effects of hypertension on children are complicated by the method by which hypertension is diagnosed in children. Again, because of the differences in blood pressure that naturally occur developmentally, there is not a universal cutoff for hypertension in children (unlike in adults, where blood pressures above 140/90 indicate hypertension). As with BMI, we have long used percentile methods by age for determining what is a "normal" blood pressure for a given age. Unfortunately, the continued use and updating of these norms allows the definition of "normal" to gradually creep up, missing individuals who previously would have been considered hypertensive because, as a whole, the blood pressure of our children is higher (in correlation with their increased weight). Most recently, the charts were updated in 1996 and again in 2005 (in the height of the upswing of obesity). For us to truly have a handle on the presence of hypertension, and therefore the need to treat children, we must stop adjusting these norms and establish unmoving, age-specific criteria that will not continue to increase with the weight of our children. Failure to do so will allow a secondary epidemic of hypertension to creep up on us, just as the obesity epidemic has, drastically increasing the rates of hypertension in adults (already standing at 30 percent[17]). The consequences of such a hypertension epidemic will be *much* more severe, as high blood pressure is linked to everything from impotence to stroke.

METABOLIC SYNDROME

A much-lesser-known complication of obesity in children and adults is referred to as the "metabolic syndrome," a collection of physical health complications created by obesity. None of the individual symptoms indicate the presence of a specific *disease*; rather, the condition entails the accumulation of multiple individual risks for a variety of diseases. Previously only defined in adults, in response to the growing need for child-specific criteria resulting from the growing obesity problem, the International Diabetes Federation recently created the first child-specific definition of metabolic syndrome.[18] This pediatrics-specific definition includes a) being classified as obese and b) having two or more of the following: elevated triglycerides (fat in the blood greater than 150 mg/dL), low HDL ("good cholesterol" of less than 40 mg/dL), elevated blood pressure (systolic blood pressure over 130 or diastolic over 85), and a fasting glucose of 100 mg/dL or higher.

While this definition may seem highly technical, the metabolic syndrome really represents a collection of symptoms that individually raise the risk of developing both diabetes and cardiovascular disease, but in concert dramatically increase that risk. Individuals with metabolic syndrome are up to three times as likely to have a heart attack and stroke, and are five times as likely to develop Type 2 diabetes.[19] The presence of this condition in our children is almost more troubling than the presence of individual diseases, because metabolic syndrome has such a wide net of associated risk.

The most troubling aspect of metabolic syndrome is how remarkably widespread it is—in 1994 (before the childhood obesity epidemic had even reached its full swing), more than two out of three children already had one symptom of metabolic syndrome, and over 10 percent of children had full-fledged metabolic syndrome.[20] To put that into a different perspective: over two-thirds of children had at least one risk factor for cardiovascular disease *in the 1990s*. This is quite simply astounding. When projecting the current prevalence of metabolic syndrome in children, recent research places the nationwide estimate at a staggering 30 percent.[21] *That is one in three children with significant, pronounced risk of developing both heart disease and diabetes.*

Again, a repeating hope emerges: if a child loses weight, the metabolic syndrome can be reversed, thereby decreasing the physical health risks associated with it. This by no means makes it less severe, as success rates for weight loss are low at best, but it does offer the chance to counteract the severe physical effects of the condition. And, also like diabetes and hypertension, preventing weight gain in the first place can completely prevent the onset of the syndrome.

ADDITIONAL HEALTH-RELATED EFFECTS

There are additional biologic findings in overweight children that may not in and of themselves constitute a medical condition, but are still worthy of mention. Because they have never before been seen in children, the long-term effects of these anomalies are unclear. For instance, obese children have been found to have lower iron availability (not because of dietary factors, but simply because the iron is not circulating at appropriate levels).[22] Because of iron's integral role in the creation of red blood cells, this finding could indicate higher levels of anemia and resulting complications could emerge in the future. Overweight children also have significantly higher rates of bed-wetting (it is nearly seven times as likely); although the reasons for this connection are still unclear. It could be tied to general metabolic processes, or even to psychological outcomes associated with obesity.[23]

Another potentially troubling finding is that in overweight children as young as ten years old, there are indications of "cardiovascular adaptations."[24] In other words, the heart has had to adjust so much to the difference in weight that there are measurable differences in heart function, and even in the size of certain portions of the heart. Again, the long-term implications are unclear, but it stands to reason that any condition that leads to a measurable change in the actual structure of the heart has the potential for devastating consequences.

In a repeated finding that still defies explanation, there is also a substantial overlap between childhood obesity and asthma.[25] While it is still unclear if the relationship is causal or simply a result of overlapping risk, the fact remains that overweight children are twice as likely to be asthmatic as children who are normal weight.[26] Not only does asthma require medical care, it can also decrease the likelihood and ability of children to engage in the kinds of physical activity that best lead to weight loss. One possible link with asthma is the overwhelming association between childhood obesity and sleep-disordered breathing. Children who are overweight are nearly five times as likely to have sleep-disordered breathing (including sleep apnea, where breathing stops, and hypopneas, where breathing becomes too shallow),[27] the result of the upper airway becoming blocked during sleep. This can cause a temporary decrease in the flow of oxygen throughout the body with a simultaneous buildup of too much carbon dioxide in the blood. Together, these can lead to nocturnal hypertension, and in the long run, can lead to general hypertension, increased cardiovascular disease, and even an increase in cardiovascular and cerebrovascular death (for example, heart attacks and strokes). Commonly treated with Continuous Positive Airway Pressure (CPAP) machines that force air into the nose to keep breathing passageways open, apnea can require decades of sleeping with a cumbersome, noisy, and uncomfortable contraption strapped to the head. Again, the presence of this condition in children is something physicians are not used to seeing, and its increase is quite troubling—literally, our children have gotten so overweight it impacts their ability to *breathe*, the most fundamental body function that exists.

THE QUICK-FIX OBSESSION: WEIGHT-LOSS SURGERIES

With the growing knowledge of the direct impact that being an overweight child has on immediate health, there has been a surge of interest in weight-loss surgery (bariatric surgery) in increasingly younger groups. While bariatric surgery typically takes place at an average age of forty years old,[28] weight-loss surgeons are increasingly being faced with the decision of whether or not a young teenager should undergo complex surgery in which the digestive system is quite literally altered and rerouted.

There are several variations of bariatric surgery, but the two most common are gastric bypass and gastric banding. In gastric bypass surgery, the stomach and part of the intestines are "bypassed," literally disconnected from the digestive process, thereby shrinking the amount of food able to be taken in at any given time and decreasing the amount of calories absorbed by the body. When you perform a pediatric gastric bypass, for all intents and purposes you have removed the stomach of a child (something most would view as drastic). In gastric banding, a silicone ring is placed around the stomach, squeezing it to reduce its size to around one ounce (about two tablespoons). Both methods have been shown to lead to dramatic weight loss, which is not surprising given you have physically redesigned the way the body interacts with food. The lingering question, however, is about the long-term consequences of such major surgery when performed on children and adolescents. We simply don't know what they are yet, but that isn't preventing widespread increase in the surgeries.

The complication rates for bariatric surgeries vary by the type of surgery conducted and range from simple nutrient deficiencies to fatal outcomes. The mainstream media began publicizing the high fatality rates of early gastric bypass procedures in the late 1990s—before laparoscopic (minimally invasive) methods were developed, nearly 1 in 100 gastric bypass patients died as a result of their surgery.[29] Newer methods have cut that rate in half, but it remains a risky surgery because patients are by definition already at increased risk of complication because of their severe obesity (something that can, in other situations, disqualify someone from a surgery).

As bariatric surgeries became more prominent and increasing numbers of celebrities (such as Randy Jackson, Al Roker, Roseanne Barr, Sharon Osbourne, Star Jones, and Carnie Wilson) publicized their own procedures, the general public became more aware of this possible weight-loss strategy. Between 1996 and 2002, bariatric surgery rates increased seven-fold among adults in the United States,[30] reaching an estimated annual cost of $2 billion. In the late 1990s, weight-loss surgery in children and adolescents was exceptionally rare; in 1997 there were only 51 documented child bariatric surgeries.[31] While the rates of childhood bariatric surgeries stayed relatively stable until the year 2000, rates of bariatric surgery in youth increased 300 percent just between 2000 and 2003.[32]

The criteria for which surgeons will consider bariatric surgery vary, but typically involve having a BMI of 40 or higher (or a BMI of 35–40 accompanied by sleep apnea, high blood pressure, or diabetes) and at least six months of continuous failed weight-loss attempts (typically doctor-supervised).[33] When considering bariatric surgery for children, physicians must consider a host of additional factors, including the child's psychological readiness for the life changes associated with such major surgery and the presence of a supportive family environment that will allow for weight losses to be maintained (increasingly rare given the rates of adult obesity).[34]

In a concerning trend, more than three-quarters of adolescent bariatric patients are female,[35] indicating the pressure to turn to surgery as an option for weight loss may be influenced unduly by social notions of thinness. There are well-recognized links between a desire for thinness and cultural influences, particularly in girls (search "Dove Onslaught Beauty Pressure" on YouTube to watch a fantastic visual representation created by Tim Piper of the "onslaught" that young girls face from the beauty industry), but the consistent difference in weight-loss surgeries by sex indicates a flawed system is in place. There should be no difference in weight-loss surgeries by sex given equal rates of complications and equal long-term consequences of uncontrolled weight.

Although still controversial, the weight-loss results of bariatric surgery in young adults are convincing—on average, patients eleven to twenty undergoing weight-loss surgery can expect to lose over sixty-five pounds[36] within one year of the surgery (with the best weight-loss results seen in gastric bypass patients). Social and psychological improvements have also been documented in children undergoing bariatric surgery.[37] When deciding upon weight-loss surgery for children and adolescents, though, one of the main concerns of the medical community is that there simply hasn't been enough time to see what the long-term effects of having weight-loss surgery at a young age will be. The complications and long-term side effects are well known in adults, whose bodies and metabolisms are fully developed. For children, however, it is plausible that the radical changes bariatric surgery brings about, coupled with their timing in the midst of growth and development, could lead to unforeseen negative effects. Given the lack of long-term follow-up studies, it is even more troubling that while the weight-loss success of bariatric surgery is not in question, the long-term benefits still are. In a recent study published in the revered *Journal of the American Medical Association,* a study of more than 40,000 men showed that there was no difference in mortality between men who had bariatric surgery and men who did not.[38] Given the widespread concern over fatal surgery complications, in the face of limited evidence of long-term benefits, parents and pediatricians are in a quandary—what to choose?

In summary, the health effects of childhood obesity range from the familiar to the obscure, but regardless combine to impact quality of life in severe ways, and as the effects spill into adulthood, impact the very length of children's lives. The next chapter explores how the health effects of childhood obesity have repercussions into adulthood.

FIVE

Once Fat, Always Fat

Physical Impact in Adulthood

Seth awoke to the sound of his alarm, his eyes flying open at the insistent screech. As he flailed for the clock on his nightstand, he tangled his arm in the tube of his CPAP, nearly ripping the expensive mask off his face and pulling the machine to the floor in the process. Once he steadied himself he was able to extricate his arm from the hose enough to turn off the alarm and carefully take the contraption off his head. He had been sleeping much better since his doctor put him on the machine for his sleep apnea, but as he turned off the machine and reached across the bed for his wife he encountered the not-yet-familiar feel of a cold, empty bed. Although she had tried valiantly, she simply hadn't been able to get accustomed to the noise of the machine, and they had been sleeping in separate bedrooms for almost a month now. While the machine was necessary for his health, and with it his sleep had improved more than he ever thought possible, it completely disrupted her own ability to sleep and they'd been forced to sleep apart.

As he had begun to do, he waited for his wife's alarm to go off next door. Once he heard it, he smiled and quietly snuck into the bedroom they had shared for more than twenty years. He crept into bed, wrapped his arms around her, and before he knew it he had fallen asleep again. He woke himself just a few minutes later with a loud snore; loud enough that Joanne hadn't needed the backup snooze. She smiled at him, still not used to the marks the mask left on his face. She quietly slipped out of bed and into the bathroom. A few minutes later she emerged carrying his diabetes testing kit. Having done this routine every morning for more than ten years now, she opened the strip, inserted it in the meter, and reached for her husband's hand completely by rote. He reached out to her, and

she quickly engaged the lancet to draw enough blood for the strip.
She held his finger to the strip to absorb the blood, and the meter
chirped a few seconds later.
"You're a little high this morning—shredded wheat for you."
Seth frowned. He hated shredded wheat. What he hated more,
though, was sleeping alone.

We have known for many years that heart disease is the number one killer in America, followed closely by cancer, and then by other diseases that jockey for the remaining places (including stroke, accidents, and chronic lower respiratory diseases). We have launched campaign after campaign to raise awareness of these diseases, such as the tremendously successful Relay for Life events to raise money for and awareness about cancer, and more recently the "Wear Red" events that raise awareness about heart disease in women. When we raise awareness about these conditions, though, we are only focusing on the end result: the disease that has already occurred. While, yes, more than a half million people die per year from heart disease, what led to that heart disease? In essence, what *really* killed them? And what role does obesity play in that?

In a landmark study that revolutionized how "causes of death" are viewed, the Centers for Disease Control and Prevention (CDC) compiled what the "actual" causes of death were in the United States. They based their findings upon their comprehensive mortality data for the year 2000,[1] drawn from a national database maintained by CDC containing information from every death certificate in the United States. Instead of examining the ultimate cause of death, such as heart failure or lung cancer, the researchers took a step further back to see what the outcome was ultimately tied to—if someone had died from lung cancer after decades of smoking, it wasn't the cancer that killed them, it was the smoking. There is much less we can do to prevent the biologic causal pathways of cancer, but if we can remove that *underlying* cause, then we can truly impact these causes of death. Once they had teased out the actual underlying causes of death, the results of the study were staggering: the leading actual causes of death were *all* linked to individual behaviors—in essence, people *choosing* to engage in behaviors that were quite literally killing them. Their analysis showed that tobacco use was the number one cause of death, accounting for over 18 percent of all deaths in the United States. Put into perspective, that means that one out of every five people who died in 2000 died because of their use of tobacco. Following only slightly behind tobacco was poor diet and physical inactivity, which led to 365,000 deaths, accounting for 15 percent of the nation's mortality. Nearly one out of every six deaths was linked directly to diet and exercise, and by extension, obesity. From there, every other underlying cause of death followed, having less impact than obesity.

The magnitude of this finding cannot be overstated: this study showed that obesity kills more people every year than alcohol, infectious diseases, poisonings, motor vehicle crashes, firearm accidents, sexual behaviors, and illicit drug use *combined*.

Now think for a moment of our focus on diet and exercise with our children: do we put as much focus on these behaviors as we do on all the others combined? Do we focus on preventing obesity with the same combined energy that we devote to preventing and treating alcoholism, avoiding catching infectious diseases, promoting motor vehicle safety and gun safety, engaging in STD prevention activities, and controlling the drug trade?

The impact of obesity upon mortality comes from its association with so many adult chronic diseases. As we saw in the previous chapter, obesity is linked to several diseases that are emerging in children, diseases that for the most part were previously considered adult diseases. These diseases continue in adults who have not reached a normal adult weight, as is the case for the 80 percent of overweight children who become obese adults.[2] In addition, they are joined by a collection of other diseases that are seen in overweight and obese adults, often worsened by—if not the direct result of— the physical harm caused to the body during childhood. The effect on physical health is so strong that obesity has been estimated to constitute nearly 10 percent of all medical care costs (amounting to almost $150 billion per year).[3] The diseases that follow will have a crushing effect on our society, as they will rapidly become the norm for health. If current trends continue, it is estimated that up to 37–44 percent of 35-year-olds in 2020 will be *obese* (the generation currently just exiting childhood),[4] not to mention the additional adults who will be overweight once they reach adulthood. The vast majority of the conditions described are *preventable* if a normal weight is able to be established and maintained—they should motivate us all to examine how important the weight of our children truly is.

While we have focused on particularly impactful diseases in this chapter, we do not want to undersell the physical health impact that obesity has on adult health. Adults who are overweight have higher rates of arthritis, birth defects in their children, cancer, congestive heart failure, coronary heart disease, diabetes, erectile dysfunction, gallstones, high blood pressure, high cholesterol, infertility, menstrual irregularities, miscarriages, sleep apnea, stroke, and countless other outcomes. The health impacts touch nearly every aspect of our lives, and as a result have a significant impact on life expectancy, shortening lifespan by up to ten years for the most obese individuals.[5] And, most tragically, the effects of these diseases lead to premature death and disease for those who were overweight children, *regardless of their adult weight.*[6]

As scientists have begun to try and examine the health effects that childhood obesity will have, leading researchers have concluded that if you want to know what's happening as a result of childhood obesity, you should look at what's happening in young and middle-aged adults,[7] as they are facing the consequences of having grown up the fattest generation ever. These effects are strong and have severe consequences: childhood obesity has already been shown to lead to higher death rates in *middle age* due to heart attack (3–4 times the risk), colon cancer (twice the risk), respiratory diseases (2.5 times the risk), and sudden unexplained death (2–3 times the risk), and we have only just begun to examine all of the long-term physical health impacts of having been an overweight child.

HEART (NOT-SO) HEALTHY: CARDIOVASCULAR DISEASE

Representing a variety of outcomes ranging from the traditional heart attack to progressive narrowing of the arteries, cardiovascular disease (encompassing heart diseases and stroke) has risen to become the number one cause of death in the United States. It's so common that children born in recent generations have between a 25 percent and 40 percent chance of having their eventual cause of death be cardiovascular disease.[8]

Obesity was classified in 1998 as a "major, modifiable risk factor" for coronary heart disease.[9] It was labeled as one of the most important factors in developing a major heart disease, but also one that could be changed (unlike age or family history). In addition, obesity has been shown to increase the odds of having a stroke fourfold, particularly in those *under* the age of 65.[10] While today the average age at first heart attack is 66 years for men[11] and 70 years for women,[12] and for stroke, the average age is 68.4 years across both genders, the ages at which these cardiovascular events are occurring is getting *younger.* For instance, the average age for a stroke is *down* nearly three years from an average of 71.3 years in 1994 to 68.4 years today. This gradual move toward an earlier age of stroke parallels the nationwide increases in obesity—when looking at younger populations (those most hit by the obesity epidemic), the rates of stroke more than doubled in twenty- to forty-five-year-olds in the same time span.[13] This directly contradicts the argument that some demographers make that the reason we are seeing higher rates of cardiovascular disease is because of the marked decreases in other causes of death; after all, everyone dies from something—if we no longer die from smallpox and tuberculosis, we are able to reach an age to die from chronic diseases. While this certainly plays a role, the shift to *younger* ages of cardiovascular outcomes cannot be explained in this way—we are suddenly doing something that is placing us at a much higher risk for death by these diseases at younger ages, and the culprit is resoundingly agreed to be obesity.

The impact of obesity in adulthood starts from its presence in childhood—obese children overwhelmingly become obese adults, and these adults face seemingly insurmountable odds of being impacted by heart disease. Studies have shown that being overweight as a child increases the risk of having coronary artery disease as an adult by more than one-third, which may not seem that significant, but it equates to thousands upon thousands of additional cardiac episodes. What is most troubling, however, is that being an overweight child not only increases the amount of risk, but also lowers the age at which events are seen—leading to an increase in cardiovascular events in adults as young as twenty-five years old.[14] Overweight children are starting to have heart attacks and plaque buildup in their twenties—which is almost incomprehensible.

Without drilling down into the complex biochemical processes that underlie obesity's relation to heart disease, think of the circulatory system as similar to an automotive engine. If you take the engine from an intermediate sedan (an "average" weight car) and place it into an Escalade, you immediately place undue and ultimately unsustainable strain upon the engine. Similarly, being overweight places the heart under too much strain, causing it to constantly have to work harder. For those with high blood pressure on top of weight gain, the effect is worse (think of it in terms of your engine trying to work effectively under too much engine pressure—operating at the risk of "blowing a hose," which, in your body, would distinctly not be good).

The second strain that obesity places on the circulatory system is similar to engine gunk buildup in hoses and chambers. People who are obese tend to build up plaque in their arteries, narrowing the passageways and forcing the heart to work harder to move blood throughout the body. Even more troubling, though, is the little-known fact that in obese individuals, fat builds up not only in the gut and on the thighs, but also directly around the heart itself. This "pericardial fat" directly in the core of the circulatory system is even more strongly linked to plaque buildup in vital arteries, essentially choking blood vessels from within.[15]

One of the biggest risk factors for having a cardiovascular event is high blood pressure, strongly associated with obesity. While hypertension is a serious illness in children, in adults it becomes even more so. Most complications of hypertension are indirect, related to the stress and damage caused within the body by having long-term elevated blood pressure. So it isn't hypertension itself that causes long-term harm, but rather the accumulation of all the microscopic damage it causes over the years. For the one out of three adults in the United States with hypertension, this can lead to damage in the heart, blood vessels, kidneys, and many other parts of the body that ultimately increases the risk of coronary heart disease, heart failure, stroke, and kidney failure. One of the most troubling aspects of hypertension is that often people do not realize they have it, even when the damage to their bodies is already occurring.[16] Even for adults with diagnosed hypertension, less than half have their condition under adequate control,[17] despite the dozens of effective hypertension medications on the market. Even beyond the physical risks, hypertension has a significant impact on the economy itself, having been projected to cost the United States *$93.5 billion per year* in medical care, medicine, and lost productivity (days missed at work).[18]

While high blood pressure ultimately has many causes, an estimated 26–28 percent of all cases are linked directly to obesity.[19] Whether the underlying cause of hypertension is weight or not, though, weight control measures can reduce or even eliminate hypertension. This effect is so strong that the National Heart, Lung, and Blood Institute (the agency that oversees much of the federal research into hypertension) lists diet, exercise, and weight as the first three of only five factors that can be used to prevent (and even treat) hypertension in adults.[20] For prevention in children and teens, the *only* prevention methods recommended are diet, exercise, and weight management—meaning we have an extraordinary degree of control over our health that we simply aren't using at this point.

The ironic part is that, for something we have so much control over, cardiovascular disease remains the number one killer in the country. Very rarely are we presented with an opportunity to prevent the exact thing that is most likely to kill us, and until we embrace our fundamental power in the process, we will continue to see skyrocketing rates of heart disease deaths as the childhood obesity epidemic continues to feed its mirror epidemic of cardiovascular disease in adults.

A LITTLE SUGAR: DIABETES

As discussed in the previous chapter, diabetes is a serious consequence of obesity that remains largely both preventable and curable through weight control. While the effects of diabetes in children are frightening, in adults they are even more severe. The issue in adults is becoming so severe that diabetes could quickly become a leading cause of death. The CDC recently projected that by the year 2050, when today's children are in the prime of adulthood, up to *one in three* adults will be diabetic, as compared to the "mere" 10 percent of adults who are diabetic today.[21] This increase, like so many things we've examined, is directly tied to increases in childhood obesity.

Complications from diabetes in adults include impacts across the entire body,[22] summarized in Table 5.1 below. The most striking complications involve cardiovascular diseases and related conditions. Nearly two out of three adult diabetics have hypertension,[23] and *two out of three* adult diabetics will die from a stroke or from heart disease.[24] Given diet and exercise's role in preventing or reversing not only diabetes, but also heart disease itself, these deaths are doubly preventable.

Diabetes impacts more than an adult's physical health; it also leads to increased risk for mental health concerns. Adults who are diabetic are twice as likely to develop depression,[25] linked both to the severity of the complications of the disease (in particular erectile dysfunction, blindness, and amputations), and also to the systemic, lifelong changes required as a part of the diagnosis. Facing a lifetime of sugar-testing, doctor's visits, and low-sugar meals can often lead newly diagnosed diabetics toward depression, or depression can gradually emerge as patients continue to struggle with their disease. Depression is not only a serious health condition in its own right, but also can interfere with a person's ability to effectively manage their disease, further increasing the risk of remaining overweight as an adult.[26]

TABLE 5.1: PHYSICAL HEALTH COMPLICATIONS OF DIABETES

Outcome	
Erectile dysfunction	Hypertension
Stroke	Hearing loss
Eating disorders	Gum disease and tooth loss
Polycystic ovarian syndrome	Kidney disease
Blindness (glaucoma, cataracts, and retinopathy)	Heart disease
	Foot/leg amputations
Nerve damage	

The effects of diabetes in those who were overweight children are just now being realized. While weight loss is the front-line defense against the progression of diabetes, the fact remains that the vast majority of diabetics remain that way for the rest of their lives. For diabetic children, if weight is not lost and diabetes remains into adulthood, the risk of long-term complications is elevated: the longer the course of diabetes, the more likely it is that complications will arise. When considering their treatment options, adults who had early-onset Type 2 diabetes are 80 percent more likely to end up requiring medical insulin,[27] and are more likely to have their medicines stop working.[28] Emerging evidence also shows that adults with childhood-onset Type 2 diabetes face increased complications, including erectile dysfunction,[29] coronary heart disease (including narrowing and hardening of the arteries),[30] eye damage,[31] and death.[32] In particular, while adults whose Type 2 diabetes developed in adulthood have four times the risk of having a heart attack when compared to non-diabetics, adults who had early-onset Type 2 diabetes are *fourteen times as likely* to have a heart attack when compared to non-diabetics, placing them at increased risk even in comparison to their fellow diabetics simply because of their earlier age at diagnosis.[33]

Diabetes is a chronic disease, which causes many people to lose sight of its wide-ranging complications—after all, if people have it for decades, it can't be that bad, right? But the body-wide impact it has directly contributes to severe medical consequences and, ultimately, earlier death.

THE BIG C: CANCER

A variety of cancers are independently associated with obesity, and for now these seem to be restricted to adult cancers. While the exact pathway by which obesity causes cancers is not fully known, chronic tissue inflammation and general physical stress on the body have been hypothesized to contribute.[34] There is also the general association of obesity with poorer nutrition and lower levels of physical activity (both of which independently increase the risk of a variety of cancers). The effects of obesity upon cancer are far reaching, so much so that obesity is viewed as the third-largest contributor to the development of cancer (behind only smoking and alcohol).[35] The link between obesity and cancer is so strong that scientists estimate that *one-third of all cancer deaths could be prevented* if obesity rates were reduced.[36]

Being obese as an adult increases the risk of a variety of cancers up to 500 percent. These cancers include everything from the much-feared pancreatic cancer to the entirely preventable colon cancer. Together, cancers impacted by obesity represent 58 percent of all cancer diagnoses.[37] The individual increases in cancer death risk associated with obesity are presented in Table 5.2.

TABLE 5.2: INCREASE IN CANCER DEATH RISK DUE TO OBESITY[38]

	Men	*Women*
All Cancers (smokers and nonsmokers)	52%	88%
All Cancers (nonsmokers only)	68%	151%
Uterus	—	525%
Kidney	70%	375%
Liver	350%	68%
Cervix	—	220%
Pancreas	160%	176%
Esophagus	91%	164%
Gallbladder	76%	113%
Breast	N/K*	112%
Non-Hodgkins Lymphoma	40%	95%
Colorectal	84%	46%
Multiple Myeloma	71%	44%
Ovary	—	51%
Prostate	34%	—

*While men can develop breast cancer, sufficient studies have not been conducted to estimate the influence of obesity on its development in men.

The rates on the previous page apply to adults who are over-weight, regardless of their weight status as children. Given the chronic nature of cancer and the unknown methods through which obesity impacts cancer, it is still unclear to what extent having been overweight as a child will influence these percentages. It is highly likely that the age at which obesity-related cancers will begin to occur in previously overweight children will gradually decrease (similar to stroke rates described previously)—we just haven't been looking at it for enough time to determine what this long-term effect will be. Similarly, we currently are not able to assess whether losing weight will reduce the associated cancer risks—if children who are able to lose weight before making it to adulthood will continue to have elevated cancer risks or not. For other cancer-causing factors the long-term risk can be diminished by stopping harmful behav-ior. So if a smoker stops smoking, their cancer risk goes down. But it is still debatable as to whether or not these risks ever drop to what they would have been if the person had never smoked. Because of obesity's role in so many cancers, it is likely that the effects will differ across the various cancers, but regardless, chances are that the risk can be diminished if weight is lost, but only eliminated if weight is never allowed to reach the level of obesity.

TRIGGER POINTS—THE GREAT UNKNOWN

As mentioned above, one of the greatest sources of uncertainty is the fact that researchers have not been able to adequately determine the role that having been an obese child will play in the develop-ment of diseases that emerge decades later—we simply haven't been watching long enough. There could be a link between childhood obesity and Alzheimer's disease, for all we know, but we haven't had enough people move from being an obese child through the sixty to eighty years it takes to reach such a long-term disease to examine its effects. While many people hold out hope that if children are able to bring their weights to a normal range, the effects will disappear, thus far this remains largely an unfounded hope. As we all know, the human body and its associated systems are incredibly complex and there is much more we *don't* know about it than we actually *do*.

Not everyone who starts smoking eventually develops lung cancer, but similarly, not everyone who *stops* smoking instantly removes their risk of developing lung cancer. What happens is that the body gradually accumulates a level of exposure to the harmful influence that sets into place a cascade of bodily processes that will lead to the development of the disease. Chronic disease experts call this the "trigger point." For smokers, there comes a point (different for each person) at which their body succumbs to the harmful effects of the habit and the cancer begins. Even if the individual stops smoking, the cancer development process has already begun; it is too late. They don't have cancer yet, but they have passed the proverbial point of no return and their body is in the process of "developing" cancer.

Where this becomes especially troubling in the case of childhood obesity is that, for the most part, we have no clue as to what a typical trigger point is for obesity-related diseases. We do not know how many years at what level of obesity will trigger the onset of diabetes, heart disease, cancers, and other diseases. As we start to see these diseases trickle down into children themselves, though, it becomes apparent that the level of exposure needed is obviously quite low (they do not even have to make it out of childhood before the *outcome* is reached, much less the trigger point). The upcoming decades will shed much light onto this process, as young adults continue to face diseases that they were never given the option to prevent themselves. The current lack of knowledge regarding when that point of no return is reached leaves us rudderless in a river of consequences, with our only remaining option being to try to stay out of the river entirely—only by doing everything we can to prevent the exposure entirely can we be sure that we will not reach that ultimate trigger point.

CONCLUSION

In this chapter and the preceding one, we have explored several of the physical health effects associated with obesity, both in childhood and in adulthood. While the biologic processes we've already examined are complex, they are clearer than many of the more psychological consequences that we explore in the following chapters. Compared to physical health we know precious little about mental and social health in general, and with regards to its relation to obesity, we are even further in the dark.

Despite often not knowing the exact mechanisms at play, there is no doubt that being an overweight child has strong and enduring effects on psychological and social well-being. The remainder of this book explores these effects, taking a critical eye to the emotional, psychological, and social ramifications of having been an overweight child. This line of inquiry as a well-developed area of science is relatively new, but, as we will see, the findings are already very troubling.

SIX

Fat Brain

Mental Health Impact in Childhood

"Fatty Mattie, two by four—can't get through the bathroom door…"

Mattie closed her eyes, screwing them shut against the barrage of insults flying her way. With every ounce of her resolve, she resisted the urge to cover her ears. Her back was to the group of bullies, and she would not give them the satisfaction of seeing her react to their taunts.

It had been the same ever since her family had moved and she had started at the new school. At her old school, she had grown up with everyone in her class and they all got along for the most part. At her new school, though, no one knew her, and she had been singled out her first day because of her weight. She had harbored a growing depression as her self-worth eroded.

The taunts continued as she thought to herself desperately— "why won't they just leave me alone?"

Her teacher saw what was going on and came over to ask if she needed help—ironically, the last thing Mattie wanted. As she fought back tears she insisted she was fine and kept her hands wrapped firmly around the chains of the swing. Her teacher looked at her with sympathy, and scattered the group of children with a single glare. Her attention was quickly pulled in another direction by a wailing child, though, and the bullies reassembled. As Mattie had feared, her teacher's concern only brought on a harsher litany of jokes calculated specifically to hit her where it hurt most. More to distract herself than anything, she started to swing again.

Mattie blocked out all the sound, ignoring everything around her to the extent that she didn't even hear when the recess bell rang and she was supposed to follow her classmates back into the building. She was so focused on just breathing and swinging that she saw nothing but the rhythmic rise and fall of the horizon and heard nothing but the slow creaking of the rusty old swing set.

Suddenly, her teacher's face appeared in front of her and the swing came to an abrupt stop.

"Mattie, what are you doing? You know better than to stay out here when the bell rings." In reality, her teacher was more concerned about Mattie being cornered by the bullies, but she couldn't exactly express that to her young student.

Mattie looked at her teacher, inexplicably crushed by the mild reprimand. Crestfallen, she launched off the swing in tears, running for the schoolhouse entryway. Her teacher frowned, thinking to herself, "that child seems to spend more time crying than smiling."

C hildren are not blind to weight—they see it, discuss it, and ridicule it. For children, weight is one of the most salient features of a person, and one that frequently leads to judgment and dislike. This effect is much stronger than many realize and has been recognized within the research community for over half a century. In one of the seminal studies on weight bias among children, a 1961 study of hundreds of school-aged children presented study subjects with six pictures of children. Participants were asked to rank the pictures in order of whom they would want to form friendships with. The six pictures included an average-weight child with no disabilities, an overweight child with no disabilities, a child in a wheelchair, a child using crutches, a child with an amputated hand, and a child with a facial disfigurement. Overwhelmingly, the overweight child was ranked last of the six figures—labeled by peers as being the "least likeable."[1] While this study is over fifty years old, it was recently replicated and not only did the overweight child continue to rank last, the distance between the highest ranked child and the lowest ranked child (the overweight child) had increased by 40 percent; while they were still last, overweight children were even less desirable as a friend today than fifty years ago.[2] Weight, it seems, is standing out more in children's minds, and apparently in an increasingly negative light.

As a result, overweight children are growing up surrounded by peers who have absolutely no problem with pointing out that they are overweight, an observation frequently coupled with an accompanying disdain for the overweight person. Children have been shown to view overweight children as being less disciplined, more self-indulgent, and less popular[3]—things that dramatically impact a child's fragile psychological well-being in a time of particular vulnerability to the influence of peers. It places them at particular risk of being bullied, which we discuss in much more detail later in this chapter. And it's not just kids who are bullied—overweight *adults* report that the most frequent weight-related harassment they experience is a *child* making fun of them for their weight (more common than hearing comments from adult strangers, being stared at, and being ignored or excluded because of weight).[4] If children are this relentless with adults, who typically command at least a shred of respect, imagine how harsh the treatment of fellow children is.

Recently, researchers have begun to look beyond physical health symptoms of obesity and have started to place increasing focus on the potential impact upon mental health and psychological well-being. While the evidence in this area is still emerging, by applying well-known principles of cognitive development and social psychology, it is easy to see how widespread and far-reaching the impact will be on children's psychological health if the childhood obesity epidemic continues. One of the driving forces behind examining the mental health impact of obesity in childhood is the fact that, despite all the physical limitations obesity imposes, when children are asked about what they feel the most immediate consequence of being overweight is, they overwhelmingly point to the differential treatment they receive from not only their peers but also from society at large.[5] The large mental health burden faced by overweight children is further reinforced by findings that the largest increases in medical care utilization associated with childhood obesity are actually tied to mental health, with overweight children 50 percent more likely to seek out mental health care than their normal-weight counterparts.[6]

Childhood is a time of growth, of development, of learning how to interact with the world and find our own place within it. When you think about the sheer amount of learning that occurs during the span of kindergarten to twelfth grade, it's quite astonishing: we go from not being able to read at all to being able to examine the complexities of eighteenth-century British literature—no small feat! While our schools' neat agendas and class rotations show us exactly the types of knowledge our children are gaining, what is often misperceived is the amount of emotional growth and social learning that is occurring during the same amount of time. During childhood and adolescence, we go from not even knowing what genders are to having gendered behavior so socialized into us that we don't even realize when we are yielding to social pressures. We learn how and when to laugh, when not to cry, how to make other people happy, and all the while feel the pressure that this places on us to fit in, to conform to an arbitrary social image. And all this occurs before the government considers us mentally capable of selecting the leader of our own country.

Because of all the pressures and the inexperience in handling those pressures, we are extraordinarily vulnerable during these times, as any parent can tell you—simply wearing the wrong color outfit at school can seem like a traumatizing experience to kids. So when we start to look at the ways in which overweight children are treated during their childhood, it should come as no surprise that they face increased risk of an entire host of mental health issues. Unfortunately, many of these problems lay the groundwork for further psychological challenges faced in adulthood (as described in the next chapter).

These factors increase the risk of several psychological disorders for overweight children. Problems with anxiety in particular are very common, with up to 40 percent of obese children having a diagnosable anxiety disorder.[7] Overweight children have also been shown to have higher rates of depression, general feelings of worthlessness and inferiority,[8] and, tragically, higher rates of suicide as well.[9]

The effects of these insidious mental health challenges are much more difficult for parents to detect. If our children suddenly have trouble breathing from asthma or pass out due to elevated blood sugar, it's easy for us to spot that something is wrong and intervene as needed. But it is much more difficult for parents, loved ones, and even teachers to notice that a child is facing mental health concerns. Adolescents are notoriously "moody," and discriminating between what is developmentally expected and what is indicative of a true problem can be very difficult. Given the fact that both overweight boys and girls have higher rates of psychological disorders (particularly depression[10]), it is crucial for parents to understand not only what the psychological effects of obesity are, but more importantly, why those effects are there (so they can help kids overcome them).

These effects are real and pose significant threats to the happiness and well-being of our children. Long-term studies tracking children over time have shown that because of the psychological strain placed upon them, overweight children have higher rates of behavior problems.[11] Some argue that psychological problems fuel weight gain, and not vice versa (for example, it's been proven that weight gain can be both a cause and an effect of depression). However, behavior problems are highest among overweight children who were previously normal weight: these children face the social pressures of being an obese child for the first time without having developed any coping strategies along the way, and so they act out.[12]

Because of all the factors described in this chapter, overweight children view themselves in general as fundamentally having less worth than their normal-weight peers[13]—while we might expect overweight children to have a negative body image, for them to view themselves as less-valuable people is simply unacceptable. These effects only increase with increasing weight—children who are extremely obese have been described by leading experts as having their day-to-day lives "globally and severely impaired," a result of obesity's dramatic impact upon their emotional, social, academic, and psychological functioning.[14] This impairment stems only partially from the physical effects of obesity—the remainder centers on the intense psychological strain that being an overweight child places on a fragile, developing psyche.

Below we have presented two main sources of the psychological impact that results from being an overweight child. There are countless others, but these two have consistent, profound, and direct impact on the mental health of overweight children.

A TWENTY-FIRST-CENTURY EPIDEMIC: BULLYING

Recently, bullying has been thrust to the forefront of the public's attention, and deservedly so. Nearly 25 percent of boys and 17 percent of girls report being bullied,[15] and these numbers are anticipated to grow even higher as bullies find an ever-increasing array of opportunities to harass others through social media and other means of cyber bullying. Being bullied has been tied to everything from increased use of substances to increased risk of suicide, and in general, those who are bullied have greater health problems, poorer emotional adjustment, and fewer social interactions.[16] Bullying captures some of parents' worst fears for children—that something will happen to them when they are away from us and therefore away from our ability to protect. When bullying takes place in the school setting, it becomes even more upsetting to us—we send our children to school for learning and development, not for exposure to hostility and potential physical injury. And, unfortunately, bullying all too often becomes a long-term, consistent issue—if a child is bullied once, it increases their chances substantially of being repeatedly bullied throughout their childhood.[17]

Bullying behaviors extend far beyond physical bullying into verbal and psychological bullying.[18] Bullying has traditionally been viewed as relentless harassment, taunting, or physical aggression toward someone perceived to be "weak" or "different." When examining what types of differences lead to bullying, the most common "reason" for bullying is someone's appearance.[19] There is a robust literature that supports both a) the increased risk of being bullied for those who are overweight or obese, and b) the resulting negative impacts that bullying has on psychological effects.

Overweight children report being bullied more often than average-weight children (at rates at least 50 percent higher than their average-weight peers),[20] and the effects become even more pronounced the more overweight a child becomes. For those at the highest end of being overweight, 63 percent of obese girls and 58 percent of obese boys report being teased or bullied about their weight by their peers.[21] Even more upsetting, almost half of obese girls and one-third of obese boys report being teased about their weight *by their own families*. This high rate of teasing in what should be a child's refuge and place of safety is astonishing and only serves to worsen the negative impacts of being bullied in the first place.

These impacts are far-reaching and serve to exacerbate many other negative effects of childhood obesity discussed throughout this book. From a social standpoint, children who are bullied are more lonely in the school setting, have lower academic achievement, have fewer friends, and have worse relationships with their classmates.[22] Victims of bullying have higher rates of anxiety, depression, psychosomatic symptoms, and eating disorders (likely a result of trying to control their weight, the source of their bullying).[23]

The psychological impact of weight-related bullying is not just about these children feeling "sad" or "lonely" at school—bullying leads directly to clinical levels of psychological illnesses. The effects of bullying-related depression and anxiety are so strong that *one in five* victims of childhood bullying has clinical levels of depression or anxiety.[24] These conditions require complex psychological or psychiatric intervention and can lead to lifelong struggles with these mental illnesses—over a third of all teenagers who experience an episode of major depression will have another within four years.[25] The effects of these disorders are amplified by *earlier* onset, so a child bullied into depression before the age of fourteen has a longer expected course of depression than a child with onset later in the teenage years. Because bullying is most intense during middle school years,[26] the impact on anxiety and depression is even more troublesome.

While these effects hold for all types of bullying, overweight children face both general bullying (being pushed and shoved, tripped in the hallways, ostracized from classmates) and weight-specific bullying (being called names about their weight, having their bodies photographed and posted on social media, and so on). Weight-specific bullying has been strongly tied to childhood depression[27] as well as overall lower self-esteem and stronger feelings of body dissatisfaction.[28] The negative effects on self-esteem and body image come from many other sources besides bullying, and are associated with so many additional problems that they are covered in their own right later in this book, but to briefly summarize: the impact on self-esteem and body image opens the door for even more complications, ranging from criminal behavior to increased risk of sexually transmitted diseases. Unfortunately, children who have been bullied because of their weight get a double whammy to their self-esteem: they are impacted by the general effects of being overweight, compounded by the effects of having been bullied.[29]

The effects of bullying are not just psychological—bullying is also tied to physical problems, including headaches, stomachaches, bed-wetting, and sleeping problems.[30] In a desperate attempt to control the weight that is the source of their bullying, overweight children are increasingly developing eating disorders,[31] the most fatal of all psychological disorders. And in an ironically cruel relationship, children often report receiving the harshest bullying when they are actually engaged in physical activity, leading them to further avoid engaging in the very thing that could help them reach a normal weight.[32]

While it might be easy to think that children will "outgrow" bullying and that it won't cause any long-term damage, this couldn't be further from the truth. As it seems with nearly everything we've examined with childhood obesity, there are long-term effects that extend well into a bullied child's adult life, even decades after the bullying has ended. Adults who were bullied as children have higher rates of depression and lower self-esteem in their twenties, despite being no more likely than others to be harassed or socially isolated in their adulthood (this represents a strong carry-over of the effects of having been bullied as a child).[33] When trying to determine why these effects would linger, it has been suggested that those who have been bullied view their poor treatment by others as proof that they are "inadequate and worthless,"[34] and thereafter internalize those perceptions to the point that they become "automatic thoughts" or beliefs about one's self that are no longer questioned—they are simply accepted as fact. Again, given how often overweight children are bullied (even by their families), it comes as no surprise that they end up fundamentally viewing themselves as being worth less than others. The long-term psychological effects of bullying are so severe that adults who were bullied as children are twice as likely to both attempt and complete suicide later in life[35]—even for bullying that occurred as young as age eight.[36]

Unfortunately, along with the skyrocketing rates of obesity, an entirely new form of bullying has appeared in the shape of cyber bullying. Online social networking has exponentially expanded the reach of bullies, allowing them to not only bully inside and outside of the school setting, but in front of an entirely new audience. By interacting with social media outlets, bullies can now spread their impact directly to children's friends and families, even inside their own homes, infiltrating what for many used to be their only safe haven. While the full effects of cyber bullying on overweight children are not yet known, the effects discussed previously can only be expected to increase.

Bullying prevention is complex and the subject of much scientific inquiry. The unfortunate thing is that nearly 20 percent of adolescents—which equals more than ten million kids—report that they bully other children.[37] With numbers so high, intervening in each individual case is not very feasible, and bullying frequently goes unreported (further complicating efforts to intervene). Given obesity's direct impact on the risk of being bullied, actions to remedy obesity itself are an important companion strategy to bullying prevention.

We are in no way saying that it is any child's fault that he or she is bullied, and we vehemently assert every child's right to live a bully-free life—but it is a brutal fact that weight is an extremely common reason for bullying behavior. Parents cannot readily control the actions of another child who is acting as a bully, but they do have power to help their child reach a healthy weight (which would in turn hopefully diminish both the occurrence and psychological impact of the bullying behaviors).

FRIENDSHIPS AND SOCIAL INTERACTIONS

Whether a child is bullied or not, overweight children face struggles with establishing and maintaining friendships. Studies have repeatedly shown that children who are overweight are socially marginalized[38] and receive less social support,[39] and as a result, overweight children report feeling that they are less liked than their normal-weight classmates.[40] They also directly report having fewer friends, and feeling less cared about by the friends they do have.[41] The impact of weight on their friendships is evident to the children themselves, as nearly 70 percent of overweight kids believe they would have more friends if they could only lose weight.[42] All these perceptions combine to lead overweight children, particularly girls, to feel they have less social status,[43] which can lead to low self-esteem.

The feeling of being less liked stems from two sources. First, because overweight children are more likely to be socially outcast in the first place, associating with overweight children places other children at increased risk of becoming outcast or bullied— driving children away before they even have a chance to establish friendships with overweight children. Second, children have been shown to generally dislike their overweight peers more than their average-weight peers.[44] This effect has been strongly tied to notions of "weight blame," in which children have internalized messages from parents and the media that it is a child's "fault" that they are overweight because they are lazy and have no self-control.

The effects of weight blame and weight bias on children's acceptance appear to be strongest during preschool,[45] when children are gaining their first exposure to other children and laying the groundwork for social interaction styles that will persist for the rest of their lives. Because overweight children do not have as much opportunity to learn how to properly establish and maintain friendships during this time, they are set up for a lifetime of difficulty in one of the areas that is most important not only for social development but for overall psychological well-being.

Weight bias is not new; it has permeated our culture for centuries. Even Shakespeare passed judgment on overweight individuals in his masterpiece *Julius Caesar*, intimating they are simpleminded and lacking in ambition when Caesar himself says to Marc Antony:

> Let me have men about me that are fat, sleek-headed men and such as sleep a-nights. Yon Cassius has a lean and hungry look. He thinks too much. Such men are dangerous.

This bias has been shown to impact employment, education, health care, and interpersonal relationships. While most forms of bias and resulting discrimination are frowned upon by society at large, there is a pervasive "social acceptability and cultural tolerance"[46] toward weight bias, significantly complicating any efforts to ameliorate its impact. The effects of this culturally accepted bias and discrimination are so severe that overweight children are described as growing up in a "hostile cultural climate"[47] that can only result in severe psychological consequences.

Even more upsetting, weight bias has even been found in those who are supposed to be allies, who are in direct positions to help kids achieve a normal weight. For instance, both physical education teachers[48] and obesity-specializing health professionals[49] have been found to exhibit weight blame and anti-fat bias, describing overweight children as "lazy," "stupid," and "worthless."[50] If these professionals, entrusted with shaping our children's education and health, are themselves biased against overweight children, how can we ever expect children to gain the support they need to reach and maintain a healthy weight?

CONCLUSION

As suggested throughout this chapter, the psychological effects of childhood obesity are severe and widespread, and will impact overweight children not only when they are young, but also in their adult lives. The factors described here infiltrate the very underpinnings of their psychological health. The next chapter not only discusses what these life-long impacts will be, but also explains the fundamental ways in which being overweight as a child impacts adult functioning.

SEVEN

In a Fat State of Mind

Mental Health Impact
in Adulthood

"Because I'm worthless."

Jennifer glared at her therapist, frustrated by her insistence on going over and over the same small detail.

"I've heard you say that before, Jennifer. What makes you think you're worthless?"

"It's not something I 'think,' it's something I know."

"But how do you know it?"

"Because—if I wasn't worthless, someone would care about me. I would care enough about myself to get healthy, to not be so fat that no one wants to even get near me," Jennifer snapped, frustrated with her therapist for harping on the issue.

Her therapist knew she was frustrated, but pressed the point.

"So no one cares for you?"

"Well, it's not really that no one cares for me. My parents care for me, and my friends, but no one will ever love me."

"Do your parents and friends love you?"

"That's not the same. How can anyone really love me, be 'in love' with me, when I'm this fat?"

"So what you're really feeling is that you won't find someone to love you because you think you're 'fat'—not that you aren't worth loving."

Jennifer paused—she'd never really thought of it that way before.

"I guess so—since I'm fat, why would anyone want me? Why would anyone want to marry me?"

Her therapist smiled gently. "Do you know anyone who is over-weight and married?"

"Of course I do; but I'm worthless."

"But you're not, you only feel that way. It seems that you're tying your own sense of worth to your weight itself, and they have nothing to do with each other."

Jennifer stared at her therapist, temporarily dumbstruck. Tentatively, hope seemed to emerge in her eyes, but was quickly extinguished by years of negative experiences.

"But I've felt that so long, how do I change it? It's not something I think anymore, it's just something I feel; it's a part of me."

The tentacles of being an overweight child extend into adulthood, fostering and sustaining avenues of psychological distress even beyond the childhood mental health challenges described in the previous chapter. The combination of all the factors discussed in this book serves to drastically impact the fundamental ways in which adults who were obese children view themselves, and as a result, it impacts their mental well-being. These effects are so strong that overweight and obese adults are much more likely to end up in the mental health-care system than their normal-weight counterparts, at rates up to 50 percent higher than would otherwise be expected.[1] The effect has been recognized for some time by researchers—to the extent that obesity has been referred to as a "psychological handicap" since the 1940s.[2] The public, however, has not yet become fully aware of the severe psychological consequences associated with being obese; their intrigue thus far has been captured almost entirely by the more predictable, familiar, and understandable physical effects of diabetes and hypertension.

In perhaps the earliest documentation of the psychological effects of being an obese adult, Dr. Wilhelm Ebstein—one of the earliest recognized experts in nutrition—defined three "technical" classifications of obesity in his 1887 book *Die Fettleibigkeit und ihre Behandlung* (*Obesity and Its Treatment*). Much to the surprise of our "modern" sensibilities, Ebstein's categories of obesity were:

enviable, laughable, and pitiable.[3] By these definitions, a slightly overweight person was to be *envied* for their financial ability to put on a few extra pounds, a fully overweight person was to be *laughed* at, and those who were obese were to be *pitied* for the ways in which their weight impacts all aspects of their lives. These were not tongue-in-cheek categories; they were intended to accurately describe the experiences of those who are obese—often ridiculed, and eventually viewed as something pitiful. While our current notions of body shape would not lend themselves to ever having an "enviable" stage of overweight, it still highlights the fact that for at least 135 years we have considered overweight individuals to be objects of ridicule and/or pity.

Ebstein's categories were perhaps influenced by William Banting's infamous 1863 "Letter on Corpulence, Addressed to the Public"—still in print 150 years later (now even available on Kindle). Having successfully lost a significant amount of weight, Banting became one of the first people to publish about successful weight loss, and in the process, he described the psychological experiences of an overweight person. Banting is often credited with being the author of the first ever "diet book," and his very name became a British slang word for "diet." In his "Letter," which was the first exposure many individuals had to what the daily life of an overweight person was like, he stated:

> Of all the parasites that affect humanity I do not know of, nor can I imagine, any more distressing than that of obesity...No man laboring under obesity can be quite insensible to the sneers and remarks of the cruel and injudicious in public assemblies, public vehicles, or the ordinary street traffic; nor to the annoyance of finding no adequate space in a public assembly if he should seek amusement or need refreshment, and therefore he naturally keeps away as much as possible from places where he is likely to be made the object of the taunts and remarks of others.

These feelings are echoed nearly the world over by individuals who have either grown up overweight, or experience being overweight for the first time as an adult. From a general psychological perspective, the impact of obesity on mental health is so strong that mental health professionals have been shown to *expect* their overweight clients to have more psychological problems—even when presented with identical case reports, they ascribe more negative psychological outcomes to overweight patients.[4] This comes from years of experiencing just that in their clients—an excess burden of psychological distress tied directly to their repeated negative reception from and treatment by society at large.

The relationship between weight status and psychological distress has seen decades of debate, with a broad range of findings regarding causal pathways and strength of the association. The results seem to vary by race, by gender, by socioeconomic status—every which way, to the point that it has become difficult to find a consistent relationship. In fact the only well-defined connection is with depression and anxiety disorders (described in this chapter). Interestingly, recent research has begun to tease out some of the reasons for discrepancies found in various studies. Overweight individuals are under intense societal pressure to bring themselves to a healthy weight, and in the process are rejected and maltreated—hypothetically, it is this alienation that impacts mental health. Fortunately for their mental health (although not their physical health), many individuals who are overweight do not actually perceive themselves to be so. In fact, 8 percent of obese individuals and 38 percent of overweight individuals do not even consider themselves to have a weight problem at all.[5]

This is a large reason why so many psychological studies have had conflicting findings—if an individual does not consider him or herself to be overweight, then he or she would not be subject to all of the emotional and social stressors we have discussed; in essence, their own ignorance of their actual weight status buffers them. They do not internalize the negativity they see surrounding being overweight because they do not believe themselves to be a member of that mistreated and stigmatized group. While research focused just on weight has been inconsistent, a parallel body of research has consistently shown that those who *perceive* themselves to be overweight have a strong and lasting negative consequence to their mental health—increasing their risk of moderate psychological distress by 50 percent, and their risk of extreme psychological distress by up to 120 percent.[6] This effect grows stronger with age, as the years of psychological distress build and continue to exert their cumulative pressure.[7]

This leads to one important point: the psychological ramifications of obesity are, unlike their physical health counterparts, almost entirely *socially* constructed. There is no universal underlying biological mechanism that explains the significantly higher levels of depression seen in the obese—it is instead largely tied to our *society's* accepted negative and discriminatory behaviors toward overweight individuals. This makes these effects all the more sinister, because they are inflicted *intentionally*. We have decided to permit a society in which such extreme psychological pressure is placed on overweight individuals that they frequently crack under the pressure. And by continuing to hold permissive attitudes toward those who enact the worst forms of weight bias, discrimination, and bullying, each of us serves to uphold the very system inflicting the harm.

As an example of the widespread cultural presence of this effect, consider television and movies. Shows such as *Drop Dead Diva*, in which a dead model comes back to life in an overweight woman's body, depend upon the inherent understanding of the audience that simply being fat makes her life worse. Former television shows such as *Ugly Betty* (centering on a young woman working at a fashion magazine whose size and style did not make for a "good fit") made frequent reference to weight as a source of "ugliness." Even though these shows focused somewhat on trying to counteract some of those stereotypes, they still relied on those stereotypes for the humor of the show. The same occurs with the stereotypical "fat" characters you find in movies: they are expected to be larger than life and often ridiculous in action (consider films such as *Bridesmaids* in which the one "plus-size" bridesmaid is the most ludicrous in the bunch). Whenever a theater roars in laughter at a fat character being humiliated in a movie, we implicitly (and vocally) support these very attitudes.

A change in the culture of "fat bashing" would require a nearly unprecedented shift in fundamental cultural views, something that we as a society have rarely been able to do. In the meantime, overweight individuals will continue to shoulder the burden heaped upon them by their often judgmental and critical normal-weight counterparts. And in turn, their underlying psychological health will continue to be compromised.

ANXIETY AND DEPRESSION

While many psychological sequelae of obesity have been examined, the two that emerge most strongly and frequently are anxiety and depression. Being overweight or obese has been tied directly and repeatedly to anxiety problems, not only in clinical samples examining the most extreme cases of weight, but also in community samples where the general public is surveyed to find more commonplace links.[8] And while weight-linked depression is stronger in women than in men, weight-linked anxiety is so extreme that both overweight women and men are more likely to be on prescription anti-anxiety medications and sleeping pills in order to overcome the bodily reactions of chronic anxiety (difficulty falling asleep/ staying asleep, heartburn, and so on) than their normal-weight counterparts.[9] The impact of weight on anxiety has been shown in a variety of specific disorders, including phobias and even post-traumatic stress disorder.[10]

While the exact reasons for the connections have not been completely explained by researchers, it stands to reason that years of bullying, mistreatment, and over-concern for the opinions of others lead to a general anxiety-prone approach to life. If you are accustomed to being ridiculed, you may easily develop social anxiety. If you have been physically or emotionally harmed enough and in increasingly violent and derisive ways, post-traumatic stress reactions may occur. In essence, the mind's defenses have been so assaulted for so many years that the defenses slip, opening the door to increasingly negative psychological consequences.

Beyond anxiety, weight status as an adult has also been tied strongly to depression—one of the most costly and debilitating psychological disorders. In addition to having overall poorer psychological well-being than normal-weight adults,[11] obese patients are more likely to be on antidepressants[12] and *nearly 90 percent have clinical levels of depression*[13] (with 25 percent having clinically *severe* depression). This only serves to further debilitate individuals who are already struggling with so much, and in the cruelest twist of all, makes them both less likely to be successful at a weight-loss attempt and also more likely to regain any weight that they take off.[14] In a ray of hope, while weight loss is more difficult to achieve and maintain for those who are depressed, depression does appear to lessen in those who are able to sustain weight loss.[15]

When looking at general community samples, among women in particular there is a demonstrated link between obesity and depression, even when taking into account other social differences that could lead to depression.[16] While there is some debate about the strength of this association, there is no doubt that obesity itself exerts some kind of influence on depression. The impact on self-esteem (described in more detail in following chapters) has a direct influence on depression, but so too do the general feelings of hopelessness and helplessness that many overweight individuals express. For people who no longer feel in control of their lives or destinies, it is easy to slip into a depression stemming from a lack of conceivable change. If an overweight individual feels lonely, but does not feel they have the skills (self-efficacy) to change their situation, an already depression-prone state becomes even more pronounced—compounding issues to the point that they become clinical.

Interestingly, evidence points to the fact that the depression experienced by obese individuals, and again among women in particular, is qualitatively different from the depression experienced by individuals who are average weight—for obese women, their depression is more likely to be "atypical,"[17] heavily influenced by the perceived likelihood of changing the circumstances that underlie it. This atypical form of depression is less connected to typical notions of "sadness" and more with symptoms related to overeating, sensitivity to rejection, and significant social impairment (each of which is easily tied directly back to weight status). Fundamentally, the depression is different—it's not a more intense version of the types of depression women are already more prone to; it's an entirely different kind of depression that particularly affects overweight women.

This atypical depression has a more transitory effect on mood—meaning that the sufferer can be clinically depressed but still have periods of "normal" emotion and happiness; unfortunately, this can disguise the presence of the underlying atypical depression because people may think that if you can be happy and experience positive emotions regularly, you can't simultaneously be depressed. This could prevent depressed overweight women from receiving help early in the course of their depression, which in turn can lead to longer, more challenging cycles of depressive symptoms.

COPING

The negative mental health consequences of having been an overweight child or being an overweight adult lead to a variety of coping strategies. Unfortunately, these strategies are not always healthy, and in some cases only serve to reinforce barriers to achieving a normal weight. When asked about ways that they protect themselves from the psychological effects of being overweight, adults are more likely to report eating (sixth most common out of twenty-one reactions) and intentionally avoiding dieting (eighth) than actually dieting (seventeenth).[18] This tug-of-war between eating and dieting can lead to an intense love/hate relationship with food (described in a later chapter) that only further undermines attempts at weight loss.

When overweight individuals do find themselves restricting their food intake in an attempt to lose weight, the inevitable "blips" that occur in a diet plan often lead to self-criticism and self-blame, which drive individuals into the familiar, comforting arms of food to cope with their disappointment and self-imposed shame. The increased food intake makes them feel like even more of a failure, and the coping mechanism perversely becomes the stressor itself.[19]

Women in particular have been shown to struggle with ways to effectively cope with weight. Women often find themselves repressing their weight-related emotions to prevent those feelings from negatively impacting their male partners' feelings toward them. In other words, men don't want to "deal with" their girlfriends' or wives' insecurities regarding weight, so in an effort to placate *their partners' needs*, women suppress their own negative feelings. Unfortunately, doing so has been shown to increase food intake, as the suppressed emotions are soothed with an alternative coping mechanism (again, trying to ameliorate their feelings with food, thereby promoting weight gain, and repeating the vicious cycle).[20]

Weight has also been associated with substance use, both in children and adults.[21] Use of substances can be a coping response (as in drinking away the pain), or a replacement for the desired "substance" of choice—food. The issues at play in substance use are similar to those for overeating—both require daily control in the face of temptation. While obesity is not and should not be considered an addiction (and we discuss this in more detail in Chapter Ten), there is no doubt that similar brain pathways are at play in both conditions. For individuals with both overeating and substance abuse conditions, it almost becomes an issue of competing addictions—as one is addressed, the other can rear its head to fill in the gap.[22] Interestingly, the presence of a substance use disorder in parents has been shown to increase the risk of a type of early onset, fast-progressing form of binge-eating disorder in their children,[23] indicating that there is a yet-to-be-identified link between these disorders (be it genetic or environmental).

BRAIN WIRING: AUTOMATIC THOUGHTS AND COGNITIVE DISTORTIONS

In the next few chapters, we will examine broader mental health concerns that overweight children and adults face. But to more fully understand the impact of having been an overweight child and the further impact of being an overweight adult on mental health, we have to first explore how our thoughts and actions are impacted by the patterns of thinking and behaving that are established during childhood. It is through these processes that the broader mental health consequences of childhood obesity occur. It's been said that you spend the rest of your life getting over your childhood, and in the case of obese children, this is most definitely the case.

While there are countless psychological theories and entire paradigms focused on this topic, one of the most widely accepted and utilized frameworks is the system employed by cognitive behavioral therapists. Cognitive behavioral theory holds that many psychological concerns are rooted in underlying cognitions (or thoughts) that then lead to our emotional and behavioral responses. Although this might seem like common sense today, when cognitive behavioral theory was being developed it was quite radical. Until that time, Freud's psychoanalysis had pretty much reigned supreme with its use of abstract, mystery-laden Oedipal complexes and penis envy theories. Rather than shrouding our psychology in a tri-layered hierarchy of id, ego, and superego, cognitive behavioral theory laid out the simple (yet still revolutionary) idea that thoughts underlie almost everything we do. And our thoughts can be trained, modified, and even changed in ways that can impact our emotions and behaviors.

To see the role that obesity can have on our thoughts, and therefore our emotions and behaviors, one must first understand the concept of "schemas." In cognitive theory, a schema is a pattern of thoughts and behaviors rooted in repeated personal experience—typically early childhood experiences, but it can be any series of experiences that begin to form a pattern in our minds. Schemas represent a basic assumption about the way things work, if you will. Our schemas, based on "data" we have accumulated about the way the world works throughout our entire lives, essentially form a "rule book" by which we view the world. We take the information we have learned throughout the years and apply this rule book to the way we view other things in our lives. So, for instance, if we learn that men tend to be more aggressive than women, we will end up anticipating more aggression in our interactions with men. As time goes on, the rule book fades into the background as these tried-and-true rules become automatic beliefs about the way the world works. As an analogy, while we are learning how to drive, we have to consciously remember what each pedal, lever, and dial represents, but as we drive more and more we automatically know what to do when situations occur—our foot automatically slams on the brakes when we need to stop, our hand automatically flips up the blinker as we prepare to turn. We don't have to stop and think "gee, that person is stopping suddenly, what should I do?"—we just do it. While the behaviors have become automatic, they are still based in a rulebook that we learned, absorbed, and now automatically use to guide our actions.

The schemas of overweight kids are formed during a time when the children are at odds with the world around them, frequently ostracized, ridiculed, and shamed. It is easy to see how readily negative schemas could be formed that carry directly into adulthood—if we come to learn that others will be cruel to us (resulting in an inner schema of "people are cruel"), we expect cruelty. And frequently, we get the outcome we expect, sometimes even subtly and unconsciously bringing about the very outcome we anticipated through our approach to the given situation. For instance, say we expect someone to be aloof and distant, and we therefore don't engage with them. Their coolness toward our lack of conversation can be perceived as the aloofness that we had originally expected. This is the concept of the self-fulfilling prophecy[24] in psychological theory.

The true tragedy of schemas is that they can eventually produce what are referred to as "automatic thoughts"—essentially, extensions of these acquired rules into specific thoughts that are so ingrained, we don't even realize we are having them. In the case of Jennifer at the beginning of this chapter, her schemas (rooted in her childhood experiences and cultural knowledge) told her that overweight people are not worthy of love. By extension, since she is an overweight person, it must mean that she is not lovable (automatic thought). This can then lead her to act (or *not* act) in ways that prevent her from achieving the very things she desires. If she believes that she is not lovable, will she even seek love out?

The danger with automatic thoughts is that they are just that—*automatic*. It is not a conscious process through which an individual examines herself or himself and consciously comes to a thought of "I am worthless." Instead, through the automatic application of years of experience, they come to *believe* they are worthless, without ever going through the thought process that would allow them to counter that belief.

These automatic beliefs can abound in individuals who were overweight as children—any type of schema generated from years of social pressure and negative individual experience can bring about a host of dysfunctional automatic thoughts. Table 7.1 below provides examples of the types of schemas and associated automatic thoughts that could result from being an overweight child.

Negative schemas do not sit at the forefront of our minds at all times—they rest in the background until what is referred to as a "critical incident" activates them. Both for individuals who remain overweight as adults and for those who have lost weight, these automatic thoughts can lie just beneath the surface, waiting to be "activated" in everyday life. For instance, if someone puts on an outfit and realizes that it is snugger than it used to be, it can activate the

TABLE 7.1: POSSIBLE SCHEMAS AND ASSOCIATED AUTOMATIC THOUGHTS FOR OVERWEIGHT CHILDREN

Schema	Automatic Thought
Fat people are unattractive.	I am ugly.
Fat people should be laughed at.	Other people have the right to make fun of me.
Fat people will always be lonely.	I should not expect to find love or companionship.
Nobody wants to be friends with a fat person.	I am better off alone.
Being fat is shameful.	People will make fun of me if they see me eating.

underlying weight-related schemas they have acquired, suddenly putting forth automatic thoughts of "I am ugly" or "no one will be attracted to me." It is not a linear, transparent process that occurs— we do not put on the outfit, consciously combine our underlying belief that "I've been told that overweight people are unattractive" with the sudden input of "I feel overweight today" and then say, *ipso facto*, "I am unattractive." This processing occurs entirely behind the scenes, leaving the person feeling ugly and unable to attract a partner without knowing why they feel this way. This is the unfortunate power of automatic thoughts—the person experiencing them does not realize where they are coming from.

These automatic thoughts can impact multiple factors, all rooted in the same schema. These thoughts can influence depression, loneliness, motivation, self-esteem—any number of psychological outcomes. To help visualize the process, Figure 7.1 on the next page shows the flow of how early experiences as an obese child can trigger the formation of automatic thoughts that, in this example, can lead to depressive symptoms (modeled after Ivy-Marie Blackburn's cognitive model of emotional disorders[25]).

Because the thoughts become automatic, they are that much more difficult to counteract. These automatic thoughts can remain even if the underlying schema is ruptured—after a time the automatic thoughts have a life of their own and sustain themselves even without the root upon which they are based. Going back to our car example, even if we learn that our new car's blinker is on the opposite side of the steering wheel, we will still automatically reach on the familiar side for it until we have gone through a long-term, repeated "re-training" process to adapt our automatic behaviors. And even then, sometimes we will still reach automatically for that turning indicator despite knowing full well it's not there. So even if a person's negative automatic thoughts ("I am unattractive.") are rooted in their weight, and they lose weight, the thought can remain—requiring intensive psychological treatment to overcome.

FIGURE 7.1: THE ROLE OF EARLY EXPERIENCES IN NEGATIVE AUTOMATIC THOUGHTS

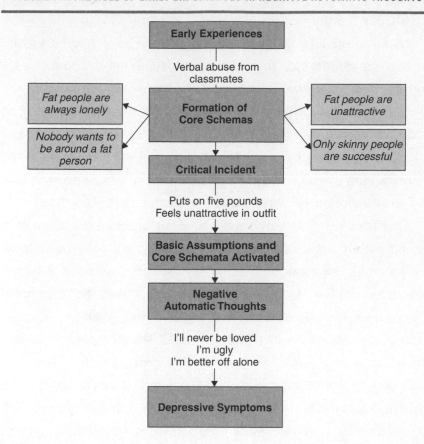

And because the link between the automatic thought and the negative psychological outcome is seemingly so removed, an individual on their own is very unlikely to understand why the thoughts remain.

While this discussion may seem a bit complex, think for a minute about all of the truths, the heuristics, the "rules of thumb" that we develop in childhood. For instance, we learn that if someone approaches us smiling, they are typically a nice person. We don't consciously think "gee, that person is probably nice" when we see someone smiling at us; rather, we automatically assume they are nice. Childhood is the time when we learn how the world works, and if we are fat while we are learning, we will shape our view of the world from the perspective of a fat person.

As these schemas are formed, nurtured, and etched into stone during our childhood, these automatic thoughts become deeply ingrained, to the point that it can take immense amounts of therapy to counteract their effect. The formerly obese child attempting to undo decades of evidence of worthlessness, substandardness, and inferiority will face an intense uphill climb that will leave them prone to everything discussed earlier: depression, anxiety, substance use, and so many other things discussed in the following chapters.

This framework briefly shows how our childhood experiences can ultimately shape our psychological nature as adults. In the next few chapters, we explore specific psychological and social implications of childhood obesity and the impacts that they can have. Throughout the discussions that follow, remember how deeply ingrained these effects can be and how difficult they are to change (even if weight is lost). We would never venture that weight loss itself is easy, but at least it is a more concrete transformation and can directly result in improved physical health. Changing a person's fundamental underlying psychology is much more difficult, and will not come automatically just because a person has lost weight.

EIGHT

"Does This Make Me Look Fat?"

Body Image

Thomas stepped out of the shower, grabbing his towel and starting to dry himself off. As usual, he was relieved to see the mirror fogged over. Overweight as long as he could remember, he had become so ashamed of his body that he did not even want to see it anymore— the mirror had long since started mocking him in the ways children had for so long. Even closing his eyes, he still saw his protruding stomach and rounded chest in his mind, hearing the years of taunts they brought him—lard-o, Mrs. Man-Boobs—so many names he couldn't even remember them all. The derisive laughter of girls at a summer pool party echoed in his ears, and he renewed his frantic drying. Once dry, he quickly grabbed his underclothes and put them on forcefully. Suffocating in the humidity of the room, he tore open the door and fled the bathroom, the only room in his house in which he ever went naked.

* * *

Mandy looked in the mirror, turning from side to side. Her eyes critically scanned her 28-year-old body from head to toe, skipping over her long, flowing hair, glowing skin, and slender neck, seeing instead the body of an overweight thirteen-year-old girl staring back. The slight indentation of her skirt around her waistline conjured images of rolls of fat overhanging her belt. The skin pressing flat as her relaxed arms crossed over her chest invoked images of flabby arms betraying her secret: she had once been fat. But despite years of being a slender, beautiful woman, she still saw the bullied, insecure girl she had been for so long staring back at her. Slight imperfections were magnified to the point of being glaring flaws,

*and any suggestion of body fat visible through her clothing was
seen as a sign of failure, of immense shame. She had not been fat in
many years, but long after her body had changed, her view of herself was still the same. Sighing, she turned her back to the mirror,
steeling herself to face the world that she was convinced saw her as
unforgivably fat, but in reality saw her as a thin, beautiful woman.*

Look at yourself in the mirror. What do you see? Take a mental
Polaroid, then think of the way that you would describe that
picture to someone who had never met you, painting a mental image of yourself. Now think for a moment—if we gave your
Polaroid to someone else and asked them to describe what they saw
in your picture, would your descriptions end up being the same?

Your mental Polaroid and the way you describe it are your body
image. Typically, our body image is fairly similar to reality—we see
the things that are "attractive" and "unattractive" about ourselves
with relative truth. While our bodies may fluctuate slightly over
time (putting on a few pounds here, losing a few there), that mental snapshot stays relatively stable in our minds, and for the most
part reasonably accurate. In other words, our own description of
the Polaroid would tend to match that of others. While women generally tend to view themselves as slightly heavier than they actually
are, the effect is fairly minor and usually reflective of that seemingly near-universal feeling of needing to lose five to ten pounds.

However, for many people who are described as having "body
image distortions," the self-image is twisted, and the version of themselves that they see in the mirror is not at all accurate. Instead of seeing positives and negatives, they may only see negatives. Even then,
those negatives may be imagined, or so exaggerated as to make minor
imperfections or natural variations something to be loathed and
concealed at every opportunity. Particularly for women (although
recently increasingly for men), this effect is greatly influenced by the
media through their impossible standards of beauty: the advertising

industry's "ideal" body has been shown to be possessed naturally by only 5 percent of the adult female population.[1] It is no wonder that the other 95 percent of the population ends up feeling overly critical and negative toward their own bodies—the media leads them to believe that *they* are the atypical ones.

Most of us are familiar with the implications of body image distortions through their strong impact on the development of eating disorders such as anorexia and bulimia (discussed in more detail in Chapter Ten). In many individuals with these disorders, their body image is that of a "fat" person, even if they are actually normal weight (or in the case of anorexia, severely *under*weight). For these individuals, it often takes years of therapy for them to be able to see their bodies in a healthy light.

Interestingly, studies have shown that anorexics and overweight individuals have similar distortions in body image—both groups see themselves as being significantly heavier than they actually are.[2] The effect is even more magnified in overweight adults who were overweight as children, as if the distortion grows with time. These distortions are so strongly ingrained that unfortunately they remain even after weight loss—adults who were overweight as children but have achieved a healthy adult weight are highly likely to retain their negative self-image, setting themselves up for a host of complications that are at that point entirely mental.[3] It is not that they still see themselves as being the same weight they were prior to weight loss; they do understand that they have lost weight and adjust their body image to that of a lighter person, but they do not adjust it far enough—they still view themselves as being much heavier than they actually are. Their years of knowing what they would see in the mirror have led to them see themselves through "fat-tinted" glasses, and they are unable to objectively look at their own bodies and see them as others would.

The challenge for adults who were overweight children is that they generally fall into two camps: overweight adults who have a negative body image because of both their childhood and current weight (thus partially having a currently "founded" negative body image that has been distorted even further), or healthy-weight adults who have a negative body image from having been over-weight as a child despite having a normal current weight (thus having a currently "unfounded" negative body image grounded in the previous views of themselves). These two scenarios have very different implications if one is trying to overcome the distortion—for the currently overweight adult, the focus on improving body image would either be on accurately viewing their actual weight (removing the distortion in favor of a truer perception of actual body size) or on engaging in behaviors that would promote weight loss and hopefully help somewhat reduce the distortions in the process. For the formerly overweight adult, the change is much deeper—it requires a systemic psychological shift that is very challenging to achieve. Unfortunately, as in Mandy's case, formerly overweight individuals are comparable to currently overweight individuals in almost *every* body image measure, still viewing their bodies as fat and as less attractive than those of other people[4] (even people who are their exact same weight). Their negative body image has remained, bolstered by the combination of many years of self-criticism along with criticism from others.

Why does this occur, though? What leads previously overweight individuals to still view themselves as fat?

It all goes back to the underlying development of body image. An individual's self-image develops throughout their life and is strongly influenced by the way their body is viewed when they are children and adolescents. It is during this time that children truly discover their bodies as an evaluable aspect of themselves, like hair color or eye color, and generally for the first time begin to view their bodies *through the eyes of others*. A five-year-old rarely comments on their appearance at all, much less states their concerns over what others think they look like. Contrast that sharply with the experience of teenagers, who seem sometimes to be completely consumed with what others think of how they look.

Increasingly, and particularly in girls, this leads to what is referred to as "self-objectification," in which our bodies only come to represent to us what *others* see in them. In essence, our views of ourselves shift from "what do I see in the mirror" to "what do other people see when they look at me?" This shift from an inward, personal view to an external, evaluative process fundamentally changes the way we see ourselves: it is no longer about what *we* see, and more about what we think *others* see. This is the critical point at which our body image can become detached from reality—even if our actual bodies change, our internal notion of how others see us may not. And if that internal notion is negative, it has repercussions that affect us throughout our lives.

Children who grow up overweight are told by peers, the media, physicians, and even potentially their parents that they are overweight, that their bodies are "wrong." While it is important for children to realize when they are overweight, and to be aware of the need for change, the constant messages can ingrain in them a sense of "wrongness" of their bodies. When children then turn to the media and are taught that overweight bodies should be hidden, masked, and concealed, it is easy for body shame to develop.

There is a delicate balance faced here—no one wants to undermine the development of a healthy body image, but, given everything we have discussed in this book, it is critical for children to realize the importance of maintaining a healthy body weight. Otherwise, weight losses generated mainly through the actions of parents will be lost once the child becomes autonomous and begins making their own diet and exercise decisions. But should parents risk creating a body image distortion by telling their children they are overweight? It truly is a catch-22, but the best strategy is to keep controlled, individual feedback (that is, from parents or doctors) objective and non-judgmental. The media will always exert judgment, and peers likely will as well, but the development of body shame may be somewhat tempered through *supportive* (rather than critical) encouragement of weight loss by trusted family members and medical professionals.

For those who have developed body shame (either because of society at large or excessive negative-focused pressure from well-intending caretakers), the shame sets into motion a series of habits around "hiding" their fatness that can persist into adulthood. For instance, you can often tell when an individual is uncomfortable about their body by certain tell-tale signs: an unconscious habit of pulling one's shirt away from the body, a tendency to cross one's arms over the body when seated, a compulsion to hug a pillow or lounge under a blanket when seated on a couch. All these habits are based upon a body image that tells the individual that they are fat, and it is something shameful—something that should be hidden—indecent for others to see. These habits persist regardless of current weight—formerly overweight women, for instance, have been shown to have the same levels of dysfunctional obsession with ensuring that they appear to be lighter than they are as do currently overweight women.[5]

For the overweight child, the "fat" self-images and habits can end up so ingrained that they become second nature. The child views themselves as fat at a fundamental level, and as a result develops body shame—they are afraid to take off their shirt in public, uncomfortable wearing clothes that show their body shape. The long-term effect that arises, though, stems from the fact that these body images become almost etched in stone by the time we reach adulthood, and it becomes very challenging to alter those self-images. Therefore, even if a previously overweight child has been able to bring their weight into a normal range, body image distortions are likely to persist—coined the "phantom fat" phenomenon.[6] These distortions can create a situation in which individuals, even if they are overweight, perceive themselves as being even "fatter" than they actually are—so someone who is slightly overweight feels grossly overweight because of the resulting body shame; this not only impacts their psychological well-being and risk for eating disorders, it also ironically places them at increased risk for avoiding both physical activity and healthy eating.[7] This effect emerges likely because they feel that they are unable to overcome an obstacle that in reality is much *smaller* than perceived—"If I'm so overweight as to be disgusting, I'll never lose enough weight to be attractive, so why even bother?" This only serves to further reinforce a vicious cycle: lower motivation leads to weight gain, which in turn leads to even lower motivation.

Regardless of current weight, these ingrained body image distortions will shape the way overweight children approach many aspects of their lives. These effects are so profound that some of the earliest research conducted into the psychological effects of obesity centered on the long-term impact on body image. In 1967, long before childhood obesity reached the public's awareness, researchers found that body image disturbances are "not affected by weight reduction."[8] This creates a permanent effect—unlike diabetes or hypertension, body image will not revert back to a healthy baseline. While we have known this for some time, the problem is just now becoming large-scale enough for it to have population-level implications.

The psychological consequences of body image disturbances are notable mainly for their impact on self-esteem and physical intimacy, discussed in more detail below.

MENTAL HEALTH'S FOUNDATION: SELF-ESTEEM

A person's self-esteem forms the foundation of a healthy outlook on life. Encompassing notions of self-worth, personal capabilities, and the potential to reach goals and enact change, a person's self-esteem guides the way they view themselves, and how (and if) they interact with those around them. A similar but distinct concept is that of self-efficacy, or one's belief in her or his own abilities to do something. Self-esteem directly influences self-efficacy—the higher our opinion of ourselves, the more likely we are to believe that we have the ability to effect change.

Unfortunately, overweight children and adults have consistently been found to have lower self-esteem than their normal-weight counterparts, placing them at risk for a host of negative outcomes, discussed in more detail in this chapter. Yet more troubling, even if an overweight child manages to maintain a healthy self-esteem in childhood, there can still be a separate impact on *adult* self-esteem[9]; if poor self-image doesn't get you as a child, it gets you as an adult.

The loss of self-esteem has been related to poor body image.[10] Our bodies are the one thing that we cannot ever truly hide from someone else—so even if a child feels that their body is "wrong," they have no choice but to have that "wrongness" be their public face—in fact, one of their most memorable aspects. This constant exposure quickly begins to degrade a child's view of him or herself—it erodes their self-esteem.

Considering all the discussion we've had to this point, this shouldn't be shocking: after facing years of bullying and negative media images, it is no surprise that overweight children tend to view themselves as "less" than other children. The disparity in self-esteem is particularly strong when considering not only physical appearance and physical competence, but also social functioning.[11] These combined impacts mean that overweight children are particularly insecure about their strength and ability to use their bodies effectively, about the way that they appear to others, and about the ways in which they are fundamentally able to interact with other people. These first two findings are not too surprising—an overweight child will very likely be insecure about their body, and because being overweight is often associated with lack of exercise, physical power is likely lower among this group. The third finding, though, begins to show how the decreases in self-esteem spill over into other areas of life. The mere fact of being overweight makes a child less confident in their ability to interact with others in a social setting. This has huge potential ramifications in friendships, relationships, and careers—timidity is not often associated with success.

Compounding the effects of lower self-esteem is the associated impact on self-efficacy, leaving an individual feeling as if they are unable to be successful at making changes in their life. Most over-weight individuals have attempted and failed to achieve/maintain a healthy weight, and often have scores of failed attempts. This per-sistent "failure" rapidly degenerates a person's self-efficacy—"if I haven't been able to do it the ten times I've tried so far, what's going to make me successful this time?" This feeling of failure leads many overweight adolescents to feel that they have no control over their lives in general. Subsequently, this increases the chance that they, along with their parents and teachers, feel that they do not have *self*-control.[12]

The lack of efficacy also leads them to explore more danger-ous options for weight loss—overweight adolescents with low self-esteem have been shown to be at significantly increased risk for developing an eating disorder when attempting to control their weight.[13] Overall, more than half of overweight adolescent girls and more than one-third of overweight adolescent boys engage in unhealthy weight-control behaviors such as fasting, eating very lit-tle food, skipping meals, or using food substitutes (weight-loss bars/powders, and so on not designed for use in children). Disturbingly, more than 10 percent of girls and 5 percent of boys exhibit extreme weight-loss behaviors such as taking diet pills, inducing vomiting, using laxatives, or using diuretics.[14]

Being overweight leaves a child insecure in more than just their body—it also makes them insecure in their fundamental abilities as a person. While the origins of much of the self-esteem and self-efficacy effects of childhood obesity stem from the original weight issue, associated negative self-views can begin to reach into other areas of an overweight individual's life: "If I'm not able to lose weight, I obviously have trouble achieving my goals—what makes me think I'll be able to get that job?" "Since I'm not attractive, why would that woman ever want to go on a date with me?" The effects can permeate an individual's life, no matter what their current weight is. The lack of self-esteem, self-efficacy, and perceived self-control have been linked to shorter life expectancies, worse career success, and fewer years of education—the fundamentals many of us would want for our children.[15]

Even if an overweight child is able to lose weight as an adult, the negative impacts on self-esteem and self-efficacy are in place, no longer anchored entirely in weight. As you can imagine, this effect is quite durable—a significant amount of research has gone into specific interventions and treatments that can boost self-esteem, but they all face an uphill battle. Once we have decided on what our core abilities are, a process that takes place as we emerge into adulthood, it is exceptionally difficult to re-imagine one's self to the extent required to reshape self-esteem. This can lead to a lifetime of missed opportunities and self-doubt.

The impact of low self-esteem is systemic and severe—its effects are seen in outcomes ranging from depression to criminal behavior. The table on the next page highlights the most concerning outcomes related to having reduced self-esteem.

It is *critical* to avoid these life-altering impacts. Many have argued that the solution to weight's impact on self-esteem is to engage in self-esteem exercises and workshops to help overweight children maintain positive self-images. While this is very valuable

TABLE 8.1: SELECTED OUTCOMES ASSOCIATED WITH
HAVING LOW SELF-ESTEEM

Outcomes of Low Self-Esteem
Depression
Aggression
Antisocial behavior
Delinquency and criminal behavior
Poor health
Limited economic prospects
Lower life satisfaction
Mental health problems
Substance dependence

and these children deserve full support, by the time they are old enough to understand the intervention, *it is too late*. The negative impact is already in place. While gains in self-esteem levels may be achieved during a workshop or temporary intervention, workshops do not take place in a vacuum, and once the child leaves the safety of that supportive environment she will be right back in the exact system that told her she was worthless in the first place. The only way to curb the effect of obesity on self-esteem (and the resulting plethora of subsequent impacts) is to prevent the weight gain in the first place.

LEAVING THE LIGHTS OFF: PHYSICAL INTIMACY

Sexual intimacy involves some of the most intense emotions we experience, and we are seldom more vulnerable than in situations involving sexuality. For children who have developed poor body image that persists into adulthood, significant impacts on sexual functioning follow. Those with poor body image go into sexual interactions expecting them to be unrewarding,[16] likely due to both founded and unfounded expectations. Women who are dissatisfied with their bodies engage in less sexual activity, have less satisfactory sexual experiences, feel less confident in giving their partners sexual pleasure, and are more likely to avoid being seen naked during a sexual encounter.[17] These barriers to sexual functioning can decrease sexual satisfaction both in the person with low body image and in their partner. Sex is an important part of any romantic relationship, and this strain can impact the quality of the relationships themselves. Unfortunately, research has failed to show any consistency in findings with regards to the impact of weight loss upon sexual functioning; that is, even for overweight adults who lose weight, there is not a consistent, predictable improvement in sexual functioning—the effects can continue indefinitely even after weight loss.[18]

Even more alarming, there is robust evidence emerging that both men and women with poor body image are at increased risk for engaging in unsafe sexual practices. So despite being *less* likely to engage in sexual activity altogether, individuals with poor body image engage in riskier sexual practices when they actually do have sex. Adolescent girls who are dissatisfied with their body begin engaging in sexual activity at an earlier age and are more likely to feel that they have fewer options for sexual partners (which in turn makes them more afraid to engage in condom-use discussions).[19] Overweight women have also been shown to be more likely to have a sexually transmitted disease.[20] Much of this can be tied back to a perceived fear of "losing" a sexual partner—the body image issues, combined with associated low self-esteem, can leave an individual feeling as though they are "lucky" to have found someone to be intimate with, therefore making them less conscious and assertive about safe sex practices. This has implications not only for sexually transmitted diseases, but also for unintended pregnancy—both of which have obvious lifelong ramifications.

Rewriting the sexual scripts that are established during adolescence and early adulthood is exceptionally difficult and requires significant intervention. While the average age of first intercourse is around seventeen for both men and women, by their late teenage years at least three-quarters of all men and women have had some form of sexual experience—and over two-thirds of all sexually experienced teenagers have had more than one partner.[21] For the high proportion of teenagers who are overweight, this places their "anchoring" sexual experience firmly in the midst of psychological struggles with body image and self-worth. Further complicating attempts to relearn how to approach sex as an adult is the simple fact that most people have an abject fear of discussing the issue openly, not only with partners but also with therapists.

In summary, self-esteem is the building block of success, but millions of overweight children have a negative body image that undermines the development of robust self-esteem. Unfortunately, body image and its effect on self-esteem aren't the only factors that create a lifelong psychologically based struggle; further difficulties can have a negative impact on developing personalities, the topic of the next chapter.

NINE

Fat Personality

Social Impact

Ryan smiled nervously at the imposing woman across from him on the subway. He hadn't seen her before and wondered what she did for a living. She was wearing an expensive suit and a set of fairly high heels, but, making little grunts of relief, she pulled off the uncomfortable shoes and traded them for a pair of Uggs she pulled from a beat-up backpack. She literally let her hair down, running her fingers through her previously tightly wound locks, and unbuttoned her sleeves, shaking her arms to relieve the tension of the day. As the "professional" melted away, she became an increasingly ordinary, and for most people, approachable woman.

She smiled briefly at him, and he laughed nervously. He closed his eyes and imagined introducing himself, asking her about her obvious disdain for high-heeled shoes. He opened his eyes and knew, though, that he would never be able to speak to her. Despite being a successful graphic artist with a rapidly expanding client base, he considered her far out of his league, and anyway, he didn't really like interacting with people because they always seemed to be mean to him. He liked his life of hiding behind a computer screen, sending beautiful images to clients from the relative anonymity of cyberspace, able to hide his obese body from the prying eyes of others.

With one last glance at the woman, he withdrew to the latest novel he was reading, as he had done his entire life, preferring to live out his dreams vicariously through the safety of the predetermined adventures of imaginary characters.

* * *

Ashley laughed raucously, drawing attention from nearly every corner of the restaurant. Boisterous and loud, she was almost always the center of attention.

"Shhhh, Ashley! Why do you have to be so loud?" her friend pleaded.

"Because I like the attention!"

"But everyone's staring!"

"Let them stare! I'm used to it."

And she was. People had been staring at her for her entire life. Originally it had been because of her weight, but as she grew older she developed a larger-than-life personality to match her larger-than-average frame. Now, when people stared, she was able to place it on her behavior, not her size. The buffer protected her well, and she allowed herself to revel in the attention that otherwise could have pushed her to tears.

"I don't know why I ever take you out in public," her friend teased.

As we have discussed, being overweight impacts all aspects of a child's growth and development. As these effects draw together during childhood and adolescence, they begin to impact the child's developing personality (one of our most enduring psychological characteristics) as well. The effects of obesity upon personality are so strong that overweight adults, particularly obese adults, have higher rates of personality disorders,[1] or underlying patterns of personality that are inherently dysfunctional and cause significant impairment or distress to one's self or those with whom they have relationships. While not all obese individuals have personality disorders, there are many aspects of personality that are affected by being overweight, or having been overweight.

Researchers have been interested in the relationship between personality and obesity since the 1940s. Hilde Bruch, one of the earliest and most prolific researchers in the field of obesity and eating disorders, posited in 1948 that:

Many of the personality features of obese people, their shyness and over-sensitivity, their easy discouragement in the face of difficulties or when confronted with the slightest rejection, their tendency

to depressions and their phlegmatic manner may be considered
sequels to their constant concern with the impression they make
on account of being obese.[2]

While Dr. Bruch's hypotheses held that being overweight had
a negative impact on personality, others have argued the opposite.
One of the earliest studies done on the relationship between obesity and personality in the 1970s developed the controversial "jolly
fat" hypothesis,[3] which holds that those who are in the overweight
range have negative psychological outcomes, but that those who are
obese often develop a "jolly" personality that helps buffer them
against those psychological risks—in essence, they have embraced
their weight and shunned the negative social messages in favor of
"living jolly." Although it became somewhat popular, the "jolly
fat" hypothesis was in direct contradiction to earlier work that had
shown that overweight individuals were more likely to act imma-
turely, to be rigid, and to be suspicious of others.[4] The hypothesis
has since largely been rejected by the scientific community, but
the debate over obesity's impact on personality has continued for
sixty years in the research world. While people may disagree as to
exactly *how* obesity impacts personality, there is a general agree-
ment that it does.

While a fair amount of research has been done into the personality characteristics associated with obesity, little attention has
been paid to how this represents some of the most damaging long-
term consequences of childhood obesity. Almost the entire literature focuses on how personality is associated with obesity—that is,
what personality traits lead individuals to become overweight or
obese. The underlying assumption, therefore, is that personality is
set *before* weight gain occurs. For the past twenty to thirty years,
that may have been an appropriate assumption, as childhood obesity rates were quite low. However, now that children are becoming overweight and obese not only in staggering numbers but at

increasingly younger ages, we can no longer assume that personality characteristics are leading to obesity; rather, we must now begin to explore the impact that obesity will have on children's still-developing personalities.

Personalities shape our entire lives—how we treat others and how they see us, some of the most defining features we possess—and the direct impact that obesity may be having on personality should not be viewed as just an academic investigation. It has real-world implications on the mental health and well-being of millions of overweight children, and because personality is by definition enduring once established, the effects of childhood obesity upon developing personalities are exceptionally important. While much less attention has been paid to this recently, as early as the 1960s scientists had recognized the negative impact that being overweight could have on personality and, subsequently, life satisfaction. In a paper published in 1967, authors Sidney Werkman and Elsa Greenberg concluded that "obesity appears to be regularly accompanied by consistent personality difficulties of a serious nature" including "restriction of social and occupational horizons."[5] Since that time, various studies have found personality-related differences associated with childhood obesity but have still yet to fully realize the permanent effects they will have on future generations and the complex role that obesity has in actually contributing to certain personalities.

This chapter begins with the most widely used theory of personality to conceptualize how being an overweight child influences each aspect of personality, then examines individual personality traits that we are all familiar with and explores how being an overweight child can impact these individual traits as well. The chapter ends with a summary of how these personality factors influence many aspects of adults' lives, such as success and happiness.

SHAPING PERSONALITIES: THE FIVE-FACTOR
MODEL OF PERSONALITY

To fully appreciate the deep impact that childhood obesity can have on personality, we first need to examine what personality actually is. Typically viewed as an enduring set of tendencies to behave in a certain way, a person's personality shapes their approach to life, the way in which they are received by others, and, as we will see in this chapter, everything up to and including how happy and successful they are.

While there are many ways in which personality is conceptualized in the field of psychology, the most widely used model is the Five-Factor Model of Personality, developed by Robert McRae and Paul Costa. Their model is based upon decades of research to find groups (or factors) of personality characteristics, and it argues that nearly all personality traits can be explained by a person's level of alignment with five certain traits: extraversion, neuroticism, openness, agreeableness, and conscientiousness. How high or low a person falls within these five factors can in general be used to describe their overall personality. Table 9.1 below shows some of the personality characteristics associated with these five factors of personality.

An individual's own breakdown of the "Big Five" can provide insights into multiple aspects of their life. For instance, higher

TABLE 9.1: COMMON PERSONALITY CHARACTERISTICS ACROSS THE FIVE FACTORS[6]

Extraversion	Neuroticism	Openness	Agreeableness	Conscientiousness
Outgoing	Anxious	Curious	Sympathetic	Diligent
Sociable	Hostile	Flexible	Trusting	Disciplined
Upbeat	Self-Conscious	Fantasy	Cooperative	Organized
Friendly	Insecure	Imaginative	Modest	Dependable
Assertive	Vulnerable	Artistic	Straightforward	
		Unconventional		

degrees of agreeableness and openness are both strongly tied to marital satisfaction.[7] These factors do not all exert "positive" influences, though—individuals with higher openness, who are therefore less "by the book," have been shown to have lower-paying jobs than those with lower levels of openness.[8] In general, when looking at quality of life, high extraversion, low neuroticism, and high conscientiousness are all associated with being happy and satisfied.[9]

There has not been sufficient attention paid to the topic to determine definitively what the impact of having grown up overweight is on the five personality characteristics. We simply haven't been tracking overweight children long enough to have examined the impact on personality fifteen and twenty years down the line. However, we can easily see how years of bullying, social isolation, and depression could encourage personalities that are correspondingly shy and withdrawn (low on extraversion). This is supported by the increased loneliness and decreased levels of friendships exhibited by overweight children, one of the first personality differences demonstrated between overweight and normal weight children (particularly boys).[10] The already demonstrated relationship between childhood obesity and anxiety, poor body image, and low self-esteem means that overweight children tend to be high on neuroticism.

Not all effects are necessarily negative—because overweight children tend to have to explore unique ways of gaining social interactions and are frequently drawn to the fantasy found in books and other media, openness may be correspondingly increased. The impact on agreeableness will likely vary based upon the individual's experience—some overweight children will develop into highly sympathetic, compassionate individuals who strive to go against the cruelty shown to them as children. Others may internalize the negativity and in turn lash out at the world. The final factor, conscientiousness, has been shown to be lower in those who are overweight—perhaps reflecting years of feeling as though they do not have control of their own weight and, therefore, their lives.[11]

As research into the impact of childhood obesity continues to evolve, it will be very interesting to see what personality types emerge as the result of increasingly younger ages of becoming overweight. Even beyond broader personality factors, though, childhood obesity has already demonstrated impact on specific, individual personality traits.

THE SMALLER IMPACTS: PERSONALITY TRAITS

In addition to the larger-picture personality differences found between those who are overweight and average weight, several trait-level variations have been demonstrated. These individual traits do not represent big, sweeping differences in personality in the same way a difference in agreeableness would, but they are differences that are more readily detected and can help enlighten certain behaviors and tendencies. People who are overweight have been shown to have lower impulse control,[12] to be more distrustful of others,[13] and in general to have less "order" in their lives,[14] something very important in maintaining mental health.

In the broader sense, those who have been overweight and have a resulting decrease in self-esteem (covered in more detail in Chapter Eight) will be more prone to developing dependent personality characteristics that stem from underlying insecurities regarding their own worth. Because of their constant awareness of a physical "difference" from others, they will also be more concerned about the opinions of others regarding their physical appearance, leading to a more external sense of self-worth (recall our earlier discussion of self-objectification in Chapter Eight as well). Along with the timidity described above will come concomitant issues with being assertive and a tendency to be somewhat avoidant. All of these characteristics limit self-efficacy, success, and a productive adult life.

Interestingly, the "fat personality" is internalized not only by the overweight, but also by those of average weight. In a fascinating study exploring people's views of the overweight,[15] a researcher at the University of Cincinnati asked a group of study participants to write short stories based on prompts. The story prompts varied only by the weight of the main character. Without any further instruction, those who wrote about overweight individuals were significantly more likely to create stories that were not only sad or negative, but that gave the main character an overall unpleasant personality. Such studies show that both experience and stigma are so strong that people *expect* certain personalities from overweight individuals.

The psychological theory of the "self-fulfilling prophecy"[16] shows that even if a group of people do not possess a characteristic, if they are expected to have it, and are therefore treated in a way that ultimately elicits the characteristic, expectation alone is enough to bring about an expected response (for example, negativity or shyness). If you expect someone to be hostile toward you, you approach that person more defensively, which could elicit the hostility by making the other person distrust your motives and intentions. For the overweight, if they are expected to be negative, in general people will ignore, avoid, or even be rude in advance to them, which can elicit the negative response originally expected.

In an interesting twist, starting in 1976, some researchers have hypothesized that being overweight, and obese in particular, can actually be *protective* against negative psychological outcomes if the individual fully "embraces" their weight status, due to the "jolly fat" phenomenon mentioned earlier. Originating in a study that demonstrated lower rates of anxiety and depression in obese individuals (contrary to almost all other studies conducted), this theory holds that individuals who are at extremes of weight *and have accepted their weight*, thereby rejecting society's rejection of them, have effectively shucked off the negative social consequences associated with being overweight. This (according to the theory) bolsters self-esteem and may protect them from the negative psychological consequences discussed throughout this book. While a few follow-up studies have found similar results, the overwhelming bulk of the literature does not support this "jolly" hypothesis.

Despite this fact, a sub-stereotype of the "funny fat guy/girl" has emerged, in which overweight people are stereotyped as having "great personalities" and in particular being riotously funny. Consider classic sitcom characters such as Roseanne Barr, George on *Seinfeld,* Homer Simpson, Robert on *Everybody Loves Raymond,* and countless others—fat people are seen as funny, both as something to be laughed at, and as someone able to make others laugh. This has perpetuated the "jolly fat" hypothesis in ways the original authors of the concept likely never anticipated. In fact, it is likely that there is a distinct subset of overweight individuals who develop a protective humorous approach to shield themselves from the effects of weight bias. However, on the whole, the direct impact of being overweight on developing personalities is not positive.

LIVING THE FAT LIFE: SUCCESS, HAPPINESS, AND HEALTH

The personality challenges described in this chapter combine with prevalent psychological problems as well as outright societal discrimination to impact the ability of overweight children to become successful, happy, healthy adults. This effect is so strong that there are numerous demonstrated implications of obesity on everything from the accessibility of health care and educational opportunities to employment opportunities and social treatment.[17] Starting very young, overweight children face challenges that can impede their educational progress. Despite the stereotype of the overweight nerd with big glasses being the "brain" of the class, overweight children have been shown to have impaired cognitive functioning[18] and are more likely to consider themselves poor students, to think that they will probably drop out of school, and to actually be held back a grade in school.[19] This leads, either by decreased ability or decreased motivation, to overweight children being less likely to get into college,[20] one of the most important predictors of career success.

When looking at common measures of success and happiness, overweight adults are less likely to be married and more likely to get divorced. These effects stem from childhood obesity and are not anchored in weight as an adult—for instance, men who are overweight at age eighteen are only half as likely as their normal-weight peers to be married by the time they reach their thirties and forties (and thus also less likely to have children).[21] This comes as a direct effect of dating patterns in adolescence—obese adolescents are less likely to have ever had a date,[22] largely due to the way that they are viewed by normal-weight peers (described earlier in Chapter Six). The stigma against overweight adolescents is so strong that most adolescents directly express an actual *discomfort* with dating an overweight peer that directly impacts their actions: only 12 percent of adolescents have *ever* dated someone who was overweight (despite the fact that more than 33 percent of children are overweight).[23]

Overweight adults also have more difficulty buying or renting a home,[24] have overall lower incomes, and (if they do marry) marry people with lower incomes.[25] The financial effects in particular are quite durable—even if an overweight child or adult is able to lose weight, the weight loss is not accompanied by a corresponding increase in income.[26] This has been largely attributed to the widespread (and legal) presence of outright weight discrimination.

TOO FAT TO WORK? THE (LEGAL) CULTURE OF
WEIGHT DISCRIMINATION

Carla braced herself, and walked into the executive's office at one of the most successful health product companies in the nation. She was prepared: well-dressed, familiar with the company's history and current strategies, and she knew every achievement her interviewer had ever made. She had cleaned up her own Facebook page and gotten an expensive, yet simple, manicure—all the necessary job interview touchups.

She smiled at the executive, who quickly eyed her and reached out for the proffered résumé. They went through the typical interview process, and he asked her about her degree, where she had worked previously, who her best references were, what book she had been reading lately, and so on. Carla's answers were spot on, and she knew it. Top of her class at the leading business school in the state, previous employment history at an even more successful company than the one she was interviewing at, her direct supervisors and even the CEO at her current company were references, and she had just finished reading Sam Walton's autobiography (which she had specifically read just to be able to use it as her answer in interviews such as this). She succinctly laid out her vision for the position and where she could see the company headed.

"Now, Ms. Gunner, a significant portion of this job involves interacting with the public and key shareholders, as well as potential investors. Do you feel that you would be able to do this successfully?"

"Absolutely—I am great with people, and have no problems with public speaking."

"Our company has a very carefully constructed and monitored public face; as a health-product based company, we have a very defined image to uphold. Do you feel that you can portray our corporate brand when interacting with investors?"

"Yes, absolutely."

"Are you sure? How much do you weigh?"

Carla was so stunned by the question, she wasn't sure how to respond. She impulsively glanced down at her body, eyeing her 180-pound physique. She was overweight, but was also a tall woman and had never in her life been obese. Her head tilted to the side, asking her unspoken question—how can you ask me that?

"I'm just asking because it's important to our company to portray the proper image. Many people respond negatively to people who are overweight, thinking that they just can't control themselves, and investors may question if you are the best representative of our multi-million dollar health brand. As you can imagine, our image is everything."

Carla stared at her interviewer, dumbfounded. As she struggled to find an appropriate response, the executive smiled perfunctorily. "Thanks for your interest. We'll be in touch."

Carla left the room, her mind reeling. As she neared the elevator, she realized that from the instant the executive saw her, he had no intention of hiring her.

Most people are surprised that Carla's experience is not only completely legal, it is fairly common. Discussions around weight are not protected like age or marital status (which you can't ask about at a job interview without opening yourself up to substantial liability). In the hiring process, if an interviewer can construct even the loosest reasoning for why an individual's weight could impact job performance, it can be discussed and subsequently considered when making hiring decisions.

Weight can also legally impact advancement within an already secured job. Imagine the following: you are interviewing for a promotion at your job. You and your coworker Ted are both up for the position. Compared to Ted, you've been at the company longer, pulled in more customers in the past year, and have more training and experience. After starting the job five years ago, you put on about fifteen pounds in the first year as you adjusted to the stress of the position—not enough to make you have to buy new clothes, but enough that you can tell a difference when you look in the mirror. You haven't put in the effort to lose the weight, instead focusing on being the best employee possible. Following several promotion interviews, your boss brings you both in at the end of the work day to let you know who has received the job. After sitting you both down, she looks you square in the eye and tells you, "You've been a great employee, but you've just let yourself go, so you're obviously not as responsible. I'm giving Ted the promotion since he's better able to control himself." Floored, you stagger from the room. As you head toward the elevator, you get angrier with every step—by the time you get home you ask your husband if he knows of a good discrimination attorney. All fired up to sue your boss for discrimination, you call the attorney first thing the next morning. After hearing your story, he simply states, "You have no case. Weight discrimination is legal. She could have looked at you and said 'you're fat so you're not getting it,' and you would have no recourse."

As surprising as this is to many, it is entirely true. While there are laws that protect gender, age, and race, there is no federal law that prohibits employers from discriminating against their employees based upon their weight.[27] This is true at the initial hiring, assignment of base pay, and decisions about promotions. As long as employers apply this discrimination "equally" (that is, they don't just discriminate against female employees based on weight), there is little recourse for someone who feels that they have experienced weight discrimination.

The problem has become so widespread that weight discrimination is now as common as race discrimination,[28] with overweight employees making less than their average-weight counterparts even when qualifications and experience are identical.[29] In researching this book, we even stumbled upon business news websites that *encourage* weight discrimination (just Google "Here's Why You Should (Quietly) Discriminate Against Fat People"), stating that an overweight (and presumably less healthy) employee can cost the company more than $6,000 per year in lost productivity, in addition to health costs that can be up to seven times as high as the cost of a normal-weight employee.[30] While there is evidence that obesity is linked to increased absenteeism from work, this effect is explained entirely by obese individuals' tendency to be in poor health—if an obese person is healthy, there is not an increased risk of absenteeism.[31]

This discrimination is not always conscious—innovative studies have shown that a person's weight unconsciously impacts the way that people perceive their general competence. One study in particular asked people to rate a potential job candidate on employment characteristics. Pictures of the exact same individual, pre- and post-bariatric surgery, were attached to identical resumes.[32] The raters who received the overweight image rated the candidate as significantly lower in likelihood of career success, a notion that would definitely factor in hiring a potential employee.

Overweight adults are twelve times as likely as their normal-weight counterparts to experience employment discrimination of any type, and the discrimination only grows stronger with increasing weight: obese adults are thirty-seven times as likely, and morbidly obese adults are one hundred times as likely.[33] These experiences are not intermittent—obese individuals report *daily* experiences with discrimination.[34] For adults already struggling with psychological and physical health concerns, the added stress of not being able to progress appropriately in the workplace can only worsen their other existing problems.

The effects of weight discrimination are only growing and are becoming increasingly unabashed—in early 2012, a Texas hospital became potentially the first employer (other than appearance-based employers such as professional dancing troupes) to publically institute a weight limit for their job candidates.[35] The hospital issued a statement that overweight employees would project the wrong image about their health-focused organization and implemented a policy that would not allow anyone with a BMI over 35 to be hired at the hospital. Perhaps most surprising is the fact that the ban was not based upon a concern over fitness or ability to complete job duties—it was based entirely on appearance and perception. In effect, due to discrimination and biases both hidden and overt, overweight adults are facing a "flab ceiling" in the workplace, one that systematically impedes their success at every turn.

As we discussed earlier, weight bias does not only appear in the workplace—overweight children are described as "lazy" and "worthless," even by medical professionals who specialize in weight loss.[36] For either fear of mistreatment or embarrassment, overweight adults who have experienced weight discrimination or weight bias are less likely to seek out preventive care services, despite needing those services more than normal-weight adults.[37] This only serves to continue the vicious cycle that limits opportunities for overweight adults: if they are less likely to seek preventive care, they will be more likely to develop medical conditions that then make them further prone to discrimination in the workplace.

TEN

I Love You, I Hate You

Relationship with Food

"I just can't do it anymore."

Landon stared resolutely at the wall behind his trainer, desperate for a change he felt he had earned, but no longer expected. He just couldn't make eye contact.

"I fought so hard to lose all my weight. It took me years, but I kept myself going with this idea that everything would change, that I would be attractive and popular and happy. Now all I am is hungry and embarrassed all the time."

His trainer looked at him calmly. "What are you embarrassed about?"

"I've told you, I lost over 100 pounds. I got down to 165, and I'd never felt better in my life. I've put 10 pounds of it back on, and now I just can't stand for anyone to see me eat anything. I never felt this ashamed of food, even before I lost weight. Sometimes I think I'd be better off if I'd never lost it. So many people ask me how I did it, almost look at me like a role model. It's just so much pressure, and now I feel so fat again."

"Even with putting back on 10 pounds, how much weight have you lost overall?"

"105 pounds."

"So still over 100 pounds, right? And you've had it off for six years now. You're right—people probably do look to you as a role model because you've managed to do what very few people have done. You've lost weight, and you've kept it off."

"So you're saying I should feel happy, that I've won?"

"That's not what I'm saying—you should feel proud about what you've done, but to keep the weight off you always have to realize that the work is never done. Your body will want to go right back to the weight you were before if you let it."

Landon put his hands in his head, sighing loudly.

"So it never ends?"

"No, it doesn't, but that's okay—it lets you realize how hard you've worked to get where you are."

"But it doesn't change the fact that just because I've put on a few pounds I can't even stand to be seen eating in public. I can't enjoy the foods I'm eating because all I can think of is the lower-calorie alternative I should have chosen over what it is that I'm actually eating and should be enjoying…how can I hate something that I love so much?"

As overweight children reach adulthood, having faced years of ridicule, shame, and self-blame, it should come as no surprise that many overweight children can develop a classic love/hate relationship with food. Because food is one of the few things in our existence that is absolutely necessary, it is not possible to simply cut it out of our lives—no other emotional trigger is intimately associated with our daily functions in the way that food is. Multiple times a day we must encounter it, whether we want to or not. And previous strategies for weight loss in children, such as "inpatient starvation,"[1] certainly do not improve a child's relationship with food.

Unfortunately for overweight children, there is increasing evidence that our bodies are altered in fundamental ways by being overweight.[2] There are documented transitory effects on base metabolism associated with weight loss, meaning that an individual's metabolism temporarily becomes more "efficient" following weight loss. In turn, this means the body requires fewer calories than would be expected and thus makes weight re-gain easier. This effect is temporary, but others are not; in fact, the basic metabolic pathways of the body are permanently altered in overweight individuals, such that even if they lose weight, there are several chemical processes designed to maintain the fat levels that remain.

Recent research has dispelled the myth that the cells of the body that store fat are permanent (which may sound like a good thing), but this means that as our fat cells die when we lose weight, the new ones that are produced cry out for our bodies to provide the fat needed to allow them to mature into "healthy," functioning fat cells.[3] The combination of these effects serves to drive individuals losing weight back toward their "original" weight. This leads overweight individuals to feel constant biological pressure to maintain their "overweightness" and leads those who have lost weight to feel constant biological pressure to put the weight back on. This can obviously lead to severe and impairing emotions when it comes to food.

This love/hate relationship can exert its influence in a variety of ways, ranging from the development of eating disorders to lifelong struggles with yo-yo dieting. Each has its own implications for long-term physical and psychological health—setting up our overweight children for a lifelong food-related minefield.

WHEN FOOD IS THE ENEMY: EATING DISORDERS

Eating disorders have been formally recognized as a cluster of psychological disorders since 1987, when the American Psychiatric Association first listed a separate section of "Eating Disorders" in the Diagnostic and Statistical Manual of Mental Disorders (the "bible" of diagnosing mental health conditions, used by both psychiatrists and psychologists).[4] Eating disorders are almost exclusively a disorder of the young—95 percent of all eating disorders occur between the ages of 12 and 25.[5] While many think that depression is the most "fatal" mental health disorder, eating disorders actually are, with mortality rates associated with eating disorders far exceeding those seen in depression. Women with an eating disorder have mortality rates approaching one in twenty, associated with a twelve-fold increase in the risk of death for young adults.[6] As we have discussed throughout this book, overweight children are at particular risk for eating disorders, which are tied to attempts to achieve and maintain a normal weight, to a history of bullying, and to low self-esteem.

As with all psychological disorders, diagnostic criteria are used to determine the presence of eating disorders (rather than the more straightforward lab tests that would be used for most physical health conditions). The criteria for eating disorders were most recently updated in 1994, at which point only two formal eating disorders were recognized: anorexia nervosa and bulimia nervosa. Characterized by an inability to maintain a normal body weight due to an intense fear of being "fat," anorexia is the eating disorder that likely receives the most attention today. This is partly because the disorder is so "public"—it is almost as difficult for the severely underweight to hide their weight as it is for the severely overweight. Although typically associated with binge eating and subsequent induced vomiting, bulimia actually involves binging paired with any inappropriate behavior to try and counteract the calorie intake of the binging (vomiting, laxatives, excessive exercise, fasting the following day, and so on). Unlike in anorexia, many bulimics maintain a normal weight and some are even overweight—the disorder is literally with the *eating* process and does not extend to physical weight in the way that anorexia does.

Although the methods and results of anorexia and bulimia are very different, they both involve an inappropriate behavior in the face of food (either avoiding it wholesale or overindulging and subsequently purging it from the body as if it were a toxin)—in essence, viewing food as the enemy and engaging in some behavior to counteract its effects. At first it might seem that these disorders couldn't be more separated from overweight and obesity, but there are surprising connections between them. While it is by definition impossible to be both anorexic and overweight, it is possible for bulimics to be overweight (although it's relatively rare in comparison to rates in the general population). However, nearly one in five bulimics has a *history* of having been overweight.[7] Interestingly for our discussion, these bulimics have a later age of onset of bulimic symptoms than normal-weight women who develop bulimia—implying that for previously overweight bulimics, their weight struggles led to their bulimia, which then "allowed" them to lose weight into a normal range (as opposed to normal-weight women who develop bulimia as a way prevent weight gain). By "acquiring" the habit of inappropriate compensatory behaviors, previously overweight bulimics create a dangerous self-rewarding system—if bulimia worked to lose the weight, why not continue it to maintain the weight loss?

Anorexics and bulimics may have different weight outcomes, but their diseases stem from distorted "self-evaluations" that are inappropriately influenced by the shape and weight of their bodies. As we have discussed, being a fat kid heightens such awareness, making overweight children focus on the size of their bodies more than a normal-weight individual typically would. In essence, by growing up overweight, a child becomes predisposed for an eating disorder. This is increasingly being seen in mental health treatment settings, where overweight children are presenting more and more frequently with accompanying eating disorder pathologies in desperate attempts to control their weight.[8]

Unfortunately, the intersection of overweight/obesity and eating disorders leads to increased complications. For bulimics with a history of being overweight, treatment may be greatly complicated by the fact that they are not only more dissatisfied with their bodies, but they also exhibit greater fear of going back to the weight they were prior to their bulimia.[9] Because of the likelihood that the bulimia developed as a weight *loss* method in overweight children (not just a weight *maintenance* method as in normal-weight individuals), the fear of weight gain is amplified. A typical psychological intervention will have to first address these fears before being able to address the other factors underlying the eating disorder itself, slowing treatment and forcing therapists to address a much more fundamental construct than the compensatory behaviors themselves.

When you examine the current definitions of "eating disorders," ironically the only types of disorders fully recognized are inappropriate behaviors to *control* weight—what, then, about inappropriate behaviors that either lead to or maintain weight *gain*? Our country has obviously lost its ability to control food intake, and the lack of an official psychiatric method of recognizing this is surprising. There is movement in this direction, however— in the face of increasing evidence of the impact of pathological eating (not just pathologically *restricted* eating), the American Psychiatric Association has proposed significant changes to the ways that eating disorders are classified and diagnosed in the first large-scale revision of mental health diagnostic categories in nearly twenty years.

As of late 2012, there are several new eating disorders proposed that will begin to represent the experience of many overweight individuals. The most relevant is the diagnosis of "binge-eating disorder," frequently eating much more than is typical paired with a sense of an inability to control the amount being eaten. Previously considered an ancillary eating disorder on the "fringe" of psychological diagnoses, it has been proposed to be "promoted" to the level of a fully recognized and characterized eating disorder in the 2013 revision of the Diagnostic and Statistical Manual of Mental Disorders. This will represent the first time that binge eating will be viewed as a psychological disorder in and of itself. Never before has the field fully acknowledged the underlying *pathological* nature of an inability to control one's eating (no longer relying on compensatory behaviors to merit an eating disorder)—this will open the door not only for additional research on how to treat the disorder, but also for people suffering from the disorder to more readily get treatment for their now fully diagnosable condition.

While there are many different theories surrounding what leads an individual to manifest binge-eating disorder, it is easy to see how it could be directly related to an underlying failed food control system put in place in an attempt to lose weight—if an individual attempts to overly restrict their intake in an unrealistic approach to losing weight, then suddenly "caves," this repeated pattern can establish a habit of binging periodically to satisfy mounting cravings. Some preliminary studies into factors associated with binge-eating disorder have shown that low self-efficacy, the lack of an internal sense of being able to accomplish a goal discussed in Chapter Eight, is strongly tied to binge eating.[10] In essence, those who don't *believe* they have control over their eating ultimately do not.

Interestingly, the proposed diagnostic criteria do not just focus on behavior; rather, there must be a component of distress or impairment associated with the binge eating for it to reach "clinical" significance. Specifically, the proposed criteria require the presence of several markers of distress associated with the binge eating, such as eating faster than normal or eating large quantities of food despite not feeling hungry.[11]

Many of these signs of distress can be directly tied to topics we have discussed in this book—for those experiencing food shame, the desire would be to eat the food quickly to end the process. In a diet-binge-diet cycle, individuals will be pulled toward eating beyond their capacity until they are uncomfortably full. Because of the associations between food and comfort, the food may easily be a self-comforting mechanism leading sufferers to eat when they are not even hungry.

The connection between these social experiences and the onset of binge-eating disorder yields surprising results that speak to the power of the combination of socially related effects of being overweight and the resulting diminished self-efficacy: while it might be intuitive to assume that these individuals are overweight *because* they are binge eaters, the vast majority develop binge-eating disorder *after* they become overweight.[12] This strongly indicates that binge eating is a *consequence*, not a *cause* of overweight and obesity. This is particularly important for overweight/obese children: their weight is placing them at risk for development of this eating disorder, but with appropriate intervention, it may be possible to prevent its onset. If binge-eating disorder is developed, it will only sabotage any attempts to lose weight as the overweight child moves through life. For those whose continued weight gain (or inability to lose weight) anchors on binge-eating episodes, binge-eating disorder presents a clinically recognized, scientifically supported manifestation of all the topics we have discussed in this book. It will be very interesting to see, as the criteria are officially put into place and diagnoses begin, what the prevalence of the disorder is and what underlies its development—we anticipate that it will relate directly back to the topics of this book.

THE GOOD, THE BAD, AND THE DANGEROUS: DIETING

A simple Google search for "diet" brings up approximately 115 million websites, and as we discovered in writing this book, will place a whole host of tracking cookies on your computer that will then bring up endless ads for diet programs and weight-loss techniques when you visit *other* websites. A similar search on Amazon .com instantly brings to you almost 125,000 products you can buy to help you reach your weight-loss goals. Guaranteed!* (*Disclaimer:

by use of the word "guaranteed" we do not assert any guarantee of accuracy of the statement.)

In all seriousness, our country's nonstop struggle to lose weight has led the diet industry to regularly cash in on the staggering $40 billion per year that Americans spend on weight-loss programs and products.[13] That is well over $125 for *every* man, woman, and child in the nation—three times what we spend going to the movies.[14] While it might be great business for many companies, the simple fact remains that 95 percent of all dieters will regain all of their lost weight within five years.[15] You have better odds of winning money in a lottery scratch-off than you do of sustaining weight loss. And this is part of the reason for the mammoth size of the weight-loss industry—they're almost guaranteed a return customer.

At first, this might seem hard to understand. If someone has been able to successfully lose weight, why would they not then have the knowledge and skills they need to keep it off? In reality, *losing* weight and *maintaining* weight are two very different things. If we knew how to properly maintain weight, none of us would ever be overweight in the first place.

We all understand how to lose weight on a diet—simply restrict eating to the point that we take in enough calories to sustain our bodies, but less than our body actually needs for a given day so that it has to turn to our stores of energy (that is, fat) to keep the body's metabolism process going. During this "diet" phase, it is relatively easy for us to refuse food—no one typically questions a response of "no thanks, I'm on a diet" when someone refuses to eat food that is offered. You might even get looks of sympathy and a few words of encouragement.

"Diets," though, are by definition temporary restrictions of intake in food with the express purpose of losing weight. Once that weight has been lost, and the diet ceases, weight will automatically trend back in the direction it came from. After all, the eating and exercise habits in place before the diet are what led to the pre-diet weight. Some people on diets think that if their weight was stable before they went on a diet (for instance, they had been overweight for ten years, but had stayed at the same weight for those ten years), all they have to do is go on a diet to reach a new, lower weight, and then when they go back to the way they ate before the diet, they will similarly hold at this new weight. This represents a fundamental misunderstanding of weight.

As we've discussed, weight is a balance: calories in to calories out. The heavier a person is, the more calories their bodies will actually burn over the course of day-to-day activity—it takes more energy for me to move around if I am 200 pounds than if I'm only 150. The dietary patterns that sustained someone at 200 pounds represented a balance of that scale—on average, the person took in exactly enough calories to support their 200-pound body. If they went on a diet to reach 150 pounds, then returned to the way they ate before, they are still eating exactly the right number of calories to maintain their weight. But at 200 pounds, not 150. Furthermore, if the diet is so extreme as to trigger the body's starvation response, it can cause metabolic damage that ultimately leads to even further decreased caloric needs than those from before the diet began.

Despite the thousands of studies that have been done on successful weight loss by countless individual researchers, the only thing that they would likely all agree upon is the fact that, as a construct, diets do not work. The *only* way to lose weight and keep that weight off is to make systematic *permanent* changes to either food intake or exercise (and preferably both). This is truly what makes weight loss so hard—you have to *change*. And people do not tend to change easily.

Because of this propensity to *not* change, as mentioned above, only one in twenty successful *dieters* becomes a successful weight *maintainer* (and that's not even counting those who were *unsuccessful* dieters). The difficulties with weight-loss maintenance lead people to try ever-more-bizarre weight-loss strategies, ranging from not eating any carbohydrates (the most fundamental source of nutrition in animal metabolism) to only drinking fruit juice spiked with cayenne pepper. Not only are these diets potentially dangerous in and of themselves, but they lead to what is now ubiquitously known as yo-yo dieting. The effects of yo-yo dieting (referred to by scientists and nutritionists as "weight cycling") include both psychological consequences (depression, lower self-efficacy, and binge eating) and physical consequences (such as coronary heart disease). In an ultimate irony, the impact of yo-yo dieting on future weight gain is so strong that some studies have even found that one of the strongest predictors of weight *gain* is a history of weight *loss*.[16] This effect applies to adults, but is even rooted in childhood: children who have dieted have been shown to have *larger* increases in body fat over the next eight years of their lives than children who have not dieted.[17]

Part of the problem ties to weight-loss self-efficacy (the internal feeling that one is fundamentally capable of losing weight). Individuals who experience weight cycling also experience a directly linked decrease in their weight-loss self-efficacy,[18] undermining their future attempts at weight loss in a vicious cycle—the more they fail, the more they believe they will fail. And unfortunately as they fail more and more, they are less likely to even try again, and more likely to develop binge eating patterns.[19]

The continued ups and downs (both physical and psychological) associated with the weight-loss hamster wheel can leave overweight children and the resulting overweight adults spiraling toward increasingly unhealthy food habits. Given the fact that one-fourth of women and over 15 percent of men are on a diet at any given time,[20] the variety of diets that have been "developed" to meet this broad demand are of questionable quality at best, and certainly have limited to no scientific basis.

Moving down the spiral, unfortunately more than one-third of dieters will progress to the point of pathological dieting (engaging in diet behaviors that are inherently unhealthy or harmful), and a further one-quarter of these will develop a partial or complete eating disorder.[21] This effect is not just seen in adults—when asked about unhealthy dietary restriction, more than 10 percent of high school students report having fasted for at least one 24-hour period *in the past thirty days* to control their weight.[22] For overweight children, who begin dieting even earlier in life than overweight adults, the path toward engaging in unhealthy weight loss/ weight maintenance strategies is moved up, leading to an increased likelihood of true physical harm in attempts to reach a new weight. In a cruel twist of fate, overweight individuals who have been most impacted by the social effects of being overweight (and have developed negative emotional states as a result) are the *least* likely to be successful at losing weight, even in intensive, medically based weight-loss programs[23]—particularly women, who feel the most social pressures.

All of these factors combine to unfortunately leave overweight individuals in a true lose-lose situation: it is not enough to do the seemingly impossible and actually lose the weight; this becomes the *beginning* of the weight-loss process. The struggles of yo-yo dieting and its impact on health and well-being only serve to reinforce to overweight children and adults that food is an enemy, and one that must be encountered daily.

FOOD SHAME

As overweight children become more aware of the ways that they are seen by others, and in turn treated by them, they can begin to develop "food shame" that can persist well into adulthood. Rooted in weight blame (an underlying tendency of society to "blame" fat people for their own situation and thus provide limited support and compassion to them), food shame involves a general feeling of embarrassment or shame for eating any non-nutritious foods. In the worst of cases, it can lead to shame regarding eating food of any kind. This can apply when purchasing food or consuming it, and can lead to intense difficulties when trying to adjust one's eating habits.

While the area of food shame is still emerging in the scientific community, early evidence strongly supports its presence and widespread potential impact. Studies have shown that when asked about how much they have eaten, overweight individuals consistently say they have eaten fewer calories than they actually have. This effect becomes magnified the more calories the person has eaten, meaning that they report proportionally *fewer* calories the *more* they have actually eaten.[24] This is obviously a direct attempt to mask actual food intake, a direct manifestation of food shame.

Food shame can progress to the point that it interferes with social interactions—some overweight individuals develop such intense food shame that they are embarrassed to eat in front of other people, afraid of what others will think when they see what and how much is being consumed. Unfortunately, this effect can be strongest around people we are close to—studies have shown that food shame is heightened when eating at a friend's house and eating at work,[25] not when eating in view of the general public.

At its most extreme, food shame can ultimately lead to the onset of a full-blown eating disorder.[26] It can lead to such restricted food intake that severe weight loss occurs (anorexia), and it can lead to binging once an individual is away from the "staring eyes" of others (bulimia). As with so many other things we have discussed, the impact of food shame for children who are overweight has the potential to lead to lifelong problems. The earlier and more ingrained that food shame becomes, the more likely it is to lead to

harmful behaviors and the harder it will be to change once adulthood is reached.

ADDICTED TO . . . FOOD?

Recently, the "food addiction" movement has gained significant
momentum. This controversial viewpoint holds that much of obesity
can be explained due to a pathological addiction that many people
have to food. While we have argued earlier that our relationships
with food can be viewed through the *lens* of addiction, the food
addiction movement holds that there are *bona fide* food addicts.

The evidence comes down on both sides,[27] which only fuels
the debate. Supporters of the notion argue that the cravings and
uncontrollable behavior of overeaters, often accompanied by corresponding remorse, constitute an addiction just as one would have
to an illegal drug. They point to certain biochemical studies that
show similar brain and physiological symptoms accompanying food
withdrawal and consumption that appear close to responses seen
in "traditional" addicts, as well as the perceived inability of people
to change their behavior without intense self-exploration and often
professional intervention.

Opponents argue that illicit drugs inherently possess addictive chemical properties that elicit addiction in the vast majority of
those exposed (something that does not occur with food). They also
express concerns that formalizing a "food addiction" will lead to
patient labeling that can have consequences for both employment
and future insurability. A central theme in arguing against formalizing food addiction is also the vital nature of food itself—how can
you truly describe something as "addictive" that is fundamental to
survival? In that sense, aren't we all "addicted" to food?

Interestingly, when you examine the technical criteria for substance dependence (akin to our notion of "addiction"), they could

almost be used without modification to describe food as an addictive substance.[28]

When you look at the criteria one-by-one, (See Table 10.1 below) it is easy to see how this line of thinking could be applied

TABLE 10.1: DIAGNOSTIC CRITERIA FOR SUBSTANCE DEPENDENCE

A maladaptive pattern of substance use, leading to clinically significant impairment or distress, as manifested by three (or more) of the following, occurring at any time in the same 12-month period:

Criterion 1:	Tolerance, as defined by either of the following: a) A need for markedly increased amounts of the substance to achieve intoxication or desired effect b) Markedly diminished effect with continued use of the same amount of the substance
Criterion 2:	Withdrawal, as manifested by either of the following: a) The characteristic withdrawal syndrome for the substance (refer to Criteria A and B of the criteria sets for withdrawal from the specific substances) b) The same (or a closely related) substance is taken to relieve or avoid withdrawal symptoms
Criterion 3:	The substance is often taken in larger amounts or over a longer period than was intended
Criterion 4:	There is a persistent desire or unsuccessful effort to cut down or control substance use
Criterion 5:	A great deal of time is spent in activities necessary to obtain the substance (e.g., visiting multiple doctors or driving long distances), use the substance (e.g., chain-smoking), or recover from its effects
Criterion 6:	Important social, occupational, or recreational activities are given up or reduced because of substance use
Criterion 7:	The substance use is continued despite knowledge of having a persistent or recurrent physical or psychological problem that is likely to have been caused or exacerbated by the substance (e.g., current cocaine use despite recognition of cocaine-induced depression, or continued drinking despite recognition that an ulcer was made worse by alcohol consumption)

Reprinted with permission from the Diagnostic and Statistical Manual of Mental Disorders, Fourth Edition, Text Revision, (Copyright © 2000), American Psychiatric Association.

to food—think about replacing the word "food" everywhere the table mentions "substance," and then how this could impact the way that obesity is viewed:

Criterion 1) *Tolerance*. Many overweight individuals find themselves consuming ever-increasing amounts of food to feel satisfied and to gain the comfort previously obtained with smaller amounts of food.

Criterion 2) *Withdrawal*. Individuals who attempt to cut out certain types of food report exceptionally strong levels of craving such foods. In addition, there is a multi-billion dollar market for "substitute" foods where you can eat similar foods without the guilt: Cut out cookies? Eat SnackWells instead…

Criterion 3) *Overindulgence*. Such behavior is the core of all food-related weight gain.

Criterion 4) *Intake Control*. As we've discussed, nearly everyone in America has been a failed dieter, and the vast majority of those who are overweight have a constant desire to be thinner.

Criterion 5) *Addiction-Linked Activities*. While this criterion is a bit harder to see from the lens of overweight and obesity, one could argue that almost everything we do is in order to keep food on the table. We organize our entire lives around meals ("I don't want to work over lunch"), and for those who gain weight as a result, we spend an amazing amount of time, energy, and money trying to lose weight ("recovering from the effects" of overindulgence).

Criterion 6) *Social/Occupational/Recreational Impact*. As we've discussed, being overweight severely impacts social, occupational, and physical health. It also severely limits the ability of an individual to engage in certain occupations (the morbidly obese cannot be effective in many physically demanding jobs and simply being overweight leads to persistent issues with weight discrimination). Recreational activities are also greatly impacted, both because of decreased stamina and decreased desire to engage in many physically based activities. As we've described, food shame is also one of many potential outcomes associated with overindulgence in food that would reduce engagement in many social and recreational activities as well.

Criterion 7) *Known Physical/Psychological Harm.* And this one almost needs no comment—it is essentially the core of this entire book.

As you can see, the relationship between an overweight person and food can easily be used to satisfy nearly all (if not all) criteria for a dependency disorder. Ready for the most surprising part? If we had been diagnosing a substance dependency, *you would only have to meet three of the criteria to be diagnosed as an addict.* Criteria 4, 6, and 7 are nearly automatically met by any overweight person, so if these criteria were ever to be used to formally designate food addiction as a mental condition, you would almost inherently be diagnosing every fat person with a psychological disorder.

While the scientific community continues to debate the relative merits of establishing a formal category of "food addiction," we feel that the conversation is somewhat counterproductive—we all know that people who have trouble controlling their intake of food have some type of impulse control problem. Whether or not it is a formal addiction does not matter—what matters is how we can leverage what we know about other impulse control disorders (including addictions) to begin to make a difference in those who are ready and willing to make changes. Like addicts, the impetus for change has to come from within, or it will ultimately be unsuccessful. Once that motivation for change has been reached, the relationship with food can begin to be rebuilt.

As with our argument that obesity is a behavior and not a disease, classifying those who are obese as having a food addiction again slides the sense of responsibility away from individual choice and into a category that can easily be used as a scapegoat (both by the overweight individuals and those trying to help). Unlike other addictions, people *must* eat. The abstinence method so strongly supported for other addictions simply isn't possible, so it is almost cruel to tell someone they are addicted to something that they must partake of for the rest of their lives—good luck! Calling "food addiction" a formal disease does not change the need to teach people how to make better choices—the "cure" is still a *choice*. Proponents of the "food addiction" label argue that it opens the door for new treatments and medicines to counteract the "condition,"[29] again perpetuating the idea that obesity can be cured with a *pill*, which it cannot.

Telling someone they have a disease does not make them stronger, or better able to make the changes that are necessary. In the case of addicts, being formally diagnosed with a disease provides an avenue to receive treatment, after which they must maintain an environment free of access to their substance of addiction. This is not possible for the overweight—it's not as if you can find a store that just sells fully nutritional foods in the exact quantities you need them. Traditional addicts are not faced with cocaine in the midst of rice cakes; the overweight and obese in essence are. Nothing can change that environment, so the change must be one of behaviors in the face of temptation.

The Result

The Fat Kid Syndrome

All our discussion comes down to this: a child who grows up overweight is always the fat kid, no matter what unlikely changes they may have been able to achieve in their adult weight. Children and adolescents who grow up fat are permanently altered in a way that will impact them for their entire lives. Until now, this effect has been missed by both the general public and the mainstream media. We have continued to look at the childhood obesity epidemic as if it has a simple solution—let's just see what we need to do to help children lose weight. First, as we've seen, this will be remarkably ineffective in creating long-term weight loss. Second, it continues to take a *reactive* stance to an issue that will require preventive solutions. Last, and most important, it will not ameliorate the long-term effects we've seen throughout this book.

It is quite simply *tragic* that we have reached this place in our history. When else have we ever knowingly let the children of our nation engage in behaviors that rob them of their physical, psychological, and social futures? In this book, we've examined the impact on everything from the amount of sugar in the blood and the ability to attract and keep a mate, to cognitive performance and job earnings. How much more evidence is required before we truly buckle down as a society and take action?

While the task of curbing childhood obesity is daunting, keep in mind that we are the nation that got so upset about *chicken pox* that we implemented nationwide vaccination requirements. The likelihood of dying from chickenpox was 0.0025 percent—or 100 children per year of the 4 million who got the disease.[1] Contrast that to the simple fact that being diabetic as a child *doubles* the chances of death in any given year and you can see that our priorities are distinctly out of line. For goodness' sake, we are the nation that has so cleaned and sanitized our children's environments that one is almost looked down on as a bad parent if a toddler catches a cold! How on earth, then, have we allowed things to get so bad?

The unfortunate answer? Laziness. It is easier to give a child a shot, or to tell them to wash their hands, than to ensure they receive proper nutrition and physical exercise.

We have argued throughout this book that obesity is a behavior, not a disease. We firmly stand by this statement and feel that viewing our current climate in this way is the only way to bring about the kinds of systematic changes necessary to reverse the course of a ship that sailed decades ago. The behavior of childhood obesity occurs in more than just the children, though; in fact, it is predominantly on the part of adults. Through action, or more impactfully, *inaction,* we have allowed our environment to degrade to the point that children are being forced into early obesity.

While obesity itself is not a disease, we hope this book has thus far shown you that there is a disease of sorts sweeping through our nation: the Fat Kid Syndrome. The collection of systematic physical, psychological, and social consequences of childhood obesity discussed throughout this book is not intended to create a new *disease* to be discussed; rather, we hope it helps formalize what the broader consequences are of the most devastating public health emergency we have faced in decades, if not *ever* in the course of modern U.S. history.

As with so many health conditions, prevention is much more effective than cure. The next chapter explores some of the options available to those who are wishing to prevent the onset of Fat Kid Syndrome, or to lessen its effects in those adults who were formerly overweight children. The Resource Guide that follows also provides the programs and initiatives with the best scientific evidence behind them.

ELEVEN

What Can We Do?

We do not want anyone walking away from this book feeling as though they've received a fire and brimstone message of doom. We are at a crisis point, yes, and the effects are severe—but we can still rally together to solve the problem. Following the old adage, the first step in changing a problem is to acknowledge its presence. This book has thus far focused on taking that first step. We hope it has helped to impress upon you the enormity of the problem, and the resulting immense need for change.

We now conclude with a brief roadmap of what we as a society we must do to achieve this necessary change. We do not presume that the next 5,000 words will be a magic bullet to the problem, but if they do nothing more than open the discourse, they will serve an important purpose. The resource guide that follows this chapter can offer more specific plans for implementing change—both within a family and within a community at large.

STEP ONE: CHANGING PARENTS' MINDS

Children are born utterly helpless, completely dependent upon their parents to take care of them. In no other species are offspring dependent for so long—even in our closest relative, chimpanzees, young are dependent for around seven years before striking out on their own. The unmatched period of dependence in humans comes with immeasurable responsibility. Feeding, clothing, and preparing children for their independence requires a commitment that approaches twenty years of investment. The goal of all the love and caring poured into a child is to have them lead a healthy, productive life—and for most parents, there is an overwhelming desire for the child to have a better life than the parent had. As we have discussed, we are now failing on this front.

One of the main roles of a parent is being a protector for their children. As a society, we have continuously expanded our definition of what this protection entails. Millennia ago, this protection focused on simply keeping a child alive—no small task at the time. Over time, we have begun to focus on the overall welfare of our children, not just their basic needs—we want our children to be protected from all manners of harm, physical and emotional. Parents routinely go to great lengths to keep their children "alive and well," buffering them from the harsh realities of the world. Perceived threats and dangers are quickly addressed and eliminated—be they concerns over bullying at school or possible abduction in the streets.

The list of immediate dangers to our children is so long, though, that we have lost sight of the long-term dangers that pose a much more likely source of harm to our children. Take, for instance, the ubiquitous fear of kidnapping we discussed in an earlier chapter. The U.S. Department of Justice has found that only around 115 children are kidnapped by strangers per year in a stereotypical "kidnapping" (where a stranger or slight acquaintance takes a child with intent to keep, ransom, or harm the child).[1] Contrast that with this fact: 3,600 children are diagnosed with obesity-linked Type 2 diabetes every year.[2] So in any given day, ten children are diagnosed with obesity-linked diabetes, but a child is only kidnapped every three days—there is a thirty-times greater risk of diabetes than kidnapping. Despite this, our daily efforts to decrease the risk of diabetes (through proper diet and exercise) are dwarfed by our efforts to keep our children safe from abduction. We put elaborate processes in place to prevent kidnapping—why do we do less for something much more likely to pose a threat to our children?

The problem is that our perception of what in fact poses a direct threat to our children is intensely skewed, and as parents we fear the immediate danger much more than the long-term danger. It is easy to perceive the threat of a child abduction, but understanding the impact of too much glucose in the blood is much more difficult. In essence, kidnapping has a clear villain but obesity does not.

But when we look at children with diabetes, their risk of *death* in any given year is doubled just by being diabetic.[3] *Doubled.* That is the same increase in the likelihood of dying associated with driving under the influence of marijuana.[4] We have at minimum doubled their chances of dying—and who wouldn't want to keep the odds of their child dying from doubling? But by allowing our children to become overweight, particularly to the point of developing diabetes, we have done the equivalent of handing them a joint and pushing them behind the wheel of a car.

In order to truly change the current childhood obesity crisis, the weight of our children must be viewed as a real and present danger to their future—no less important to survival than clothing and shelter. But more importantly, it must be viewed as a *modifiable* danger—something that can be changed. The childhood obesity epidemic has become global—truly a pandemic throughout the industrialized world—and the sheer scope of the problem has left many reeling, questioning our ability to do anything to address such a widespread issue. When something seems impossible, it is human nature to avoid it—why invest the time if the outcome is already set? What can *I* do to address this crushing, worldwide problem?

The answer to that particular question is a resounding *nothing,* which stops most people in their tracks. There is nothing that any of us can do as individuals that will change the problem at the worldwide level, but there is still something each of us can do—impact the children in our own lives (whether they be our own children or those of others).

The necessary changes that must be made to prevent childhood obesity do not occur within the child—*adults* hold the key. Although challenging, complex, and difficult to change, ultimately *we do have control over the weight of our children*. With the proper focus on diet and exercise and a steel-reinforced will to enforce necessary rules (despite the temporary backlash that may result), we can reach a place where our children can grow and prosper without continuing the current trend toward being more and more overweight. Until parents fully grasp that responsibility and embrace that role, there will be no changes to the current trends. As we've discussed, the federal government has not much aided the cause of helping parents know when their children have officially reached a dangerous weight, but the underlying fact remains that most people *know* when their child needs to lose weight. What's lacking is either the knowledge of what to do, or the drive to do it.

Excuses for poor diet and exercise in children abound—it is too expensive, it takes too much time, my child doesn't like to do it, and so on. Even if a family's finances are extraordinarily tight, affordable and nutritious foods are available if one knows where to look. For those at the extremes of poverty, the federal Women, Infants and Children (WIC) program provides access to nutritious food for children up to the age of five (currently assisting over half of all infants), but it is up to the parents to make the most informed choices possible when selecting which foods to provide to their children. While WIC expenditures are often restricted to only the healthiest options, there are still choices to be made and portion sizes to be set. Even for those whose budgets are so tight as to require fast food or other low-cost convenience foods, portion control can have a huge impact. Yes, the super-sized double cheeseburger combo may only be $4, but if it is 2,500 calories then split the meal between two children (and thus make it even more economical to be healthy). For the vast majority of families who are able to afford healthy foods, though, it really does come down to a matter of choice for parents: will you bear the responsibility of keeping your child healthy despite their protests, or leave the burden on them created by a lifetime of missed opportunities and complications to their health?

Again, we fully admit that this is easier said than done, and requires determination and drive on the part of parents (who are increasingly struggling with their own weight). Part of the challenge here comes down to an underlying guilt: no one wants to deprive their child of anything, and providing sustenance is the most basic of all things we give. Withholding food from children fundamentally goes against our entire evolutionary trajectory.

The reframing of food into "regulated territory" can assist with this. Parents restrict countless things enjoyed by their children and enforce numerous "unpopular" requirements for the sake of their well-being—movies, video games, the number and kinds of toys they can play with, what kinds of friends they spend time with, not to mention the constant battles over bedtime, tooth brushing, and baths—the list goes on and on. We know how to regulate our children's behaviors and desires to meet their needs, and we know better than they do what those needs are. We must begin to take this approach with food—to view it as something to be monitored and regulated, just like TV and sun exposure.

And with food, we have the ultimate control. Fundamentally, the only way that a child eats something is if the food itself is either provided to them, or left for them to access themselves. Parents are then by definition the front line of defense. Similarly, if a child is not exercising in any way, it is the parent's responsibility to find a way for them to be active. Is it difficult? Yes, of course. But it is a parent's fundamental *duty*.

While it is important to regulate and monitor food, we are not advocating for children to be counting every calorie or to be barred outright from certain foods. Teaching children moderation with foods will help them gain the skills they will need when they are able to start making their own food choices. If they are never taught to *choose* the proper foods, they will not be able to do so once they are on their own. What is important, as with most things, is moderation. Finding the balance between making children responsible about food vs. making them neurotic about food may seem daunting, but that makes it nonetheless important.

A COMPLICATION: FAT PARENTS

As we've discussed throughout this book, more and more children are being raised by parents who are overweight themselves. In fact, given the current rates of obesity in adults, *most* children are raised by fat parents. In the long run, this is a direct after-effect of the accumulation of decades of increases in childhood obesity—fat children become fat adults, and sometimes skinny children become fat adults. It is much rarer for a fat child to become a skinny adult, or even for a fat adult to manage to become a skinny adult. The impetus is definitely in the direction of getting heavier with age, and since children are starting out heavier than ever, the ripple effects are already being seen in adult obesity rates.

Unfortunately, until *adults* begin to get a handle on weight, it will be impossible to help children. We know that children develop their relationship with food and their opinions of exercise by observing their parents, their first role models, and other important adults in their lives (grandparents, teachers, and so on). To be the best role models possible, parents and in fact all adults must do everything they can to be at a healthy weight themselves, and to *show* (not just tell) children how to live a life of proper diet and activity. Children do not respond well to "do as I say, not as I do"—they need to see their parents engaged in the same behaviors that are expected of them.

Parents who themselves struggle with weight should think about what habits they should change in their own lives *before* their children develop the same habits. And if families put in place a structure to get themselves to the right weight, their children's weight will follow. In fact, the desired results will be much more likely—families that adopt family-level changes are much more likely to bring a child's weight into a healthy range than families that focus their efforts just on the identified child—in fact, one of the strongest predictors of child success in a weight-loss program is *parent* success.[5]

Changing the weight of parents is *critical* in the fight against childhood obesity—studies show that children of obese parents are up to ten times more likely to be obese themselves, and these links are not genetic—they are environmental. Yes, they "inherit" it from their parents—but they're inheriting patterns and habits that lead to obesity, not DNA. This applies to the factors that lead to obesity as well—one of the strongest predictors of whether or not a child will engage in regular physical activity is whether or not their *parents* engage in regular physical activity.[6]

For parents who are overweight, particularly those who were overweight children, think of how the topics we've talked about throughout this book have impacted your own life. Do you have body shame? Food shame? Have you felt the effects of the flab ceiling? For overweight adults who have struggled for years with their weight, add your children to the list of motivators for losing weight—not only to increase *your* health and longevity, but, more importantly, to increase *theirs*. For adults who are overweight, particularly those who have been their entire lives, losing weight is damned hard—but so is raising a child in the first place. And wouldn't we do anything for our children?

CLIMATE CHANGE

Even beyond the influence of parents and family, children are also products of their broader environments. As we've discussed throughout, they are bombarded with advertisements, surrounded in supermarkets by cartoon characters pleading with them to eat nutrition-barren foods, and tragically seen as a target market to increase income in schools. This continued exploitation of our children must not continue—the effects are already dire and will only worsen. It is essential to cease altogether the marketing of unhealthy foods directly to children and to stop building profits off their increasing waistlines.

Opponents of such measures frequently raise questions regarding regulation of commerce and free speech—but consider for a minute all of the legislation surrounding smoking. In a series of sweeping moves considered to be aggressive (and at times called unconstitutional), the advertisement of cigarettes has become so tightly regulated that cigarette companies can no longer have any ads within 1,000 feet of a school or playground. They cannot use cartoon characters to advertise their products and cannot even put their logos on sports sponsorships. This regulation is necessary, effective, and for the most part accepted because of smoking's role in the development of cancer.

Yes, smoking is a known carcinogen, but as we've seen in this book, *so is obesity.*

Yet, despite the overwhelming data on the consequences of childhood obesity, ads specifically targeting children to purchase junk food can be seen not just at home, but even within schools while watching mandatory educational programming. Until hard decisions are made to limit this direct marketing, constant pressure will continue to be placed on our children to demand foods they should not be eating.

The problem extends to the lunchroom as well when we consider the problems posed by "à la carte" school lunches and school vending machines. Yes, if regulations and bans are put in place there could be financial repercussions for schools. School, though, is a place of *learning*, not *income*. Schools functioned before vending and will continue to function after vending. Federally supported "how-to guides," which can help school systems avoid financial losses due to vending restrictions, have been developed (see the Resource Guide for examples), but even without them, changes should occur. Hard decisions have to be made, and even if school programs were to have to fall by the wayside (unlikely given the limited financial return of vending), continuing on this path that is literally robbing children of their future, in the very environment that is charged with laying the groundwork for their future, is quite simply unconscionable. Is it all about vending? Of course not. But vending only serves to add to the climate of weight gain our children are drowning in. You can drain a pool cup by cup. It may take a lot of cups, but each one counts.

WHAT TO DO WITH FAT CHILDREN

We have helped lead community events focused on ways to reduce childhood obesity and it is always interesting to hear the ideas that emerge—ranging from the simple (giving children jump ropes) to the complex (creating a multimedia campaign that ties in mobile messaging). Innovative approaches are constantly being pursued, and finding weight-loss solutions for kids is rapidly expanding into quite a lucrative enterprise (we keep waiting to see Weight Watchers: Junior Edition or Jenny Craig for Kids! emerge any day now).

There are countless books out there that offer step-by-step guides on treating childhood obesity—we will not attempt to replicate those here. While many individuals have found these resources

helpful, they still take a very limited view of the scope of the problem, typically focusing on ways to change what is occurring with
one individual overweight child.

As we've discussed, there are so many forces at work that any
effective, long-term strategy must explore how to not only change
the child, but the family and the child's environment as well. Many
individuals who have been successful at losing weight have not
done so because they learned to exercise some extreme form of
self-control during all meal times and any time in between; rather,
success was often achieved because they learned how to modify
their surroundings to support their behavior change. A child cannot eat junk food at home if there is no junk food at home—by
exercising self-control when purchasing what will surround a child,
the temptation and availability of foods can be removed entirely.

This is not a catch-all, however, as children still eat a substantial
number of meals away from the home (be it at school or restaurants). Teaching children the importance of making proper selec-
tions and encouraging them to do so by modeling similar behavior
can definitely help make a difference. The same is true for exercise—teaching children how to exercise and encouraging them to
do so is important in the support process.

For families in which the parents are also overweight, change
becomes more complicated but can also create a unique advantage.
If an entire family commits to making the changes necessary, the
entire family unit can be transformed. This allows children to gain
support from family members going through the same weight-loss
process right along with them.

In reality, though, the solution for children who are already
overweight will be the same as described previously for prevention, just on a more targeted level. Instead of focusing on the entire
food advertising system, parents can limit the influence of those
messages on children by *not* giving in to demands for purchases of
unhealthy foods, by limiting overall exposure to television in favor

of more exercise—any number of things to try to locally minimize the impact. Sustained, healthy weight-loss efforts rarely fail—what prevents them from succeeding is typically a lapse of will.

WHAT NOT TO DO WITH FAT CHILDREN

There is one set of proposed solutions that we vehemently oppose widespread use of: medical intervention. While bariatric surgery has been revolutionary and has allowed many people to lose significant amounts of weight, it is a *reactive* approach to weight gain that fundamentally does not alter the underlying condition. It is akin to removing metastatic cancers without taking out the root tumor— without corresponding intensive behavior change, weight losses will not be maintained, only increasing frustration and decreasing weight-loss self-efficacy. For some people this is the only option, but for the *vast* majority, it is not.

Similarly, weight-loss pills only offer a short-term, temporary solution. Taking those that are not FDA approved is like playing a pill form of Russian Roulette—these drugs do not have to prove any claim of safety or efficacy, and children should *never* be allowed to take them. Those that are FDA approved are still predicated on being tied in with significant changes in diet and exercise to be effective, and many diet pills in the past have been subsequently shown to have very harmful side effects (one of the best-known being the link between fenfluramine-phentermine, or fen-phen, and severe cardiovascular damage; use of fen-phen led to abnormal cardiac rhythms in nearly one-third of patients taking the drug). Regardless, they are a temporary fix and not designed to provide long-term support. Without complete lifestyle change, results will be transient and only exacerbate the negative emotions that inherently surround weight-loss failures.

As anyone who has ever maintained weight loss for an extended period of time will tell you, losing weight is a journey, not a destination. Once a goal weight has been met, the journey has just begun—the trailhead has only just been reached. No amount of "dieting" or quick fixes will address obesity in children. Those who are overweight must be supported in any way possible in making the lifelong fundamental changes required to create and sustain weight loss.

ADULTS WITH FAT KID SYNDROME

For those who have grown up as overweight children and feel the physical, psychological, and social impacts it creates, there is no simple path to "getting over" it. There is no switch to flip that will address all of the problems it creates. As we've shown throughout this book, it will have a lifelong impact across nearly all aspects of their lives. Like grief for the death of a loved one, it will always be there.

What can be done, though, is to realize how many aspects of our lives are influenced by having been overweight. By looking at ourselves and our actions through the lens of the Fat Kid Syndrome, we can start to see what might be underlying some of our most frustrating experiences, emotions, and tendencies.

For the physical effects, it will be important to get regular checkups and to monitor signs of the most common diseases associated with childhood obesity (getting regular blood pressure checks and periodically checking blood glucose). Many of the long-term physical effects can be diminished by losing weight—the more pressing issues lie in the mental and social effects.

For the mental and social impacts, let the preceding chapters serve as a roadmap for what is occurring. Rather than being frustrated by body shame or food shame, understand that it is a natural reaction to having grown up overweight. Often, the consequences of these after-effects are mostly linked to our reactions to them, not the feelings themselves. Feeling self-conscious about eating in front of other people is very difficult to overcome, and may require therapy to truly counteract, but simply understanding *why* the feeling is there can help explain the intensity of emotions that can arise and keep us from feeling strange or broken because others do not have the same food shame issues. Also, it's important to realize that for the most part, people are not evaluating you in the same way that you are evaluating yourself—the vast majority of the time someone isn't even paying attention to what you are eating. And most importantly, knowing that these feelings are *normal* can also be liberating—there is nothing wrong with you for feeling this way, you just have to decide what to do with those feelings.

For those who become successful in their weight-loss journey yet still feel the after-effects of Fat Kid Syndrome, the same applies—the feelings are normal. Don't let it run your life—if you are at a party and are hungry, eat if the food is good and you want some. Especially if you are at a normal weight, nobody will be thinking "Doesn't he know he used to be fat? He shouldn't eat that!" You're the only one there who is thinking that.

Also, always remember that the Fat Kid Syndrome is always waiting under the surface. From personal experience, if just a few pounds are gained—enough to make us uncomfortable again with the weight we've reached—the emotional and social impacts can rear their heads faster than you can believe. Take the feelings for what they are, and use them to motivate you back to the weight you are comfortable with.

Sadly, the best piece of advice we can offer for those with Fat Kid Syndrome is not to expect it to go away on its own—it won't, and don't let that make you feel "defective." You can work on counteracting its effects by explaining the impacts to others (for instance, explaining to your partner why you are uncomfortable showing your body, or eating out with friends), and working with them to find a way to push through it. The effects can be minimized by consciously focusing on them, but don't expect them to evaporate just because of weight loss, or just because you want them to. Just like losing weight, losing Fat Kid Syndrome takes work.

THE ROAD AHEAD

The fight against childhood obesity will be epic—we have never before faced a threat to the health of our nation that directly impacts so many people; the *majority* of Americans, in fact. Change will require persistence, drive, and tough decision making. It will take years to turn the tide, and many people coming together to change our nation. Our children cannot lead this charge themselves—we must take it on for them.

This change will require *all* of us. But, after all, aren't our children worth it?

Where Do We Go From Here?

Children, parents, and community members who want to make a difference in the childhood obesity epidemic face a dizzying prospect when attempting to find reputable, reliable, accurate, and effective information, programs, and interventions. As we prepared this book, we came across hundreds of valuable resources—in the following pages, we present what we consider to be the most important and reliable, separated into three main categories: general information, data, and tools; childhood obesity prevention and intervention tips and programs; and community-level interventions that can be implemented by schools and other community groups/organizations. Each of the sites listed in this guide offers additional linked content.

As we mentioned earlier, reversing the course of childhood obesity will require concerted community effort—none of us can relegate the responsibility to an individual group. Sure, it would be easy to point at the schools and say it's their responsibility, but that doesn't impact what is happening in the homes. Similarly, changes in the home cannot affect the nutrition and physical activity environment of the school. The responsibility also isn't just on those who have kids or interact with them—we are all complicit in the society that has brought us to this point. We have exerted tremendous power on the development of the problem, yes. But that also means that if we refocus that power, we can reverse the trend. Together, we can make the difference—but we must commit to it. If you have been struck by the information in this book, and want to do something about it, these resources can hopefully help you find a way to get the ball rolling. If you are interested in making a difference, we assure you that there are others in your community who are interested as well—reach out and you will be surprised at the response that you get. We always have been. People care about this issue deeply, but they frequently just don't know where to start. Well, here is the beginning of the map. Only you can impact where it goes.

GENERAL INFORMATION, DATA, AND TOOLS

The following resources offer general information about childhood obesity, data and trends, and tools such as child BMI percentile calculators and meal planners. This basic information can help when trying to learn more about your own family or community. It can also be useful when trying to build a case for the need for change in communities. Many of the interventions and programs presented later in this resource guide depend upon community support, and the information on these websites (and within this book itself) can help in building a compelling case to decision makers whose support may be essential.

The Centers for Disease Control and Prevention (CDC) Childhood Obesity Site. As the federal agency tasked with "collaborating to create the expertise, information, and tools that people and communities need to protect their health—through health promotion, prevention of disease, injury and disability, and preparedness for new health threats," the CDC is the front line of defense against all health concerns in the United States. They have a robust, information-packed website dedicated to both childhood and adult obesity. Their childhood obesity site includes basics of the measurement and health risks largely covered in this book, but also includes up-to-date statistics on childhood obesity rates in much more detail than could be presented in this book (by state and county, by income status, and so on) as well as links to several programs (some described below) that can be implemented to improve children's health related to diet, exercise, and weight. http://www.cdc.gov/obesity/childhood/.

American Academy of Pediatrics: Prevention and Treatment of Childhood Obesity. This site compiles all of the academy's information regarding childhood obesity. It contains facts and figures, a summary of childhood obesity activities being enacted nationwide, and resources for health professionals, families, and communities who wish to address the obesity epidemic. http://www2.aap.org /obesity/index.html.

Healthy Child Care America. Developed by the American Academy of Pediatrics, this program aims to educate health-care professionals, families, and early child-care providers about ways to promote health in the infants and young children that they provide care for. For parents whose children are in day care settings, the information in the program can be put forward to your day care provider to promote a healthier environment not only for your child, but the other children in the same care setting. Those involved in child care want the best for the children they care for, and will be remarkably receptive to appropriately presented information (particularly backed by one of the leading pediatrics groups in the nation). The program includes webinars, professional development, and continuing education opportunities for child-care centers to learn more about the latest evidence-based practices for improving child health. http://www.healthychildcare.org/index.html.

Child and Teen BMI Calculator. The CDC hosts a child and teen BMI calculator that, when provided with a child's age, height, and weight, will indicate what percentile the child's BMI is in. While this method has limitations (described earlier in this book), this tool is still a good resource for approximately determining a child's weight status. In addition to providing the percentile, the website also provides its interpretation and recommendations for ways to improve weight if needed. http://apps.nccd.cdc.gov /dnpabmi/.

Fruits and Vegetables Calculator. This online "calculator" provides age-, sex-, and activity-level specific guidelines for how many servings of fruits and vegetables children and adults should eat, and provides examples of what quantities of each count as a "serving." http://www.cdc.gov/nutrition/everyone/fruitsvegetables/howmany. html.

Daily Food Plan. Based on the new FDA "MyPlate" (which replaced the food pyramid we had all come to know and love so much), this site creates an age-, sex-, weight-, height-, and physical activity-level specific food plan that lays out exactly how much of what kinds of foods should be eaten on an average day. http://www. choosemyplate.gov/myplate/index.aspx.

There are also age-specific sites for parents wanting to learn more about their child's daily nutrition: http://www.choosemyplate .gov/preschoolers.html for preschoolers and http://www.choosemy plate.gov/children-over-five.html for children over five (their section also contains a great online game called "Blast Off!" that teaches children about how to balance their nutrition).

SuperTracker. This FDA-developed free online tracking program helps develop age-specific meal plans combined with a tracking tool that helps monitor progress toward weight-loss goals (by tracking both physical activity and dietary habits). The program also contains nutritional information for more than 8,000 foods, making it much easier to accurately determine daily intake. The site also has a virtual coach that will help you and your child or entire family reach weight-loss goals and provides individually customized reports of progress and plans for reaching goals. https:// www.choosemyplate.gov/SuperTracker/default.aspx.

Nutrition Standards for Foods in Schools. Because of the integral role that schools play in the nutrition of the vast majority of children in the United States, they represent a very important intervention point for ensuring adequate nutrition is being provided to children nationwide. This website presents nutrition guides that are audience specific, explaining the appropriate standards that school foods should uphold to parents/teachers, school boards and other administrators, school nutritionists, and students themselves. Parents in particular can help use this information to lobby their school boards for increased nutrition standards in line with national evidence. http://www.cdc.gov/healthyyouth/nutrition/standards.htm.

Health Education Curriculum Analysis Tool (HECAT). More technical than the other tools in this section, the HECAT is a formal evaluation tool that can assist schools and communities in determining the quality of their health education (including diet, physical activity, and weight control). It helps determine if national health education standards are being met and can help schools identify new curricula that can improve their quality of health education. A strong feature of HECAT is its ability to be tailored to the needs of individual communities (and to operate within the broader curriculum requirements of individual jurisdictions). http://www.cdc.gov/healthyyouth/hecat/index.htm.

Physical Education Curriculum Analysis Tool (PECAT). The PECAT is the parallel program to HECAT, above, and assists schools in determining the quality of their physical education programs. http://www.cdc.gov/healthyyouth/PECAT/.

For communities that implement the PECAT and find the need to improve their physical education curriculum, a toolkit focused on the quality of physical education programs is also available, http://www.cdc.gov/healthyyouth/physicalactivity/pdf/quality_pe.pdf, supplemented by a downloadable presentation that can be customized by parents and community members for advocating for change at the local government level http://www.cdc.gov/healthyyouth/physicalactivity/toolkit/youth_pa_guidelines_schools.pdf.

Preventing Childhood Obesity in Early Care and Education Programs. This standards guide was jointly developed by the Health Resources and Services Administration's Maternal and Child Health Bureau, the American Academy of Pediatrics, the American Public Health Association, and the National Resource Center for Health and Safety in Child Care and Early Education. The guide offers "a set of national standards describing evidence-based best practices in nutrition, physical activity, and screen time for early care and education programs." This resource is particularly useful for individuals establishing or revising the approach of a preschool or day care to nutrition and exercise. http://nrckids.org/CFOC3/PDFVersion/preventing_obesity.pdf.

Food Desert Locator. Maintained by the U.S. Department of Agriculture, this interactive map allows you to see if your community is designated as a "food desert," indicating a stark lack of available, affordable fresh food options. Being designated as a food desert opens the door to certain grant programs and can help communities in advocating for additional support to improve access to healthy foods. http://www.ers.usda.gov/data-products/food-desert-locator.aspx.

Health and Sustainability Guidelines for Federal Concessions and Vending Operations. This information guide presents the various definitions and guidelines that agencies have put in place regarding what "healthy" concession and vending machine guidelines are; these guidelines can be useful when advocating for a change to vending machine contents within local schools or other child-involved settings. http://www.cdc.gov/chronicdisease/resources/guidelines/food-service-guidelines.htm.

A companion guide to help schools develop healthy beverage vending agreements is available from the National Policy

and Legal Analysis Network to Prevent Childhood Obesity http://
changelabsolutions.org/sites/phlpnet.org/files/nplan/Healthy
VendngAgrmnt_FactSheet_FINAL_090311.pdf.

Comprehensive School Physical Activity Programs Package.
This collection of position statements from the National Association
for Sport and Physical Education details what constitutes adequate
physical activity within the school setting, covering topics ranging
from guidelines for after-school physical activity programs to a
coaches' code of conduct. As with other guides listed here, it can help
parents advocating for increased physical activity within the schools
by providing evidence-based and nationally supported options to
school boards and other officials. http://www.aahperd.org/naspe
/publications/teachingTools/cspa.cfm.

CHILDHOOD OBESITY PREVENTION AND
INTERVENTION TIPS AND PROGRAMS

This section contains programs and other resources that can help
children and families enact healthy lifestyles, ranging from interactive games that teach children about the importance of nutrition
and exercise to informational pamphlets designed to help you learn
more about specific nutritional pitfalls that often impact children's
health.

BAM! (Body and Mind!). Developed by CDC as a "kids-only"
version of their website, BAM! serves as a gateway for children to
learn more about health topics that specifically affect them. Two of
the main sections of the BAM! website are "Food/Nutrition" and
"Physical Activity." Within each section are age-appropriate tips,
explanations, and interactive games to help children learn more
about establishing healthy diet and exercise habits. http://www
.bam.gov/.

Best Bones Forever! This initiative, focused on young girls, aims
to increase nutritional intake of calcium and Vitamin D, along with

daily physical activity, in order to strengthen bones. The website offers nutritional tips and exercise pointers to help girls maintain active, healthy lifestyles. http://www.bestbonesforever.gov/.

Eat Smart, Play Hard! Healthy Lifestyle. This program, which can be implemented by families, helps parents learn to eat better and exercise more to help them be healthy role models for their children. It shows parents how to track progress, make healthy food choices, make "family time active time," and other steps that will not only improve their children's health, but their own as well. The website also contains activity sheets, bookmarks, posters, comic books, and stickers to help engage children in the program. http://teamnutrition.usda.gov/Resources/eatsmartmaterials.html.

SPARK. Originally funded by the National Institutes of Health, the SPARK website provides access to free evidence-based resources for improving physical education and wellness programs for children and youth. The website offers physical education lesson plans, webinars, trainer tips, newsletters, and a grants finder to help communities bring funds to their area to support physical education improvements. The site also provides very affordable curriculum packages for more in-depth guides to implementing programs. SPARK programs include physical education, early childhood programs, after school programs, and coordinated school health programs. http://www.sparkpe.org/.

Portion Distortion! This interactive site helps teach about how portion sizes have become disguised by comparing the twenty-year differences in many common food items through a "quiz"-style game. http://hp2010.nhlbihin.net/portion/.

Healthier Food Retail. This guide helps communities engage in an assessment of the quality of the retail food available within their area in order to help highlight areas of improvement. The guide includes links to specific programs implemented throughout the country that have helped improve the food retail environment. http://www.cdc.gov/obesity/downloads/HFRassessment.pdf.

Motion Moments. Developed by the National Resource Center for Health and Safety in Child Care and Early Education, the Motion Moments website provides training videos designed to show child care and early education providers how to integrate physical activity into the classroom and daily routines of young children. Separate activity recommendations are made for infants, toddlers, and preschool-aged children, and the videos are available in both English and Spanish. http://nrckids.org/Motion_Moments/index .htm.

School Health Resource Center. Compiled and maintained by the CDC, this site provides access to webinars, implementation guides, fact sheets, and tips for addressing school health in seven areas: 1) working with school districts; 2) school wellness policies; 3) school food environment; 4) improving nutritional content; 5) joint use agreements; 6) physical activity and education; and 7) physical activity and education after school. http://www.cdc.gov/ CommunitiesPuttingPreventiontoWork/resources/schools.htm.

Leadership for Healthy Communities. In addition to links to several toolkits and other childhood obesity resources, this website contains a database of ongoing childhood obesity initiatives that parents and community members can search by geography to determine what activities are taking place in their area. http://www .leadershipforhealthycommunities.org/.

Action Strategies Toolkit. Developed by the Robert Wood Johnson Foundation through the Leadership for Healthy Communities Initiative, this toolkit organizes best practices and evidence-based programs for ten action areas within childhood obesity, broken into active living strategies and healthy eating strategies. Within active living, the toolkit provides information on implementing programs focused on: 1) active transportation; 2) land use for active living; 3) open spaces, parks, and recreation; 4) quality physical education in and near schools; and 5) safety and crime prevention. Within healthy eating, the toolkit focuses on:

1) quality nutrition in schools; 2) supermarkets and healthy food vendors; 3) farm-fresh local foods; 4) restaurants; and 5) food and beverage marketing. http://www.leadershipforhealthycommunities .org/index.php/home-toolkitnav-161?task=view.

Tips for Parents: Ideas to Help Children Maintain a Healthy Weight. Sponsored by CDC, this website lays out several ways in which parents can help their children reduce their weight in a healthy way. http://www.cdc.gov/healthyweight/children/index.html.

Physical Activity Guidelines for Children. This website details not only the appropriate physical activity levels for children, but also various ways in which that level of physical activity can be reached, how to determine age-appropriate exercises, and at what intensity level of activity children should be engaged. http://www .cdc.gov/physicalactivity/everyone/guidelines/children.html.

Types of Physical Activity for Children. This site lists the three different types of physical activity all children need (aerobic, muscle-strengthening, and bone-strengthening) and provides specific examples of several types of each activity that both children and adults can engage in. http://www.cdc.gov/physicalactivity/everyone /guidelines/what_counts.html.

Making Physical Activity a Part of a Child's Life. This site lays out specific ways in which to help children get their daily level of physical activity (for example, setting a positive example and ways to make physical activity fun). http://www.cdc.gov/physicalactivity /everyone/getactive/children.html.

How to Use Fruits and Vegetables to Help Manage Your Weight. This brochure (assembled based on the latest scientific evidence) describes the most effective and beneficial ways in which to use fruits and vegetables as part of an overall weight management program. It presents specific ways to incorporate more fruits and vegetables into everyday meals, with specific advice for breakfast, lunch, and dinner. http://www.cdc.gov/healthyweight/healthy _eating/fruits_vegetables.html.

Eat More, Weigh Less? This companion to "How To Use Fruits and Vegetables" shows how you can actually eat *more* food that has less calories, and lays out specific foods to eat or avoid to help you feel more full with less calories. http://www.cdc.gov/healthyweight /healthy_eating/energy_density.html.

How to Avoid Portion Size Pitfalls to Help Manage Your Weight. As we saw in this book, portion sizes have risen dramatically in recent years, and many of us aren't even aware of all of the changes that have been made. This resource lays out ways to help control the amount of food being eaten, including some things that may not be expected (such as *encouraging* snacking as a way to avoid overeating at meals). http://www.cdc.gov/healthyweight /healthy_eating/portion_size.html.

Rethink Your Drink. This brochure helps identify the "hidden" calories that many children and adults get from what they drink, rather than from what they eat. It lays out the number of calories in leading beverages and shows ways to make simple substitutions that can save up to 600 calories per day (that's a pound a week!). http:// www.cdc.gov/healthyweight/healthy_eating/drinks.html.

How to Understand and Use the Nutrition Facts Label. This site helps parents learn how to read the somewhat confusing food labels that are now mandated on many food items. It breaks the label down into specific nutritional components to limit and components to encourage. http://www.fda.gov/Food/ResourcesForYou /Consumers/NFLPM/ucm274593.htm.

Bright Futures in Practice: Physical Activity. This guide, developed by Georgetown University, provides families, health professionals, and communities with concrete, achievable means of "creating a lifelong foundation for physical activity." By focusing on establishing good exercise habits in early childhood, this guide helps establish patterns of behavior that can prevent childhood obesity later in life through early intervention. http://www.brightfutures .org/physicalactivity/.

Early Head Start National Resource Center. This site is a compilation of toolkits, webinars, podcasts and informational videos about early child health (focusing on birth to three years of age), including guides on nutrition and activity. http://www.ehsnrc.org/.

COMMUNITY-LEVEL INTERVENTIONS

For those wanting to make a broader impact on more than just their own family or a particular child they care about, a wide range of community-level interventions have been developed, tested, and shown to make a positive impact on childhood obesity within entire communities. These programs by definition require more effort and more collaboration among families, schools, and entire communities, but they have the benefit of impacting a broad range of children. Community-level interventions like the ones below will be key in reversing the childhood obesity epidemic, as we have long since passed the point of being able to effectively address the issue at the individual level.

Let's Move! This federal initiative, spearheaded by First Lady Michelle Obama, has catalyzed physical activity and nutrition programs across the nation. The comprehensive Let's Move! website contains information on how to encourage activity and nutrition activities in homes, schools, and communities, and offers many tips and pointers on encouraging healthy lifestyles in children. http://www.letsmove.gov/.

Let's Move Salad Bars to School. A companion to the Let's Move! Campaign, Let's Move Salad Bars to School focuses on providing grants to local communities to support the installation of salad bars in local schools. To date, the initiative has installed nearly 1,500 salad bars that have served nearly three-quarters of a million children. The goal of the program is to install 6,000 salad bars nationwide to provide access to healthier school lunch options by removing the initial cost burden of creating salad bar options. http://saladbars2schools.org.

We Can! (Ways to Enhance Children's Activity & Nutrition).
This evidence-based program developed through the National
Institutes of Health has been implemented across the country, and
is "a national movement designed to give parents, caregivers, and
entire communities a way to help children 8 to 13 years old stay
at a healthy weight." The website is filled with toolkits, programs,
and implementation guides that can help any community group
(from a school board to a concerned group of citizens) implement
community-wide change to improve weight. The site has separate
sub-sections devoted to parents/families, partners, health professionals, and the media. http://www.nhlbi.nih.gov/health/public/heart
/obesity/wecan/.

**School Health Guidelines to Promote Healthy Eating and
Physical Activity.** This evidence-based toolkit sets forth nine guidelines for ensuring that schools appropriately encourage healthy eating and physical activity:

1. Use a coordinated approach to develop, implement, and evalu-
    ate healthy eating and physical activity policies and practices
2. Establish school environments that support healthy eating
    and physical activity
3. Provide a quality school meal program and ensure that stu-
    dents have only appealing, healthy food and beverage choices
    offered outside of the school menu program
4. Implement a comprehensive physical activity program with
    quality physical education as the cornerstone
5. Implement health education that provides students with the
    knowledge, attitudes, skills, and experiences needed for life-
    long healthy eating and physical activity
6. Provide students with health, mental health, and social ser-
    vices to address healthy eating, physical activity, and related
    chronic disease prevention
7. Partner with families and community members in the devel-
    opment and implementation of healthy eating and physical
    activity policies, practices, and programs

8. Provide a school employee wellness program that includes healthy eating and physical activity services for all school staff members

9. Employ qualified persons and provide professional development opportunities for physical education, health education, nutrition services, and health, mental health, and social services staff members, as well as staff members who supervise recess, cafeteria time, and out-of-school-time programs.

The toolkit then presents specific, practical strategies for implementing each guideline. While these strategies may seem very broad, far-reaching, and potentially challenging to implement, they represent those highest-impact activities that can be used to improve children's health at the community level. Concerned citizens and community groups can work together to help implement all or some of the guidelines, but even if the entire program isn't able to be implemented, any incremental change can help improve health. http://www.cdc.gov/healthyyouth /npao/strategies.htm.

Implementing Strong Nutrition Standards for Schools: Financial Implications. One of the most frequently heard counterarguments to improving school nutrition standards is the inevitable argument of cost—healthy foods do tend to cost more, and resource-strapped schools are often highly resistant to exploring options for improving food quality because of concerns over implementing programs that will not be ultimately financially sustainable. This brief shows evidence that 80 percent of schools implementing better nutrition standards saw little to no change in overall revenues, and in fact, some schools had *higher* revenues. The brief also discusses ways to maximize revenue generated from healthier food choices (including vending machines). http://www .cdc.gov/healthyyouth/nutrition/pdf/financial_implications.pdf.

Making it Happen! School Nutrition Success Stories. This collection of success stories from across the country highlights programs actual schools have successfully implemented and sustained. Broken into a searchable database covering everything from nutrition policies to new marketing techniques, this resource documents how and why programs were implemented, challenges faced, and the impact the programs ultimately had on school nutrition and health. http://www.cdc.gov/healthyyouth/mih/index.htm.

The program also has a companion website that provides a wealth of information on how to enact the "central themes" of the successful programs, providing theme-by-theme guidance on implementation, available at http://www.cdc.gov/healthyyouth/mih/approaches.htm. Information is provided on each of the following:

1. Establish nutrition standards for competitive foods
2. Influence food and beverage contracts
3. Make more healthful foods and beverages available
4. Adopt marketing techniques
5. Limit student access to competitive foods
6. Use fundraising activities and rewards

HealthierUS School Challenge. Developed by the U.S. Department of Agriculture, this site offers information for schools (educators and food service staff) on how to increase nutrition in school children. The HealthierUS School Challenge (a feature program of the USDA) certifies schools that have gone above and beyond to increase nutrition and physical activity options within their schools. The site offers information on how schools can achieve this certification by improving the healthy options of their school lunch and activity programs. http://www.fns.usda.gov/tn/HealthierUS/index.html.

MyPlate Partnering Program. Also sponsored by the U.S. Department of Agriculture, this initiative is a country-wide effort to increase knowledge about USDA nutrition guidelines. Communities, businesses, and individuals can partner with the USDA's Center for Nutrition Policy and Promotion to become advocates for increased awareness of the importance of nutrition. http://www.choosemyplate.gov/partnering-program.html.

VERB! This highly effective program, which targeted the physical activity levels of "tweens," was a large-scale media campaign conducted by the Centers for Disease Control and Prevention to get adolescents motivated about engaging in exercise. While the media campaign has since ended, the program maintains the resources generated as part of the initiative, including handouts, planning guides, mini-magazines, and tips for engaging children in physical activity. http://www.cdc.gov/youthcampaign/index.htm.

National Farm to School Network. There is a growing "farm-to-school" movement mirroring the recent "farm-to-table" trend that focuses on improving the nutritional content of school lunches by directly engaging farms in the acquisition of fresh produce for schools. The initiative defines the movement as "a program that connects schools (K–12) and local farms with the objectives of serving healthy meals in school cafeterias, improving student nutrition, providing agriculture, health and nutrition education opportunities, and supporting local and regional farmers." There are now an estimated 2,500 schools nationwide engaged in farm-to-school initiatives, and the network provides information on how to establish such a program and support in doing so. The site contains briefs, publications, funding opportunities, research findings, and archived webinars to help communities create their own initiatives. http://www.farmtoschool.org/index.php.

A similar toolkit from the Gretchen Swanson Center for Nutrition is also available from http://toolkit.centerfornutrition.org/.

Companion guides on how to scale up farm-to-school programs are also available, offering in-depth case studies of communities that have successfully implemented such programs. https://www.food security.org/pub/Delivering_More-Scaling_up_Farm_to_School .pdf and http://www.extension.umn.edu/farm-to-school/toolkit/.

Similar programs, in which schools start their own vegetable gardens to help supply fresh produce for the cafeteria, have occasionally faced regulatory hurdles—the National Policy and Legal Analysis Network to Prevent Childhood Obesity has developed a brief explaining the regulatory climate of school garden programs http:// changelabsolutions.org/sites/phlpnet.org/files/SchoolGarden_to _Cafteria_Liability_FINAL_20110523.pdf.

Water In Schools. This initiative stemmed from a study in California that showed that nearly half of school children did not have access to free drinking water during school meals, effectively forcing children to consume calorie-laden drinks with their meals. The website offers tips for creating opportunities for children to have water, one of the most basic human needs. http://www .waterinschools.org/index.shtml.

Safe Routes to School. This nationwide initiative both documents and encourages the development of new "Safe Routes to School" that allow children to safely walk or bike to school as a means of increasing physical activity. The site contains a regularly updated interactive map that shows federally supported safe routes, and provides access to mini-grants and implementation guides to help communities establish safe ways for children to exercise on their way to and from school. http://www.saferoutesinfo.org/.

The site contains a local policy guide to assist with implementation, available at http://www.saferoutespartnership.org/sites/default /files/pdf/Local_Policy_Guide_2011.pdf.

There is also a separate guide for low-income schools and communities available at http://www.saferoutespartnership.org/ sites/default/files/pdf/LowIncomeGuide.pdf and a CDC-developed presentation that can be customized for community, school board, and local government presentations http://www.cdc.gov/nccdphp/dnpa/kidswalk/resources.htm#guide.

CDC also has its own implementation guide that can be used to promote a safe system of increasing the number of children who get daily physical activity through walking to school. http://www.cdc.gov/nccdphp/dnpa/kidswalk/pdf/kidswalk.pdf.

Partnership for Prevention Toolkits. The Partnership for Prevention, a national "nonpartisan organization of business, nonprofit, and government leaders working to make evidence-based disease prevention and health promotion a national priority" has developed three free toolkits that allow communities to implement evidence-based programs to improve physical activity. The three toolkits include 1) "Places for Physical Activity: Facilitating Development of a Community Trail and Promoting Its Use to Increase Physical Activity among Youth and Adults," which provides a step-by-step guide for changing the built environment of a community to encourage physical activity by establishing safe, accessible walking trails that are community owned and community led; 2) "School Based Physical Education: Working with Schools to Increase Physical Activity among Children and Adolescents in Physical Education Classes," which helps communities re-tailor their physical education programs to have more of a health and wellness focus (rather than the traditional sports focus), providing children with skills that will last a lifetime in controlling obesity; and 3) "Social Support for Physical Activity: Establishing a Community-Based Walking Group Program to Increase Physical Activity Among Youth and Adults," which guides communities through the process of building a community-based support network for physical activity. Each toolkit was developed with the intention of helping translate the latest in research on physical activity into actual implementable programs that communities can use to improve their health. http://www.prevent.org/Action-Guides/The-Community-Health-Promotion-Handbook.aspx.

Eat Healthy, Be Active! Community Workshops. This series of workshops, developed by the U.S. Department of Agriculture, is designed to provide community members with specific skills to help them live healthy, active lives. The workshops are broken into six themes: 1) Enjoy Healthy Food That Tastes Great; 2) Quick, Healthy Meals and Snacks; 3) Eating Healthy on a Budget; 4) Top Tips for Losing Weight and Keeping It Off; 5) Making Healthy Eating Part of Your Total Lifestyle; and 6) Physical Activity is the Key to Living Well. Each topic comes with an in-depth workshop guide that allows a facilitator to teach community members about each of the preceding topics, supported by handouts, evaluations, posters, and other materials. http://www.health.gov/dietaryguidelines/workshops/.

FitnessGram. The FitnessGram is a school-based assessment of physical activity and physical fitness levels that can be implemented by schools, school systems, and even states to provide a fitness "report card" to help parents be more aware of their child's physical health. The report details child-specific performance on a variety of fitness measures, and can even be used to track a child's progress over time in areas such as BMI, aerobic capacity, muscle strength, flexibility, and many other areas. Many states have implemented FitnessGram requirements for schools, which has helped to dramatically raise awareness of physical health needs in school-aged children. http://www.fitnessgram.net/home/.

Together Counts/Energy Balance 101. Developed and supported by the Healthy Weight Commitment Foundation, the Together Counts movement aims to encourage family- and community-level involvement in improving nutrition and exercise habits. The site includes lesson plans for teachers, resources for school nurses, community-level interventions that can be enacted by groups of community members, activities that parents can implement at home, and interactive games for children that teach them about exercise and nutrition. http://www.togethercounts.com/.

Obesity Prevention on a Budget: Low- and No-Cost Policy Options to Increase Healthy Eating and Active Living. As with the most common arguments against vending machine regulation in schools, one of the most frequent complaints about implementing any type of physical activity or healthy eating program in schools is the issue of cost. This resource guide, developed by the Robert Wood Johnson Foundation (one of the nation's leading health foundations), provides practical and specific real-world programs and policy changes that can be put in place to improve nutrition and physical activity with little or no cost to the community itself. http://www.leadershipforhealthycommunities.org/images/stories/obesity_prevention_on_budget.final.pdf.

Promoting Healthy Youth, Schools, and Communities: A Guide to Community-School Health Councils. This evidence-based approach to improving the health of school children through building community-school partnerships focused on health was developed jointly by the American School Health Association, the American Academy of Pediatrics, the National Center for Health Education, the American Cancer Society, and the Iowa Department of Public Health. The toolkit offers a step-by-step guide to forming school health councils (designed to focus on improving health in schools through better policies, planning, and programming) by providing implementation guidelines, sample policies, presentations that can be made to school boards and county commissioners, action planning assistance, and conducting a formal needs assessment and impact evaluation. http://www.cancer.org/acs/groups/content/@nho/documents/document/guidetocommunityschoolhealhcou.pdf.

Healthy School Toolkit. Developed by The Food Trust, this guide helps parents and other community members implement a comprehensive plan for evaluating and reforming the "health environment" of their schools, focusing on implementing school nutrition policies that promote healthy lifestyles. http://www .thefoodtrust.org/catalog/download.php?product_id=144.

The CDC has a companion presentation that can be used when discussing the need for improving the school health environment, available at http://www.cdc.gov/healthyyouth/npao/presentation .htm.

Healthy Schools Program Framework. Developed by the Alliance for a Healthier Generation (co-led by former President Bill Clinton in partnership with the American Heart Association), this certification program recognizes "schools that create healthier school environments that promote physical activity and healthy eating among students and staff" by promoting best practices for creating healthy school environments. The certification/award process focuses on seven key areas: 1) policy/systems; 2) school meals; 3) competitive food and beverages; 4) health education; 5) employee wellness; 6) physical education; and 7) student wellness. http:// www.leadershipforhealthycommunities.org/images/stories/07–278 _hspframework_11–12.pdf.

The Community Guide. This clearinghouse of community-based health promotion initiatives, maintained by the Community Preventive Services Task Force of the U.S. Department of Health and Human Services, provides a wealth of information on nearly every health outcome imaginable. Specific sub-sites are devoted to nutrition, obesity, and physical activity. http://www.thecommunityguide .org/index.html.

How To Start a Healthy Food Market (in schools). Following a growing movement in schools, this toolkit outlines how to start a food market "where students create, own, and operate fresh fruit and vegetable stands for fellow students, teachers, parents, and administrators." The program teaches children not only about how to grow and use fresh foods, it also improves self-efficacy for healthy eating and encourages entrepreneurial achievement. http:// www.thefoodtrust.org/catalog/download.php?product_id=124.

Key Lessons from California Schools Working to Change School Food Environments. This guide offers "lessons learned" from a group of California schools that implemented programs to improve their food environments. The guide discusses challenges faced when attempting to change school food environments, and offers specific strategies for overcoming these challenges. http://www .partnershipph.org/sites/default/files/70171_CAE_HEAC_9.pdf.

The Kindergarten Initiative. This program is designed to teach kindergarten children about the importance of healthy eating, and to introduce them to the skills needed to make healthy food choices. Using a holistic approach, the initiative brings together children, teachers, parents, schools, and communities to set children on the proper nutritional path from early childhood. An implementation guide is available from the Food Trust website at http://www .thefoodtrust.org/catalog/download.php?product_id=139.

Opening School Playgrounds to the Community After Hours: A Toolkit for Increasing Physical Activity Through Joint Use Agreements. This toolkit details the procedural, legal, regulatory, and liability issues that surround implementing "joint-use agreements" in which school playgrounds become available to the community after hours, providing detailed case studies to help communities model themselves after successful programs. Implementing such a program is an evidence-based method for increasing physical activity in local communities, and the initiative is becoming increasingly common throughout the United States. While the process may at first seem daunting, this thorough toolkit lays out everything a community needs to implement the program. http://changelabsolutions.org/sites/phlpnet.org/files/Joint_Use _Toolkit_FINAL_web_2010.01.28.pdf.

5210 Let's Go! The 5210 Let's Go! initiative is a nationally recognized prevention program that targets childhood obesity through
six programs aimed at crucial intervention points: early childhood,
schools, communities, the workplace, after school, and health care.
Separate programs for each of the sectors aim to collectively get
kids to eat five or more fruits and vegetables per day, to have less
than two hours of screen time, to have one or more hours of daily
physical activity, and to have zero sugary drinks. Free toolkits are
available to implement the program, with individualized activities
across settings and educational levels (K–5, middle and high school,
after school, and so on). http://www.letsgo.org/.

Notes

INTRODUCTION

1. S. C. Harris, A. C. Ivy, and L. M. Searle, "The Mechanism of Amphetamine-Induced Loss of Weight: A Consideration of the Theory of Hunger and Appetite," *Journal of the American Medical Association* 134(17) (1947): 1468–1475.

CHAPTER ONE: THE BATTLE OF THE BULGE

1. National Weather Service, "Medical Aspects of Lightning," http://www.lightning safety.noaa.gov/medical.htm.
2. U.S. Census Bureau, "Motor Vehicle Accidents—Number and Deaths: 1990–2009 (Table 1103)," 2012, http://www.census.gov/compendia/statab/2012/tables /12s1103.pdf.
3. U.S. Census Bureau, "Educational Attainment by Race and Hispanic Origin: 1970 to 2010 (Table 229)," 2012, http://www.census.gov/compendia/statab/2012 /tables/12s0229.pdf.
4. American Heart Association, "Overweight in Children," 2012, http:// www.heart.org/HEARTORG/GettingHealthy/Overweight-in-Children_ UCM_304054_Article.jsp.
5. S. S. Go and W. C. Chumlea, "Tracking of Body Mass Index in Children in Relation to Overweight in Adulthood," *American Journal of Clinical Nutrition* 70 (supplement) (1999): 145S–148S.
6. National Institutes of Health, "First Federal Obesity Clinical Guidelines Released," 1998, http://www.nih.gov/news/pr/jun98/nhlbi-17.htm.
7. International Obesity Task Force of the World Health Organization and the International Association for the Study of Obesity, "The Asia-Pacific Perspective: Redefining Obesity and Its Treatment," *Health Communications Australia*, 2000.
8. C. L. Ogden and K. M. Flegal, "Changes in the Terminology for Childhood Overweight and Obesity," *National Health Statistics Reports* 25 (2010): 1–7.
9. J. H. Himes and W. H. Dietz, "Guidelines for Overweight in Adolescent Preventive Services: Recommendations from an Expert Committee," *American Journal of Clinical Nutrition* 59 (1994): 307–316.
10. S. E. Barlow, "Expert Committee Recommendations Regarding the Prevention, Assessment, and Treatment of Child and Adolescent Overweight and Obesity: Summary Report," *Pediatrics: Neoreviews* 120 (s4) (2007): s164–s192.

11. C. L. Ogden, C. D. Fryar, M. D. Carroll, and K. M. Flegal, "Mean Body Weight, Height, and Body Mass Index, United States 1960–2002," *Advance Data* 347 (2004): 1–17.

12. Johns Hopkins University Bloomberg School of Public Health, "Obesity Rates Continue to Climb in the United States," 2007, http://www.jhsph.edu/news/news-releases/2007/wang_adult_obesity.html.

13. Centers for Disease Control and Prevention, "CDC Grand Rounds: Childhood Obesity in the United States," *Morbidity and Mortality Weekly Report* 60(2) (2011): 42–46.

14. E. Arias, "United States Life Tables, 2007," *National Vital Statistics Reports* 59(9) (2011): 1–61, http://www.cdc.gov/nchs/data/nvsr/nvsr59/nvsr59_09.pdf.

15. S. J. Olshanskey et al., "A Potential Decline in Life Expectancy in the United States in the 21st Century," *New England Journal of Medicine* 352(11) (2005): 1138–1145.

16. Central Intelligence Agency, "The World Factbook: Country Comparisons, Life Expectancy at Birth," 2012, https://www.cia.gov/library/publications/the-world-factbook/rankorder/2102rank.html.

CHAPTER TWO: OBESITY IS A BEHAVIOR, PART ONE

1. S. J. Nielsen and B. M. Popkin, "Patterns and Trends in Food Portion Sizes, 1977–1998," *JAMA* 289(4) (2003): 450–453.

2. L. R. Young and M. Nestle, "The Contribution of Expanding Portion Sizes to the US Obesity Epidemic," *American Journal of Public Health* 92(2) (2002): 246–249.

3. B. J. Rolls, L. S. Roe, and J. S. Meengs, "Larger Portion Sizes Lead to a Sustained Increase in Energy Intake Over 2 Days," *Journal of the American Dietetic Association* 106(4) (2006): 543–549.

4. J. P. Koplan and K. D. Brownell, "Response of the Food and Beverage Industry to the Obesity Threat," *Journal of the American Medical Association* 304(13) (2010): 1487–1488.

5. Young and Nestle, "The Contribution of Expanding Portion Sizes to the US Obesity Epidemic."

6. B. J. Rolls, D. Engell, and L. L. Birch, "Serving Portion Size Influences 5 Year Old but Not 3 Year Old Children's Food Intakes," *Journal of the American Dietetic Association* 100(2) (2000): 232–234.

7. E. Schlosser, *Fast-Food Nation: The Dark Side of the All-American Meal* (New York: Mariner Books, 2000).

8. L. E. Urban, et al., "Accuracy of Stated Energy Contents of Restaurant Foods," *JAMA* 306(3) (2011): 287–293.

9. S. I. O'Donnell, S. L. Hoerr, J. A. Mendoza, and E. T. Goh, "Nutrient Quality of Fast Food Kids Meals," *The American Journal of Clinical Nutrition* 88 (2008): 1388–1395.

10. M. E. Eisenberg, R. E. Olson, D. Neumark-Sztainer, M. Story, and L. H. Bearinger, "Correlations between Family Meals and Psychosocial Well-Being Among Adolescents," *Archives of Pediatrics & Adolescent Medicine* 158(8) (2004): 792–796.

11. A. H. Lichtenstein and D. S. Ludwig, "Bring Back Home Economics Education," *Journal of the American Medical Association* 303(18) (2010): 1857–1858.

12. U.S. Department of Agriculture, *America's Eating Habits: Changes and Consequences,* 1999.

13. M. Gamble and N. Cotugna, "A Quarter Century of TV Food Advertising Targeted at Children," *American Journal of Health Behavior* 23(4) (1999): 261–267.

14. Schlosser, *Fast-Food Nation*.

15. S. Linn and C. L. Novosat, "Calories for Sale: Food Marketing to Children in the 21st Century," *The Annals of the American Academy of Political and Social Sciences* 615 (2008): 133–155.

16. Juliet Schor, *Born to Buy: The Commercialized Child and the New Consumer Culture* (New York: Scribner, 2004).

17. J. Eggerton, "Food-Marketing Debate Heats Up: Congress to JOIN FCC and FTC in Pressing for Action," 2007, http://www.broadcastingcable.com /article/108968-Food_Marketing_Debate_Heats_Up.php.

18. Gregg Cebryznski, and Amy Zuber, "Burger Behemoths Shake Up Menu Mix, Marketing Tactics," *Nation's Restaurant News*, February 5, 2001, 1.

19. S. Thompson, "Cap'n Goes AWOL as Sales Flatten; Quaker Redirects Cereal Brand's Marketing Budget to Focus on Kids," *Advertising Age*, November 22, 1999, 8.

20. J. Berr, "Is Cap'n Crunch Easing Quietly into Retirement?" 2011, http://www .dailyfinance.com/2011/03/07/capn-crunch-easing-into-retirement/.

21. U.S. Department of Agriculture, *America's Eating Habits: Changes and Consequences,* 1999.

22. Center for Science in the Public Interest, "Class Action Lawsuit Targets McDonald's Use of Toys to Market to Children: Practice Illegally Exploits Children, Says CSPI," 2010, http://www.cspinet.org/new/201012151.html.

23. Ibid.

24. Linn and Novosat, "Calories for Sale."

25. M. Slosson, "Jack in the Box Yanks Toys from Kids' Meals," 2011, http://www .reuters.com/article/2011/06/21/us-toys-fastfood-idUSTRE75K6RZ20110621.

26. T. N. Robinson, D. L. G. Borzekowski, D. M. Matheson, and H. C. Kraemer, "Effects of Fast Food Branding on Young Children's Taste Preferences," *Archives of Pediatrics and Adolescent Medicine* 161(8) (2007): 792–797.

27. A. E. Gallo, "Food Advertising in the United States," in E. Frazao, ed., *America's Eating Habits: Changes and Consequences* (Washington, DC: United States Department of Agriculture Economic Research Service, 1999), 173–180.

28. A. Batada and M. G. Wootan, "Nickelodeon Markets Nutrition-Poor Foods to Children," *American Journal of Preventive Medicine* 33(1) (2007): 48–50.

29. L. M. Lipsky and R. J. Iannotti, "Associations of Television Viewing with Eating Behaviors in the 2009 Health Behaviour in School-Aged Children Study," *Archives of Pediatrics and Adolescent Medicine* 166(5) (2012): 465–472.

30. Sesame Workshop, "If Elmo Eats Broccoli, Will Kids Eat It Too?" 2005, http:// archive.sesameworkshop.org/aboutus/inside_press.php?contentId=15092302.

31. J. A. Hruban, "Selection of Snack Foods from Vending Machines by High School Students," *Journal of School Health* 47(1) (1977). 33–37.

32. Ibid.

33. M. C. Jalonick, "Pizza Is a Vegetable? Congress Says Yes," 2011, http://www .msnbc.msn.com/id/45306416/ns/health-diet_and_nutrition/t/pizza-vegetable -congress-says-yes/#.UDk1a6BoWSo.

34. U.S. Department of Agriculture, *School Nutrition Dietary Assessment Study II Summary of Findings* (Alexandria, VA: 2001).

35. Ibid.

36. M. Y. Kubik, L. A. Lytle, P. J. Hannan, C. L. Perry, and M. Story, "The Association of the School Food Environment with Dietary Behaviors of Young Adolescents," *American Journal of Public Health* 93 (2003): 1168–1173.

37. J. L. Wiecha, D. Finkelstein, P. J. Troped, M. Fragala, and K. E. Peterson, "School Vending Machine Use and Fast-Food Restaurant Use Are Associated with Sugar-Sweetened Beverage Intake in Youth," *Journal of the American Dietetic Association* 106(10) (2006): 1627–1630.

38. Ad Age Data Center, "100 Leading National Advertisers: 2002 Edition Index," 2002, http://adage.com/article/datacenter-advertising-spending/100-leading -national-advertisers-index-2002-edition/106669/.

39. T. Lang, G. Rayner, and E. Kaelin, *The Food Industry, Diet, Physical Activity, and Health: A Review of Reported Commitments and Practice of 25 of the World's Largest Food Companies,* City University of London, 2006.

40. J. Johanson, J. Smith, and M. G. Wootan, "Raw Deal: School Beverage Contracts Less Lucrative Than They Seem," Washington, DC: Center for Science in the Public Interest, 2006.

41. National Center for Education Statistics, "Overview of Public Elementary and Secondary Schools and Districts," 2001, http://nces.ed.gov/pubs2001/overview/ table05.asp.

42. American Academy of Child and Adolescent Psychiatry, "Obesity in Children and Teens," 2011, http://aacap.org/page.ww?name=Obesity+in+Children+and +Teens&section=Facts+for+Families.

43. Ibid.

44. WebMD/Stanford, "Parents, Kids, Doctors Balk at Talk About Weight," WebMD Health News, 2011, http://www.webmd.com/parenting/news/20110914 /parents-kids-doctors-balk-at-talk-about-weight.

45. Ibid.

46. L. Jonides, V. Buschbacher, and S. E. Barlow, "Management of Child and Adolescent Obesity: Psychological, Emotional, and Behavioral Assessment," *Pediatrics* 110(s1) (2002): 215–221.

47. E. M. Perrin, A. C Skinner, and M. J. Steiner, "Parental Recall of Doctor Communication of Weight Status: National Trends from 1999 through 2008," *Archives of Pediatrics and Adolescent Medicine,* 166(4) (2012): 317–322.

CHAPTER THREE: OBESITY IS A BEHAVIOR, PART TWO

1. Centers for Disease Control and Prevention, "Trends in the prevalence of physical activity and sedentary behaviors—National YRBS: 1991–2011," 2012, http://www.cdc.gov/healthyyouth/yrbs/pdf/us_physical_trend_yrbs.pdf.

2. Centers for Disease Control and Prevention, "Youth Risk Behavior Surveillance System: 2011 National Overview," 2012, http://www.cdc.gov/healthyyouth /yrbs/pdf/us_overview_yrbs.pdf.

3. F. W. Booth, S. E. Gordon, C. J. Carlson, and M. T. Hamilton, "Waging War on Modern Chronic Diseases: Primary Prevention Through Exercise Biology," *Journal of Applied Physiology* 88 (2000): 774–787.

4. M. V. Chakravarthy and F. W. Booth, "Inactivity and Inaction: We Can't Afford Either," *Archives of Pediatrics and Adolescent Medicine* 157(8) (2003): 731–732.

5. S. L. Gortmaker, "Innovations to Reduce Television and Computer Time and Obesity in Childhood. *Archives of Pediatrics and Adolescent Medicine* 162(3) (2008): 283–284.

6. Nielsen Wire, "TV Viewing Among Kids at an Eight-Year High," 2009, http://blog.nielsen.com/nielsenwire/media_entertainment/tv-viewing-among-kids-at-an-eight-year-high/.

7. Duke Children's Hospital and Health Center, "Monitor Your Kids' Computer Time," 2012, http://www.dukechildrens.org/about_us/newsroom/monitor_computer_time.

8. The Henry J. Kaiser Family Foundation, "Daily Media Use Among Children and Teens up Dramatically from Five Years Ago: Big Increase in Mobile Media Helps Drive Increased Consumption," 2010, http://www.kff.org/entmedia/entmedia012010nr.cfm/.

9. Ibid.

10. National Sleep Foundation, "Teens and Sleep," 2012, http://www.sleepfoundation.org/article/sleep-topics/teens-and-sleep.

11. A. Grontved and F. B. Hu, "Television Viewing and Risk of Type 2 Diabetes, Cardiovascular Disease, and All-Cause Mortality: A Meta-Analysis," *Journal of the American Medical Association* 305(23) (2011): 2448–2455.

12. Centers for Disease Control and Prevention, "Trends in the prevalence of physical activity and sedentary behaviors—National YRBS: 1991–2011."

13. H. E. Marano, "A Nation of Wimps," *Psychology Today,* Nov/Dec 2004, http://www.psychologytoday.com/articles/200411/nation-wimps.

14. R. Clements, ed., *Elementary School Recess: Selected Readings, Games, and Activities for Teachers and Parents* (Boston: American Press, 2005).

15. J. C. Lumeng, D. Appugliese, H. J. Cabral, R. H. Bradley, and B. Zuckerman, "Neighborhood Safety and Overweight Status in Children," *Archives of Pediatrics and Adolescent Medicine* 160(1) (2006): 25–31.

16. D. Martin, "That Upside-Down High Will Be Only a Memory: Monkey Bars Fall to Safety Pressures," 1996, http://www.nytimes.com/1996/04/11/nyregion/that-upside-down-high-will-be-only-a-memory-monkey-bars-fall-to-safety-pressures.html?scp=1&sq=Douglas+Martin+playgrounds+monkey+bars&st=nyt.

17. T. A. Farley, R. A. Meriwether, E. T. Baker, J. C. Rice, and L. S. Webber, "Where Do the Children Play? The Influence of Playground Equipment on Physical Activity of Children in Free Play," *Journal of Physical Activity and Health* 5(2) (2008): 319–331.

18. J. Tierney, "Can a Playground Be Too Safe?" 2011, http://www.nytimes.com/2011/07/19/science/19tierney.html?_r=1&src=me&ref=general.

19. E. J. C. Leeuwen, E. Zimmermann, and M. D. Ross, "Responding to Inequities: Gorillas Try to Maintain Their Competitive Advantage During Play Fights," *Royal Society Biology Letters,* 2008, doi: 10.1098/rsbl.2010.0482.

20. J. Viegas, "You're It! Gorillas Play Tag: African Great Apes Play That Ever-Popular Kids' Game as a Way to Earn How to Keep a Competitive Edge," 2010, http://news.discovery.com/animals/gorillas-apes-tag.html.

21. E. Bazar, "Not It!" More Schools Ban Games at Recess," 2006, http://www.usatoday.com/news/health/2006-06-26-recess-bans_x.htm.

22. G. Nielsen, R. Taylor, S. Williams, and J. Mann, "Permanent Play Facilities in School Playgrounds as a Determinant of Children's Activity," *Journal of Physical Activity and Health* 7(4) (2010): 490–496.

23. P. Gordon-Larsen, M. C. Nelson, P. Page, and B. M. Popkin, "Inequality in the Built Environment Underlies Key Health Disparities in Physical Activity and Obesity," *Pediatrics* 117(2) (2006): 417–424.

24. J. L. Frost, "The Dissolution of Children's Outdoor Play: Causes and Consequences," 2012, http://www.ipema.org/documents/common%20good%20pdf.pdf.

25. E. B. H. Sandseter and L. E. O. Kennair, "Children's Risky Play from an Evolutionary Perspective: The Anti-Phobic Effects of Thrilling Experiences," *Evolutionary Psychology* 9(2) (2011): 257–284.

CHAPTER FOUR: IT'S *NOT* JUST A LITTLE BABY FAT

1. J. M. Sorof, D. Lai, J. Turner, T. Poffenbarger, and R. J. Portman, "Overweight, Ethnicity, and the Prevalence of Hypertension in School-Aged Children," *Pediatrics* 113(3) (2004): 475–482, 475.

2. S. E. Hampl, C. A. Carroll, S. D. Simon, and V. Sharma, "Resource Utilization and Expenditures for Overweight and Obese Children," *Archives of Pediatrics and Adolescent Medicine,* 161(1) (2007): 11–14.

3. J. B. Schwimmer, T. M. Burwinkle, and J. W. Varni, "Health-Related Quality of Life of Severely Obese Children and Adolescents," *Journal of the American Medical Association,* 289(14) (2003): 1813–1819.

4. American Diabetes Association, "Diabetes Basics: Type 1," 2012, http://www.diabetes.org/diabetes-basics/type-1/?loc=DropDownDB-type1.

5. Mayo Clinic, "Type 2 Diabetes: Risk Factors," 2012, http://www.mayoclinic.com/health/type-2-diabetes/ds00585/dsection=risk-factors.

6. Centers for Disease Control and Prevention, "Diabetes Public Health Resource: Children and Diabetes—More Information," 2012, http://www.cdc.gov/diabetes/projects/cda2.htm.

7. National Diabetes Information Clearinghouse, "National Diabetes Statistics, 2011," 2011, http://diabetes.niddk.nih.gov/dm/pubs/statistics/.

8. Centers for Disease Control and Prevention, "National Diabetes Fact Sheet: National Estimates and General Information on Diabetes and Prediabetes in the United States, 2011," 2011, http://www.cdc.gov/diabetes/pubs/pdf/ndfs_2011.pdf.

9. Today Study Group, "A Clinical Trial to Maintain Glycemic Control in Youth with Type 2 Diabetes," *New England Journal of Medicine* 366 (2012): 2247–2256.

10. M. Riley and B. Bluhm, "High Blood Pressure in Children and Adolescents," *American Family Physician* 85(7) (2012): 693–700.

11. S. M. Bartosh and A. J. Aronson, "Childhood Hypertension. An Update on Etiology, Diagnosis, and Treatment," *Pediatric Clinics of North America* 46 (1999): 235–252.

12. G. G. Luma and R. T. Spiotta, "Hypertension in Children and Adolescents," *American Family Physician* 73(9) (2006): 1558–1568.

13. Ibid.

14. C. B. Ingul, A. E. Tjonna, T. O. Stolen, A. Stoylen, and U. Wisloff, "Impaired Cardiac Function Among Obese Adolescents: Effect of Aerobic Interval Training," *Archives of Pediatrics and Adolescent Medicine* 164(9) (2010): 852–859.

15. National Heart, Lung, and Blood Institute, "Chart 3—67," in *Morbidity and Mortality: 2009 Chart Book on Cardiovascular, Lung, and Blood Disease* (Rockville, MD: U.S. Department of Health and Human Services, National Institutes of Health, 2009).

16. National Heart, Lung, and Blood Institute, "The Fourth Report on the Diagnosis, Evaluation, and Treatment of High Blood Pressure in Children and Adolescents," 2005.

17. N. L. Keenan and K. A. Rosendorf, "Prevalence of Hypertension and Controlled Hypertension—United States, 2005–2008," *Morbidity and Mortality Weekly Report* 60(1) (2011): 94–97.

18. International Diabetes Federation, "The IDF Consensus Definition of the Metabolic Syndrome in Children and Adolescents," 2007, http://www.idf.org /webdata/docs/Mets_definition_children.pdf.

19. K. G. M. M. Alberti, P. Z. Zimmet, and J. E. Shaw, "The Metabolic Syndrome: A New World-Wide Definition from the International Diabetes Federation Consensus," *Lancet* 366 (2005), 1059–1062.

20. S. D. de Ferranti, K. Gauvreau, D. S. Ludwig, E. J. Neufeld, J. W. Newburger, and N. Rifai, "Prevalence of the Metabolic Syndrome in American Adolescents: Findings from the Third National Health and Nutrition Examination Survey," *Circulation 110* (2004): 2494–2497.

21. N. Gungor, F. Bacha, R. Saad, J. Janosky, and S. A. Arslanian, "The Metabolic Syndrome in Healthy Children Using In-Vivo Insulin Sensitivity Measurement," *Pediatric Research 2004* 55 (2004): 145A. As cited in Zimmet et al., "The Metabolic Syndrome in Children and Adolescents—An IDF Consensus Report," *Pediatric Diabetes* 8(5) (2007): 299–306; S. Cook, M. Weitzman, P. Auinger, M. Nguyen, and W. H. Dietz, "Prevalence of a Metabolic Syndrome Phenotype in Adolescents: Findings from the Third National Health and Nutrition Examination Survey, 1988–1994," *Archives of Pediatric and Adolescent Medicine* 157 (2003): 821–827.

22. I. Aeberli, R. F. Hurrell, and M. B. Zimmermann, "Overweight Children Have Higher Circulating Hepcidin Concentrations and Lower Iron Status but Have Dietary Iron Intakes and Bioavailability Comparable with Normal Weight Children," *International Journal of Obesity* 33 (2009): 1111–1117.

23. Y. Weintraub, S. Singer, D. Alexander, S. Hacham, G. Menucin, R. Lubetzky, et al., "Enuresis: An Unattended Comorbidity of Childhood Obesity," *International Journal of Obesity* (2012): ePub, doi: 10.1038/ijo.2012.108.

24. J. Peralta-Huertas, K. Livingstone, A. Banach, P. Klentrou, and D. O'Leary, "Differences in Left Ventricular Mass Between Overweight and Normal-Weight Preadolescent Children," *Applied Physiology, Nutrition, and Metabolism* 33 (2008): 1172–1180.

25. S. R. Lucas and T. A. E. Platts-Mills, "Paediatric Asthma and Obesity," *Paediatric Respiratory Reviews* 7(4) (2006): 233–238.

26. L. G. Sulit, A. Storfer-Isser, C. L. Rosen, H. L. Kirchner, and S. Redline, "Associations of Obesity, Sleep-Disordered Breathing, and Wheezing in Children," *American Journal of Respiratory and Critical Care Medicine* 171(6) (2005): 659–664.

27. S. Redline, P. V. Tishler, M. Schluchter, J. Aylor, K. Clark, and G. Graham, "Risk Factors for Sleep-Disordered Breathing in Children: Associations with Obesity, Race, and Respiratory Problems," *American Journal of Respiratory and Clinical Medicine* 159(5) (1999): 1527–1532.

28. A. I. Arbaje, "Determining Eligibility for Gastric Bypass Surgery," *American Family Physician* 73(9) (2006): 1638–1643.

29. Y. D. Podnos, J. C. Jimenez, S. E. Wilson, C. M. Stevens, and N. T. Nguyen, "Complications after Laparoscopic Gastric Bypass: A Review of 3464 Cases," *Archives of Surgery* 138(9) (2003): 957–961.

30. M. M. Davis, K. Slish, C. Chao, and M. D. Caban, "National Trends in Bariatric Surgery, 1996–2002," *Archives of Surgery* 141(1) (2006): 71–74.
31. P. L. Schilling, M. M. Davis, C. T. Albanese, S. Dutta, and J. Morton, "National Trends in Adolescent Bariatric Surgical Procedures and Implications for Surgical Centers of Excellence," *Journal of the American College of Surgeons* 206(1) (2008): 1–12.
32. W. S. Tsai, T. H. Inge, and R. S. Burd, "Bariatric Surgery in Adolescents: Recent National Trends in Use and In-Hospital Outcome," *Archives of Pediatrics and Adolescent Medicine* 161(3) (2007): 217–221.
33. Duke Health, "Weight Loss Surgery," 2012, http://www.dukehealth.org/services/weight_loss_surgery/about/first_steps.
34. T. H. Inge, N. F. Krebs, V. F. Garcia, J. A. Skelton, K. S. Guice, R. S. Strauss, et al., "Bariatric Surgery for Severely Overweight Adolescents: Concerns and Recommendations," *Pediatrics* 114(1) (2004): 217–223.
35. Schilling, Davis, Albanese, Dutta, and Mortan, "National Trends in Adolescent Bariatric Surgical Procedures and Implications for Surgical Centers of Excellence."
36. S. E. Messiah, G. Lopez-Mitnik, D. Winegar, B. Sherif, K. L. Arheart, K. W. Reichard, et al., "Changes in Weight and Co-Morbidities Among Adolescents Undergoing Bariatric Surgery: 1-Year Results from the Bariatric Outcomes Longitudinal Database," *Surgery for Obesity and Related Diseases,* 2012, doi:10.1016/j.soard.2012.03.007.
37. H. J. Sugerman, E. L. Sugerman, E. J. DeMaria, J. M. Kellum, C. Kennedy, Y. Mowery, et al., "Bariatric Surgery for Severely Obese Adolescents," *Journal of Gastrointestinal Surgery* 7(1) (2003): 102–108.
38. M. L. Maciejewski, E. H. Livinsgston, V. A. Smith, A. L. Kavee, L. C. Kahwati, W. G. Henderson, et al., "Survival Among High-Risk Patients After Bariatric Surgery, *Journal of the American Medical Association* 305(23) (2011): 2419–2426.

CHAPTER FIVE: ONCE FAT, ALWAYS FAT

1. A. H. Mokdad, J. S. Marks, D. F. Stroup, and J. L. Gerberding, "Actual Causes of Death in the United States, 2000," *Journal of the American Medical Association* 293(3) (2005): 293–294.
2. K. Bibbins-Domingo, P. Coxson, M. J. Pletcher, J. Lightwood, and L. Goldman, "Adolescent Overweight and Future Adult Coronary Heart Disease," *New England Journal of Medicine* 357 (2007): 2371–2379.
3. E. A. Finkelstein, J. G. Trogdon, J. W. Cohen, and W. Dietz, "Annual Medical Spending Attributable to Obesity: Payer- and Service-Specific Estimates," *Health Affairs* 28(5) (2009): 822–831.
4. Bibbins-Domingo, Coxson, Pletcher, Lightwood, and Goldman, "Adolescent Overweight and Future Adult Coronary Heart Disease."
5. G. Whitlock, S. Lewington, P. Sherliker, R. Clarke, J. Emberson, J. Halsey, et al., "Body-Mass Index and Cause-Specific Mortality in 900,000 Adults: Collaborative Analyses of 57 Prospective Studies," *Lancet* 373 (2009): 1083–1096.
6. T. Bjorge, A. Engeland, A. Tverdal, and G. D. Smith, "Body Mass Index in Adolescence in Relation to Cause-Specific Mortality: A Follow-Up of 230,000 Norwegian Adolescents," *American Journal of Epidemiology* 168(1) (2008): 30–37.

7. J. M. Lee, "Why Young Adults Hold the Key to Assessing the Obesity Epidemic in Children," *Archive of Pediatrics & Adolescent Medicine* 162(7) (2008): 682–687.

8. J. C. Warren, "Creation of a Markov Chain Model of National Center for Health Statistics 2002 Mortality Data: Examining Life Expectancies, Hypothetical Cure Scenarios, and Mortality Disparities" (Ph.D. diss., University of Miami School of Medicine, 2006), http://scholarlyrepository.miami.edu/dissertations/2392/.

9. R. H. Eckel and R. M. Krauss, "American Heart Association Call to Action: Obesity as a Major Risk Factor for Coronary Heart Disease," *Circulation* 97 (1998): 2099–2100.

10. S. Suk, R. L. Sacco, B. Boden-Albala, J. F. Cheun, J. G. Pittman, M. S. Elkind, et al., "Abdominal Obesity and Risk of Ischemic Stroke," *Stroke* 34 (2003): 1586–1592.

11. WebMD, "His Guide to a Heart Attack: Symptoms in Men," 2012, http://www.webmd.com/heart-disease/features/his-guide-to-a-heart-attack.

12. Women's Heart Foundation, "Women and Heart Disease Facts," 2012, http://www.womensheart.org/content/heartdisease/heart_disease_facts.asp.

13. Science Daily, "Stroke Incidence Rising Among Younger Adults, Decreasing Among Elderly," 2010, http://www.sciencedaily.com/releases/2010/02/100224165219.htm.

14. J. Baker, L. W. Olsen, and T. I. A. Sorensen, "Childhood Body Mass Index and the Risk of Coronary Heart Disease in Adulthood," *New England Journal of Medicine* 357 (2007): 2329–2337.

15. C. Miao, S. Chen, J. Ding, K. Liu, D. Li, R. Macedo, et al., "The Association of Pericardial Fat with Coronary Artery Plaque Index at MR Imaging: The Multi-Ethnic Study of Atherosclerosis (MESA)," *Radiology* 261 (2011): 109–115.

16. National Heart Lung and Blood Institute, "What Is High Blood Pressure?" 2011, http://www.nhlbi.nih.gov/health/health-topics/topics/hbp/.

17. N. L. Keenan and K. A. Rosendorf, "Prevalence of Hypertension and Controlled Hypertension—United States, 2005–2008," *Morbidity and Mortality Weekly Report* 60(1) (2011): 94–97.

18. P. A. Heidenreich, J. G. Trogdon, O. A. Khavjou, J. Butler, K. Dracup, M. D. Ezekowitz, et al., "Forecasting the Future of Cardiovascular Disease in the United States: A Policy Statement from the American Heart Association," *Circulation* 123 (2011): 933–44.

19. P. W. F. Wilson, R. B. D'Agostino, L. Sullivan, H. Parise, and W. B. Kannel, "Overweight and Obesity as Determinants of Cardiovascular Risk," *Archives of Internal Medicine* 162(16) (2002): 1867–1872.

20. National Heart Lung and Blood Institute, "How Can High Blood Pressure Be Prevented?" 2011, http://www.nhlbi.nih.gov/health/health-topics/topics/hbp/prevention.html.

21. CDC, "Number of Americans with Diabetes Expected to Double or Triple by 2050," 2010, http://www.cdc.gov/media/pressrel/2010/r101022.html.

22. American Diabetes Association, "Living with Diabetes: Complications," 2012, http://www.diabetes.org/living-with-diabetes/complications/.

23. American Diabetes Association, "Living with Diabetes: High Blood Pressure (Hypertension)," 2012, http://www.diabetes.org/living-with-diabetes/complications/high-blood-pressure-hypertension.html.

24. American Diabetes Association, "Living with Diabetes: Stroke," 2012, http://www.diabetes.org/living-with-diabetes/complications/stroke.html.

25. R. J. Anderson, K. E. Freedland, R. E. Clouse, and P. J. Lustman, "The Prevalence of Comorbid Depression in Adults with Diabetes: A Meta-Analysis," *Diabetes Care* 24(6) (2001): 1069–1078.

26. L. P. Richardson, R. Davis, R. Poulton, E. McCauley, T. E. Moffitt, A. Caspi, et al., "A Longitudinal Evaluation of Adolescent Depression and Adult Obesity," *Archives of Pediatrics and Adolescent Medicine* 157(8) (2003): 739–745.

27. T. A. Hillier and K. L. Pedula, "Complications in Young Adults with Early-Onset Type 2 Diabetes: Losing the Relative Protection of Youth," *Diabetes Care* 26(1) (2003): 2999–3005.

28. Today Study Group, "A Clinical Trial to Maintain Glycemic Control in Youth with Type 2 Diabetes," *New England Journal of Medicine* 366 (2012): 2247–2256.

29. C. G. Bacon, F. G. Hu, E. Giovannucci, D. B. Glasser, M. A. Mittleman, and E. B. Rimm, "Association of Type and Duration of Diabetes with Erectile Dysfunction in a Large Cohort of Men," *Diabetes Care* 25(8) (2002): 1458–1463.

30. C. S. Fox, L. Sullivan, R. B. D'Agostino, Sr., and P. W. F. Wilson, "The Significant Effect of Diabetes Duration on Coronary Heart Disease Mortality," *Diabetes Care* 27(3) (2004): 704–708.

31. K. C. Donaghue, J. M. Fairchild, M. E. Craig, A. K. Chan, S. Hing, L. R. Cutler, et al., "Do All Prepubertal Years of Diabetes Duration Contribute Equally to Diabetes Complications?" *Diabetes Care* 26(4) (2003): 1224–1229.

32. E. Brun, R. G. Nelson, P. H. Bennett, G. Imperatore, G. Zoppini, G. Verlato, et al., "Diabetes Duration and Cause-Specific Mortality in the Verona Diabetes Study," *Diabetes Care* 23(8) (2000): 1119–1123.

33. Hillier and Pedula, "Complications in Young Adults with Early-Onset Type 2 Diabetes: Losing the Relative Protection of Youth."

34. E. E. Calle, C. Rodriguez, K. Walker-Thurmond, and M. J. Thun, "Overweight, Obesity, and Mortality from Cancer in a Prospectively Studied Cohort of U.S. Adults," *New England Journal of Medicine* 348 (2003): 1625–1638.

35. B. S. Warren and C. M. Devine, "Obesity and Cancer Risk. Fact Sheet #57," Sprecher Institute for Comparative Cancer Research at Cornell University, 2007.

36. American Cancer Society, "Cancer Facts & Figures, 2012," 2012, http://www.cancer.org/Research/CancerFactsFigures/index.

37. Ibid.

38. Calle, Rodriguez, Walker-Thurmond, and Thun, "Overweight, Obesity, and Mortality from Cancer in a Prospectively Studied Cohort of U.S. Adults."

CHAPTER SIX: FAT BRAIN

1. S. A. Richardson, N. Goodman, A. H. Hastorf, and S. M. Dornbusch, "Cultural Uniformity in Reaction to Physical Disabilities," *American Sociological Review* 26 (1961): 241–247.

2. J. D. Latner and A. J. Stunkard, "Getting Worse: The Stigmatization of Obese Children," *Obesity Research* 11 (2003): 452–456.

3. R. M. Puhl and J. D. Latner, "Stigma, Obesity, and the Health of the Nation's Children," *Psychological Bulletin* 133(4) (2007): 557–580.
4. A. Myers and J. C. Rosen, "Obesity Stigmatization and Coping: Relation to Mental Health Symptoms, Body Image, and Self-Esteem," *International Journal of Obesity* 23 (1999): 221–230.
5. U.S. Department of Health and Human Services, "The Surgeon General's Call to Action to Prevent and Decrease Overweight and Obesity: Factsheet, Overweight in Children and Adolescents," 2001, http://www.surgeongeneral. gov/library/calls/obesity/.
6. P. A. Estabrooks and S. Shetterly, "The Prevalence and Health Care Use of Overweight Children in an Integrated Health Care System," *Archives of Pediatrics and Adolescent Medicine* 161(3) (2007): 222–227.
7. G. Vila, E. Zipper, M. Dabbas, C. Bertrand, J. J. Robert, C. Ricour, et al., "Mental Disorders in Obese Children and Adolescents," *Psychosomatic Medicine* 66(3) (2004): 387–394.
8. R. BeLue, L. A. Francis, and B. Colaco, "Mental Health Problems and Overweight in a Nationally Representative Sample of Adolescents: Effects of Race and Ethnicity," *Pediatrics* 123(2) (2009): 697–702.
9. P. W. Speiser, M. C. J. Rudolf, H. Anhalt, C. Camacho-Hubner, F. Chiarelli, A. Eliakim, et al., "Childhood Obesity," *The Journal of Clinical Endocrinology & Metabolism* 90(3) (2005): 1871–1887.
10. S. Mustillo, C. Worthman, A. Erkanli, G. Keeler, A. Angold, and E. J. Costello, "Obesity and Psychiatric Disorder: Developmental Trajectories," *Pediatrics* 111(4) (2003): 851–859.
11. A. Datar and R. Sturm, "Childhood Overweight and Parent- and Teacher-Reported Behavior Problems," *Archives of Pediatrics and Adolescent Medicine* 158(8) (2004): 804–810.
12. J. C. Lumeng, K. Gannon, H. J. Cabral, D. A. Frank, and B. Zuckerman, "Association Between Clinically Meaningful Behavior Problems and Overweight in Children," *Pediatrics* 112(5) (2003): 1138–1145.
13. C. Braet, I. Mervielde, and W. Vandereycken, "Psychological Aspects of Childhood Obesity: A Controlled Study in a Clinical and Nonclinical Sample," *Journal of Pediatric Psychology* 22(1) (1997): 59–71.
14. M. H. Zeller, H. R. Roehrig, A. C. Modi, S. R. Daniels, and T. H. Inge, "Health-Related Quality of Life and Depressive Symptoms in Adolescents with Extreme Obesity Presenting for Bariatric Surgery," *Pediatrics* 117(4) (2006): 1155–1161.
15. W. Craig, Y. Harel-Fisch, H. Fogel-Grinvald, S. Dostaler, J. Hetland, B. Simons-Morton, et al., "A Cross-National Profile of Bullying and Victimization Among Adolescents in 40 Countries," *International Journal of Public Health* 54(supp 2) (2009): 216–224.
16. T. R. Nansel, W. Craig, M. D. Overpeck, G. Saluja, and W. Ruan, "Cross-National Consistency in the Relationship Between Bullying Behaviors and Psychosocial Adjustment," *Archives of Pediatrics & Adolescent Medicine* 158(8) (2004): 630–736.
17. A. Sourander, L. Helstela, H. Helenius, and J. Piha, "Persistence of Bullying from Childhood to Adolescence: A Longitudinal 8-Year Follow-Up Study," *Child Abuse and Neglect* 24(7) (2000): 873–881.
18. T. J. Nanse, M. Overpeck, R. S. Pilla, W. J. Ruan, B. Simons-Morton, and P. Scheidt, "Bullying Behaviors Among US Youth: Prevalence and Association

with Psychosocial Adjustment," *Journal of the American Medical Association* 285(16) (2001): 2094–2100.

19. Ibid.

20. L. J. Griffiths, D. Wolke, A. S. Page, and J. P. Horwood, "Obesity and Bullying: Different Effects for Boys and Girls," *Archives of Disease in Childhood* 91 (2006): 121–125.

21. D. Neumark-Sztainer, N. Falkner, M. Story, C. Perry, P. J. Hannan, and S. Multert, "Weight-Teasing Among Adolescents: Correlations with Weight Status and Disordered Eating Behaviors," *International Journal of Obesity and Related Metabolic Disorders* 26 (2002): 123–131.

22. T. J. Nanse, M. Overpeck, R. S. Pilla, W. J. Ruan, B. Simons-Morton, and P. Scheidt, "Bullying Behaviors Among US Youth: Prevalence and Association with Psychosocial Adjustment," *Journal of the American Medical Association* 285(16) (2001): 2094–2100.

23. K. H. Riittakerttu, M. Rimpelä, P. Rantanen, and A. Rimpelä, "Bullying at School: An Indicator of Adolescents at Risk for Mental Disorders," *Journal of Adolescence* 23(6) (2002): 661–674.

24. D. L. Espelage and M. K. Holt, "Bullying and Victimization During Early Adolescence: Peer Influences and Psychosocial Correlates," *Journal of Emotional Abuse* 2(2–3) (2001): 123–142.

25. P. M. Lewinsohn, G. N. Clarke, J. R. Seeley, and P. Rohde, "Major Depression in Community Adolescents: Age at Onset, Episode Duration, and Time to Recurrence," *Journal of the American Academy of Child and Adolescent Psychiatry* 33(6) (2001): 809–818.

26. M. Eslea and J. Rees, "At What Age Are Children Most Likely to Be Bullied at School?" *Aggressive Behavior* 27(6) (2001): 419–429.

27. T. D. Jackson, C. M. Grilo, and R. M. Masheb, "Teasing History and Eating Disorder Features: An Age- and Body Mass Index-Matched Comparison of Bulimia Nervosa and Binge-Eating Disorder," *Comprehensive Psychiatry* 43(2) (2000): 108–113.

28. T. D. Jackson, C. M. Grilo, and R. M. Masheb, "Teasing History, Onset of Obesity, Current Eating Disorder Psychopathology, Body Dissatisfaction, and Psychological Functioning in Binge Eating Disorder," *Obesity Research* 8(6) (2000): 451–458.

29. K. K. Davison and L. L. Birch, "Processes Linking Weight Status and Self-Concept Among Girls from Ages 5 to 7 Years," *Developmental Psychiatry* 38 (2002): 735–748.

30. K. Williams, M. Chambers, S. Logan, and D. Robinson, "Association of Common Health Symptoms with Bullying in Primary School Children," *British Medical Journal* 313 (1996): 17.

31. K. T. Eddy, M. Tanofsky-Kraff, H. Thompson-Brenner, D. B. Herzog, T. A. Brown, and D. S. Ludwig, "Eating Disorder Pathology Among Overweight Treatment-Seeking Youth: Clinical Correlates and Cross-Sectional Risk Modeling," *Behaviour Research and Therapy* 45(10) (2007): 2360–2371.

32. M. S. Faith, M. A. Leone, T. S. Ayers, M. Heo, and A. Pietrobelli, "Weight Criticism During Physical Activity, Coping Skills, and Reported Physical Activity in Children," *Pediatrics* 110(2) (2002): e23.

33. D. Olweus, "Bullying at School: Long-Term Outcomes for the Victims and an Effective School-Based Intervention Program," in L. R. Huesmann, ed., *Aggressive Behavior: Current Perspectives* (New York: Plenum Press, 1994), 97–130.

34. T. J. Nanse, M. Overpeck, R. S. Pilla, W. J. Ruan, B. Simons-Morton, and P. Scheidt, "Bullying Behaviors Among US Youth: Prevalence and Association with Psychosocial Adjustment," *Journal of the American Medical Association* 285(16) (2001): 2094–2100.

35. H. Meltzer, P. Vostanis, T. Ford, P. Bebbington, and M. S. Dennis, "Victims of Bullying in Childhood and Suicide Attempts in Adulthood," *European Psychiatry* 26(8) (2011): 498–503.

36. A. B. Klomek, A. Sourander, M. D. Niemelä, M. D. Kumpulainen, J. Piha, T. Tamminen, et al., "Childhood Bullying Behaviors as a Risk for Suicide Attempts and Completed Suicides: A Population-Based Birth Cohort Study," *Journal of the American Academy of Child & Adolescent Psychiatry* 48(3) (2009): 254–261.

37. T. R. Nansel, M. Overpeck, R. S. Pilla, W. J. Ruan, B. Simons-Morton, and P. Scheidt, "Bullying Behaviors Among US Youth: Prevalence and Association with Psychosocial Adjustment," *Journal of the American Medical Association* 285(16) (2001): 2094–2100.

38. R. M. Puhl and J. D. Latner, "Stigma, Obesity, and the Health of the Nation's Children," *Psychological Bulletin* 133 (2007): 557–580.

39. M. H. Zeller and A. C. Modi, "Predictors of Health-Related Quality of Life in Obese Youth," *Obesity Research* 14 (2006): 122–130.

40. N. McCullough, O. Muldoon, and M. Dempster, "Self-Perception in Overweight and Obese Children: A Cross-Sectional Study," *Child: Care, Health, and Development* 35(3) (2009): 357–364.

41. N. H. Falkner, D. Neumark-Sztainer, M. Story, R. W. Jeffery, T. Beuhring, and M. D. Resnick, "Social, Educational, and Psychological Correlates of Weight Status in Adolescents," *Obesity Research* 9 (2001): 32–42.

42. J. W. Pierce and J. Wardle, "Cause and Effect Beliefs and Self-Esteem of Overweight Children," *Journal of Child Psychology & Psychiatry* 38 (1997): 645–650.

43. A. R. Lemeshow, L. Fisher, E. Goodman, I. Kawachi, C. S. Berkey, and G. A. Colditz, "Subjective Social Status in the School and Change in Adiposity in Female Adolescents," *Archives of Pediatrics and Adolescent Medicine* 162(1) (2008): 23–28.

44. S. K. Bell and S. B. Morgan, "Children's Attitudes and Behavioral Intentions Toward a Peer Presented as Obese: Does Medical Explanation for the Obesity Make a Difference?" *Journal of Pediatric Psychology* 25 (2000): 137–145.

45. E. A. Iobst, P. N. Ritchey, L. A. Nabors, R. Stutz, K. Ghee, and D. T. Smith, "Children's Acceptance of a Peer Who Is Overweight: Relations Among Gender, Age, and Blame for Weight Status," *International Journal of Obesity* 33 (2009): 736–742.

46. R. Puhl and J. Latner, "Weight Bias: New Science on a Significant Social Problem," *Obesity* 16 S1-S2 (2008).

47. M. J. Devlin, S. Z. Yanovski, and G. T. Wilson, "Obesity: What Mental Health Professionals Need to Know," *The American Journal of Psychiatry* 157 (2000): 854–866.

48. K. S. O'Brien, J. A. Hunger, and M. Banks, "Implicit Anti-Fat Bias in Physical Educators: Physical Attributes, Ideology and Socialization," *International Journal of Obesity* 31(1) (2007): 308–314; H. O. Chambliss, C. E. Finley, and S. N. Blair, "Attitudes Toward Obese Individuals Among Exercise Science Students," *Medicine and Science in Sports and Exercise* 36(3) (2004): 468–474.

49. M. B. Schwartz, H. O. Chambliss, K. D. Brownell, S. N. Blair, and C. Billington, "Weight Bias Among Health Professionals Specializing in Obesity," *Obesity Research* 11(9) (2003): 1033–1039.

50. D. M. Peters and R. J. A. Jones, "Future Sport, Exercise, and Physical Education Professionals' Perceptions of the Physical Self of Obese Children," *Kinesiology* 42(1) (2010): 36–43.

CHAPTER SEVEN: IN A FAT STATE OF MIND

1. S. H. Stanley, J. D. E. Laugharne, S. Addis, and D. Sherwood, "Assessing Overweight and Obesity Across Mental Disorders: Personality Disorders at High Risk," *Social Psychiatry and Psychiatric Epidemiology* (2012), ePub ahead of print, DOI: 10.1007/s00127–012-0546–1.

2. H. Bruch, "Psychological Aspects of Obesity," *Bulletin of the New York Academy of Medicine* 24(2) (1948): 73–86.

3. W. Ebstein, *Die Fettleibigkeit und ihre Behandlung* (Wiesbaden, Germany: Bergmann, 1882).

4. L. M. Young and B. Powell, "The Effects of Obesity on the Clinical Judgments of Mental Health Professionals," *Journal of Health and Social Behavior* 26 (1985): 233–246.

5. R. R. Dorsey, M. S. Eberhardt, and C. L. Ogden, "Racial/Ethnic Differences in Weight Perception," *Obesity* 17(4) (2009): 790–795.

6. E. Atlantis and K. Ball, "Association Between Weight Perception and Psychological Distress," *International Journal of Obesity* 32(4) (2008): 715–721.

7. M. Kivimäki, G. D. Batty, A. Singh-Manoux, H. Nabi, S. Sabia, A. G. Tabak, et al., "Association Between Common Mental Disorder and Obesity over the Adult Life Course," *British Journal of Psychiatry* 201(1) (2009): 149–155.

8. E. S. Becker, J. Margraf, V. Türke, U. Soeder, and S. Neumer, "Obesity and Mental Illness in a Representative Sample of Young Women," *International Journal of Obesity and Related Metabolic Disorders* 25(S1) (2001): s5–s9.

9. R. Rosmond, L. Lapidus, P. Marin, and P. Björntorp, "Mental Distress, Obesity and Body Fat Distribution in Middle-Aged Men," *Obesity Research* 4(3) (1996): 245–252.

10. K. M. Scott, M. A. McGee, J. E. Wells, and M. A. O. Browne, "Obesity and Mental Disorders in the Adult General Population," *Journal of Psychosomatic Research* 64 (2008): 97–105.

11. J. Wardle and L. Cooke, "The Impact of Obesity in Psychological Well-being," *Best Practice and Research: Clinical Endocrinology and Metabolism* 19(3) (2005): 421–440.

12. R. Rosmond, L. Lapidus, P. Marin, and P. Björntorp, "Mental Distress, Obesity and Body Fat Distribution in Middle-Aged Men," *Obesity Research* 4(3) (1996): 245–252.

13. G. S. M. Cowan, C. K. Buffington, M. Graney, S. Vickerstaff, and G. S. M. Cowan, "Psychological Status of the Morbidly Obese," *Obesity Surgery* 6(2) (1996): 107.

14. R. R. Wing and S. Phelan, "Long-Term Weight Loss Maintenance," *American Journal of Clinical Nutrition* 82(1) (2005): S222–S225.

15. J. B. Dixon, M. E. Dixon, and P. E. O'Brien, "Depression in Association with Severe Obesity: Changes with Weight Loss," *Archives of Internal Medicine* 163(17) (2003): 2058–2065.

16. J. Istvan, K. Zavela, and G. Weidner, "Body Weight and Psychological Distress in NHANES I," *International Journal of Obesity and Related Mental Disorders* 16(12) (1992): 999–1003.

17. S. L. McElroy, R. Kotwal, S. Malhotra, E. B. Nelson, P. E. Keck, and C. B. Nemeroff, "Are Mood Disorders and Obesity Related? A Review for the Mental Health Professional," *Journal of Clinical Psychiatry* 65(5) (2004): 634–651.

18. A. Myers and J. C. Rosen, "Obesity Stigmatization and Coping: Relation to Mental Health Symptoms, Body Image, and Self-Esteem," *International Journal of Obesity* 23 (1999): 221–230.

19. M. R. Solomon, "Eating as both Coping and Stressor in Overweight Control," *Journal of Advanced Nursing* 36(4) (2002): 563–572.

20. E. A. Butler, V. J. Young, and A. K. Randall, "Suppressing the Please, Eating to Cope: The Effect of Overweight Women's Emotion Suppression on Romantic Relationships and Eating," *Journal of Social and Clinical Psychology* 29(6) (2010): 599–623.

21. D. M. Eichen, B. T. Conner, B. P. Daly, and R. L. Fauger, "Weight Perception, Substance Use, and Disordered Eating Behaviors: Comparing Normal Weight and Overweight High School Students," *Journal of Youth and Adolescence* 41(1) (2012): 1–13.

22. R. S. McIntyre, S. L. McElroy, J. Z. Konarski, J. K. Soczynska, A. Bottas, S. Castel, et al., "Substance Use Disorders and Overweight/Obesity in Bipolar I Disorder: Preliminary Evidence for Competing Addictions," *The Journal of Clinical Psychiatry* 68(9) (2007): 1352–1357.

23. K. K. Blomquist, R. M. Masheb, M. A. White, and C. M. Grilo, "Parental Substance Use History of Overweight Men and Women with Binge Eating Disorder Is Associated with Distinct Developmental Trajectories and Comorbid Mood Disorder," *Comprehensive Psychiatry* 52(6) (2011): 693–700.

24. R. K. Merton, "The Self-Fulfilling Prophecy," *The Antioch Review* 8(2) (1948): 193–210.

25. I. Blackburn, "Cognitive Therapy," in A.S. Bellack and M. Hersen, eds., *Comprehensive Clinical Psychology,* vol. 6 (Maryland Heights, MO: Elsevier, 1998), 51–84.

CHAPTER EIGHT: "DOES THIS MAKE ME LOOK FAT?"

1. The Renfrew Center Foundation for Eating Disorders, "Eating Disorders 101 Guide: A Summary of Issues, Statistics and Resources," 2003.

2. D. M. Garner, P. E. Garfinkel, H. C. Stancer, and H. Moldofsky, "Body Image Disturbances in Anorexia Nervosa and Obesity," *Psychosomatic Medicine* 38(5) (1976): 327–336.

3. M. Sorbara and A. Geliebter, "Body Image Disturbance in Obese Outpatients Before and After Weight Loss in Relation to Race, Gender, Binge Eating, and Age of Onset of Obesity," *International Journal of Eating Disorders* 31(4) (2002): 416–423.

4. T. F. Cash, B. Counts, and C. E. Huffine, "Current and Vestigial Effects of Overweight Among Women: Fear of Fate, Attitudinal Body Image, and Eating Behaviors," *Journal of Psychopathology and Behavioral Assessment* 12(2) (1990): 157–167.

5. N. M. Annis, T. F. Cash, and J. I. Hrabosky, "Body Image and Psychosocial Differences Among Stable Average Weight, Currently Overweight, and Formerly Overweight Women: The role of stigmatizing experiences," *Body Image* 1 (2004): 155–167.

6. N. M. Annis, T. F. Cash, and J. I. Hrabosky, "Body Image and Psychosocial Differences Among Stable Average Weight, Currently Overweight, and Formerly Overweight Women: The role of stigmatizing experiences," *Body Image* 1 (2004): 155–167.

7. S. D. Anton, M. G. Perri, and J. R. Riley, "Discrepancy Between Actual and Ideal Body Images: Impact on Eating and Exercise Behaviors," *Eating Behaviors* 1(2) (2000): 153–160.

8. A. Stunkard and M. Mendels, "Obesity and the Body Image: Characteristics of Disturbances in the Body Image of Some Obese Persons," *The American Journal of Psychiatry* 123(10) (1967): 1296–1300.

9. R. M. Puhl and J. D. Latner, "Stigma, Obesity, and the Health of the Nation's Children," *Psychological Bulletin* 133 (2007): 557–580.

10. J. A. Pesa, T. R. Syre, and E. J. Jones, "Psychosocial Differences Associated with Body Weight Among Female Adolescents: The Importance of Body Image," *Journal of Adolescent Health* 26 (2000): 330–337.

11. L. J. Griffiths, T. J. Parsons, and A. J. Hill, "Self-Esteem and Quality of Life in Obese Children and Adolescents: A Systematic Review," *International Journal of Pediatric Obesity* 5 (2010): 382–304.

12. E. Tsukayama, S. L. Toomey, M. S. Faith, and A. L. Duckworth, "Self-Control as a Protective Factor Against Overweight Status in the Transition from Childhood to Adolescence," *Archives of Pediatrics and Adolescent Medicine* 164(7) (2010): 631–635.

13. J. V. Russo, L. Brennan, J. Walkley, S. F. Fraser, and K. Greenway, "Psychosocial Predictors of Eating Disorder Risk in Overweight and Obese Treatment-Seeking Adolescents," *Behaviour Change* 28(3) (2011): 111–127.

14. D. Neumark-Sztainer, M. Story, P. J. Hannan, C. H. Perry, and L. M. Irving, "Weight-Related Concerns and Behaviors Among Overweight and Nonoverweight Adolescents: Implications for Preventing Weight-Related Disorders," *Archives of Pediatrics and Adolescent Medicine* 156(2) (2002): 171–178.

15. M. L. Kern, H. Friedman, L. Martin, C. Reynolds, and G. Luong, "Conscientiousness, Career Success, and Longevity: A Lifespan Analysis," *Annals of Behavioral Medicine* 37(2) (2009): 154–163.

16. T. E. Davison and M. P. McCabe, "Relationships Between Men's and Women's Body Image and Their Psychological, Social, and Sexual Functioning," *Sex Roles* 52(7–8) (2005): 463–475.

17. D. M. Ackard, A. Kearney-Cook, and C. B. Peterson, "Effect of Body Image and Self-Image on Women's Sexual Behaviors," *International Journal of Eating Disorders* 28(4) (2000): 422–429.

18. S. H. Larsen, G. Wagner, and B. L. Heitmann, "Sexual Function and Obesity," *International Journal of Obesity* 31 (2007): 1189–1198.

19. G. M. Wingood, R. J. DiClemente, K. Harrington, and S. L. Davies, "Body Image and African American Females' Sexual Health," *Journal of Women's Health & Gender-Based Medicine* 11(5) (2004): 433–439; I. L. Kvalem, T. von Soest, B. Traen, and K. Singsaas, "Body Evaluation and Coital Onset: A Population-Based Longitudinal Study," *Body Image* 8(2) (2011): 110–118.

20. T. S. Kershaw, A. Arnold, J. B. Lewis, U. Magriples, and J. R. Ickovics, "The Skinny on Sexual Risk: The Effects of BMI on STI Incidence and Risk," *AIDS and Behavior* 15(7) (2011): 1527–1538.
21. Guttmacher Institute, "Sexual and Reproductive Health: Women and Men," 2002, http://www.guttmacher.org/pubs/fb_10–02.html.

CHAPTER NINE: FAT PERSONALITY

1. S. H. Stanley, J. D. E. Laugharne, S. Addis, and D. Sherwood, "Assessing Overweight and Obesity Across Mental Disorders: Personality Disorders at High Risk," *Social Psychiatry and Psychiatric Epidemiology,* 2012, ePub ahead of print, DOI: 10.1007/s00127–012-0546–1.
2. H. Bruch, "Psychological Aspects of Obesity," *Bulletin of the New York Academy of Medicine* 24(2) (1948): 73–86.
3. A. H. Crisp and B. McGuiness, "Jolly Fat: Relation Between Obesity and Psychoneurosis in General Population," *British Medical Journal* 1 (1976): 7–9.
4. M. E. Moore, A. Stunkard, and L. Srole, "Obesity, Social Class, and Mental Illness," *Journal of the American Medical Association* 181(11) (1962): 962–966.
5. S. L. Werkman and E. S. Greenberg, "Personality and Interest Patterns in Obese Adolescent Girls," *Psychosomatic Medicine* 29 (1967): 72–80.
6. W. Weiten, M. A. Lloyd, D. S. Dunn, and E. Y. Hammer, eds., "Theories of Personality," in *Psychology Applied to Modern Life: Adjustment in the 21st Century,* (Belmont, CA: Wadsworth Cengage, 2009), 33–34.
7. M. B. Donnellan, R. D. Conger, and C. M. Bryant, "The Big Five and Enduring Marriages," *Journal of Research in Personality* 38(5) (2004): 481–504.
8. S. E. Seibert and M. L. Kraimer, "The Five-Factor Model of Personality and Career Success," *Journal of Vocational Behavior* 58(1) (2001): 1–21.
9. N. Hayes and S. Joseph, "Big 5 Correlates of Three Measures of Subjective Well-Being," *Personality and Individual Differences* 34(4) (2003): 723–727.
10. A. C. Israel and L. S. Shapiro, "Behavior Problems of Obese Children Enrolling in a Weight Reduction Program," *Journal of Pediatric Psychology* 10(4) (1985): 449–460.
11. A. Terracciano, A. R. Sutin, R. R. McCrae, B. Deiana, L. Ferrucci, D. Schlessinger, et al., "Facets of Personality Linked to Underweight and Overweight," *Psychosomatic Medicine* 71(6) (2009): 682–689.
12. S. L. Werkman and E. S. Greenberg, "Personality and Interest Patterns in Obese Adolescent Girls," *Psychosomatic Medicine* 29 (1967): 72–80.
13. M. L. Held and D. L. Snow, "Personality Characteristics of Obese Adolescent Females," Presentation at the Rocky Mountain Psychological Association Convention, Denver, CO: May 12–15, 1971.
14. Terracciano, Sutin, McCrae, Deiana, Ferrucci, Schlessinger, et al., "Facets of Personality Linked to Underweight and Overweight."
15. D. V. Hiller, "The Salience of Overweight in Personality Characterization," *The Journal of Psychology: Interdisciplinary and Applied* 108(2) (1981): 233–240.
16. R. K. Merton, "The Self-Fulfilling Prophecy," *The Antioch Review* 8(2) (1948): 193–210.

17. K. K. Davison and L. L. Birch, "Predictors of Fat Stereotypes Among 9-Year-Old Girls and Their Parents," *Obesity Research* 12(1) (2004): 86–94.

18. R. G. Cosgrove, C. Arroyo, J. C. Warren, and J. Zhang, "Impaired Cognitive Functioning in Overweight Children and Adolescents," *European Journal of Nutraceuticals & Functional Foods* 20(1) (2009): 49–51.

19. N. H. Falkner, D. Neumark-Sztainer, M. Story, R. W. Jeffery, T. Beuhring, and M. D. Resnick, "Social, Educational, and Psychological Correlates of Weight Status in Adolescents," *Obesity Research* 9 (2001): 32–42.

20. F. X. Pi-Sunyer, "NHLBI Obesity Education Initiative Expert Panel on the Identification, Evaluation, and Treatment of Overweight and Obesity in Adults—the Evidence Report," *Obesity Research* 6(Supp 2), (1998): s51–s209.

21. M. Nahapetyan, "Obese Men Have Less Chance to Get Married," (2009), http://www.enotalone.com/relationships/19552.html.

22. M. J. Pearce, J. Boergers, and J. J. Prinstein, "Adolescent Obesity, Overt and Relational Peer Victimization, and Romantic Relationships," *Obesity Research* 10 (2002): 386–393.

23. J. Sobal, V. Nicolopoulos, and J. Lee, "Attitudes About Overweight and Dating Among Secondary Students," *International Journal of Obesity* 19 (1995): 376–381.

24. F. X. Pi-Sunyer, "NHLBI Obesity Education Initiative Expert Panel on the Identification, Evaluation, and Treatment of Overweight and Obesity in Adults—the Evidence Report," *Obesity Research* 6(Supp 2), (1998): s51–s209.

25. D. Costello, "The Price of Obesity: Beyond the Health Risks, the Personal Financial Costs Are Steep, Recent Studies Show," 2005, http://articles.latimes.com/2005/aug/01/health/he-obesecost1.

26. J. L. Zagorsky, "Health and Wealth: The Late-20th Century Obesity Epidemic in the US," *Economics and Human Biology* 3(2) (2005): 296–313.

27. R. M. Puhl and C. A. Heuer, "Public Opinion About Laws to Prohibit Weight Discrimination in the United States," *Obesity* 19(1) (2011): 74–82.

28. R. M. Puhl, T. Andreyeva, and K. D. Brownell, "Perceptions of Weight Discrimination: Prevalence and Comparison to Race and Gender Discrimination in America," *International Journal of Obesity* 32 (2008): 992–1000.

29. M. V. Roehling, "Weight-Based Discrimination in Employment: Psychological and Legal Aspects," *Personnel Psychology* 52 (1999): 969–1017.

30. G. Lubin, "Here's Why You Should (Quietly) Discriminate Against Fat People," *Business Insider*, 2011, http://articles.businessinsider.com/2011–10-26/strategy/30323623_1_fattest-chronic-disease-workers.

31. M. R. Frone, "Obesity and Absenteeism Among U.S. Workers: Do Physical Health and Mental Health Explain the Relation?" *Journal of Workplace Behavioral Health* 22(4) (2008): 65–79.

32. K. S. O'Brien, J. D. Latner, D. Ebneter, and J. A. Hunter, "Obesity Discrimination: The Role of Physical Appearance, Personal Ideology, and Anti-Fat Prejudice," *International Journal of Obesity*, 2012, doi: 10.1038/ijo.2012.52.

33. M. V. Roehling, P. V. Roehling, and S. Pichler, "The Relationship Between Body Weight and Perceived Weight-Related Employment Discrimination: The Role of Sex and Race," *Journal of Vocational Behavior* 71 (2007): 300–318.

34. D. Carr and M. A. Friedman, "Is Obesity Stigmatizing? Body Weight, Perceived Discrimination, and Psychological Well-Being in the United States," *Journal of Health and Social Behavior* 46(3) (2005): 244–259.

35. E. Ramshaw, "Victoria Hospital Won't Hire Very Obese Workers," 2012, http://www.texastribune.org/texas-health-resources/health-reform-and-texas/victoria-hospital-wont-hire-very-obese-workers/.

36. M. B. Schwartz, H. O. Chambliss, K. D. Brownell, S. N. Blair, and C. Billington, "Weight Bias Among Health Professionals Specializing in Obesity," *Obesity Research* 11(9) (2003): 1033–1039.

37. N. K. Amy, A. Aalborg, P. Lyons, and L. Keranen, "Barriers to Routine Gynecological Cancer Screening for White and African-American Obese Women," *International Journal of Obesity* 30 (2006): 147–155.

CHAPTER TEN: I LOVE YOU, I HATE YOU

1. K. D. Brownell and T. A. Wadden, "Confronting Obesity in Children: Behavioral and Psychological Factors," *Pediatric Annals* 13(6) (1984): 473–478.

2. M. J. Devlin, S. Z. Yanovski, and G. T. Wilson, "Obesity: What Mental Health Professionals Need to Know," *The American Journal of Psychiatry* 157 (2000): 854–866.

3. K. L. Spalding, E. Arner, P. O. Westermark, S. Bernard, B. A. Buchholz, O. Bergmann, et al., "Dynamics of Fat Cell Turnover in Humans," *Nature* 453 (2008): 783–787.

4. B.T. Walsh, "Report of the DSM-5 Eating Disorders Work Group," 2009, http://www.dsm5.org/ProgressReports/Pages/0904ReportoftheDSM-VEatingDisordersWorkGroup.aspx.

5. National Association of Anorexia Nervosa and Associated Disorders, "Eating Disorder Statistics," 2012, http://www.anad.org/get-information/about-eating-disorders/eating-disorders-statistics/.

6. P. F. Sullivan, "Mortality in Anorexia Nervosa," *American Journal of Psychiatry* 152(7) (1995): 1073–1074.

7. J. E. Mitchelle, R. L. Pyle, E. Eckert, D. Hatsukami, and E. Soll, "Bulimia Nervosa with and Without a History of Overweight," *Journal of Substance Abuse* 2(3) (1990): 369–374.

8. K. T. Eddy, M. Tanofsky-Kraff, H. Thompson-Brenner, D. B. Herzog, T. A. Brown, and D. S. Ludwig, "Eating Disorder Pathology Among Overweight Treatment-Seeking Youth: Clinical Correlates and Cross-Sectional Risk Modeling," *Behaviour Research and Therapy* 45(10) (2007): 2360–2371.

9. P. F. Sullivan, "Mortality in Anorexia Nervosa," *American Journal of Psychiatry* 152(7) (1995): 1073–1074.

10. P. M. Miller, J. A. Watkins, R. G. Sargent, and E. J. Rickert, "Self-Efficacy in Overweight Individuals with Binge Eating Disorders," *Obesity Research* 7(6) (1999): 552–555.

11. American Psychiatric Association, "Proposed Revision: Binge Eating Disorder," 2012, http://www.dsm5.org/ProposedRevisions/Pages/proposedrevision.aspx?rid=372.

12. D. L. Reas and C. M. Grilo, "Overweight, Dieting, and Binge Eating in Overweight Patients with Binge Eating Disorder," *International Journal of Eating Disorders* 40(2) (2007): 165–170.

13. R. Reisner and D. Thompson, "The Diet Industry: A Big Fat Lie," *Business Week*, 2008, http://www.businessweek.com/debateroom/archives/2008/01/the_diet_indust.html.

14. U.S. Census Bureau, "Industry Statistics Sampler: Motion Picture Theaters," 2008, http://www.census.gov/econ/industry/products/p512131.htm.

15. The Renfrew Center Foundation for Eating Disorders, "Eating Disorders 101 Guide: A Summary of Issues, Statistics and Resources," 2003.

16. A. Kroke, A. D. Liese, M. Schulz, M. M. Bergmann, K. Klipstein-Grobusch, K. Hoffmann, et al., "Recent Weight Changes and Weight Cycling as Predictors of Subsequent Two Year Weight Change in a Middle-Aged Cohort," *International Journal of Obesity and Related Metabolic Disorders* 26(3) (2002): 403–409.

17. M. Tanofsky-Kraff, M. L. Cohen, S. Z. Yanovski, C. Cox, K. R. Theim, M. Keil, et al., "A Prospective Study of Psychological Predictors of Body Fat Gain Among Children at High Risk for Adult Obesity," *Pediatrics* 117(4) (2006): 1203–1209.

18. J. P. Foreyt, R. L. Brunner, G. K. Goodrick, G. Cutter, K. D. Brownell, and S. T. St. Jeor, "Psychological Correlates of Weight Fluctuation," *International Journal of Eating Disorders* 17(3) (1995): 263–275.

19. G. D. Foster, D. B. Sarwer, and T. A. Wadden, "Psychological Effects of Weight Cycling in Obese Persons: A Review and Research Agenda," *Obesity Research* 5(5) (1997): 474–488.

20. T. Parker-Pope, "Instead of Eating to Diet, They're Eating to Enjoy," 2008, http://www.nytimes.com/2008/09/17/dining/17diet.html.

21. C. M. Shisslak, M. Crago, and L. S. Estes, "The Spectrum of Eating Disturbances," *International Journal of Eating Disorders* 18(3) (1995): 209–219.

22. Centers for Disease Control and Prevention, "Trends in the Prevalence of Obesity, Dietary Behaviors, and Weight Control Practices: National YRBS: 1991–2011."

23. J. A. Linde, R. W. Jeffery, R. L. Levy, N. E. Sherwood, J. Utter, N. P. Pronk, et al., "Binge Eating Disorder, Weight Control Self-Efficacy, and Depression in Overweight Men and Women," *International Journal of Eating Disorders* 28 (2004): 418–425.

24. J. E. Schebendach, K. J. Porter, C. Wolper, B. T. Walsh, and L. E. S. Mayer, "Accuracy of Self-Reported Energy Intake in Weight-Restored Patients with Anorexia Nervosa Compared with Obese and Normal Weight Individuals," *International Journal of Eating Disorders* 45(4) (2012): 570–574.

25. I. Steenhuis, "Guilty or Not? Feelings of Guilt About Food Among College Women," *Appetite* 52(2) (2009): 531–534.

26. E. S. Frank, "Shame and Guilt in Eating Disorders," *American Journal of Orthopsychiatry* 61(2) (1991): 303–306.

27. R. L. Corwin and P. S. Grigson, "Symposium Overview: Food Addiction: Fact or Fiction?" *The Journal of Nutrition* 139(3) (2009): 617–619.

28. *Diagnostic and Statistical Manual of Mental Disorders: DSM-IV* (Washington D.C.: American Psychiatric Association, 1994), 181–183.

29. J. A. Corsica and M. L. Pelchat, "Food Addiction: True or False?" *Current Opinion in Gastroenterology* 26(2) (2010): 165–169.

INTERLUDE

1. K. A. Bechtel, "Pediatric Chickenpox," 2011, http://emedicine.medscape.com/article/969773-overview.

CHAPTER ELEVEN: WHAT CAN WE DO?

1. A. J. Sedlak, D. Finkelhor, H. Hammer, and D. J. Schultz, "National Estimates of Missing Children: An Overview," in J. R. Flores, ed., *National Incidence Studies of Missing, Abducted, Runaway, and Thrownaway Children* (Washington, D.C.: U.S. Department of Justice, Office of Juvenile Justice and Delinquency Prevention, 2002).
2. National Diabetes Information Clearinghouse, "National Diabetes Statistics, 2011," 2011, http://diabetes.niddk.nih.gov/dm/pubs/statistics/.
3. CDC, "National Diabetes Fact Sheet, 2011," 2011, http://www.cdc.gov/diabetes/pubs/pdf/ndfs_2011.pdf.
4. M. Asbridge, J. A. Hayden, and J. L. Cartwright, "Acute Cannabis Consumption and Motor Vehicle Collision Risk: Systematic Review of Observational Studies and Meta-Analysis," *BMJ* 344 (2012): e536.
5. B. H. Wrotniak, L. H. Epstein, R. A. Paluch, and J. N. Roemmich, "Parent Weight Change as a Predictor of Child Weight Change in Family-Based Behavioral Obesity Treatment," *Archives of Pediatrics and Adolescent Medicine* 158(4) (2004): 342–347.
6. M. Fogelholm, O. Nuutinen, M. Pasanen, E. Myöhänen, and T. Säätelä, "Parent-Child Relationship of Physical Activity Patterns and Obesity," *International Journal of Obesity and Related Metabolic Disorders* 23(12) (1999): 1262–1268.

Index

INDEX